THE ORANG GANG ET AL

Loved, Hugged & Peed On

A Houston Zoo Volunteer's Diary of Love as an Orangutan "Mom"

SHERRY LUCAS

Copyright © 2011 Sherry Lucas
All rights reserved.

ISBN: 061552074X
ISBN-13: 9780615520742

FORWARD

This is a diary; a day by day account of working as a volunteer at the Houston Zoo. It's mostly about working with orangutans; helping to hand raise three babies. It's my experience learning about them; watching their interactions with each other, the keepers, other volunteers, and vet staff. They share about 97 % of our DNA and I've been amazed at how smart they are. It's also about helping to hand raise a baby siamang, and there are notes about other zoo animals that I've met in my years at the zoo.

Orangutan means "person of the forest" and that's how I've come to think about my orange ape buddies. They are my friends. Yes, they are animals and that must not be forgotten. They are also endangered animals. It's important to do all that can be done to make sure they don't become extinct in their native Borneo and Sumatra, the only place they are found in the wild. They are also very strong, being 5 to 7 times stronger than a human. Great care must be taken when working with them or near them.

I've worked with the orangutans over 13 years. There have been changes in what volunteers are allowed to do and not do in interacting with them. Occasionally, I was allowed certain privileges with supervision, such as scratching an adult's back or spoon feeding them. I've asked permission to bring edible treats. Their diets are monitored closely so extras may mean making adjustments in the diets that day. I've also learned what is and isn't allowed as enrichment.

I give thanks to my family and friends for putting up with my endless stories about the orangutans, and for encouraging me to write this book. It is not a scholarly work, and published exactly as written. Please just read it as a peek into someone's personal diary.

It's been so much fun reliving the memories. Enjoy!

Sherry Lucas

ACKNOWLEDGMENTS

This diary is dedicated to Lynn Killam, Assistant Curator of Primates at the Houston Zoo, but who was the Primate supervisor when I worked with the youngsters. Her love and concern for people and animals abounds. She shares her knowledge willingly, but humbly. I thank her for all I have learned. I appreciate the trust and confidence she has given me in working with the apes.

A special thank you goes to Barbara Lester, the Curator at the time, who not only selected me as one of the caregivers, but also gave me so much support throughout the days of caring for the little ones.

I also thank Cindy Leeson and Tammy Buhrmester, two of the keepers I have worked with extensively in the orangutan night house, for all they have taught me. I appreciate their ongoing efforts to provide all the orang gang members need for healthy, happy, and enriched lives.

And thank you to the other caregivers, who willingly gave of their time, talent, and treasure while raising the youngsters. The lasting friendships we developed mean the world to me.

Sherry Lucas

MEET THE ORANGUTANS

Cheyenne
Hybrid female, born May 13,1972 in Colorado Springs, CO, and arrived at the Houston Zoo, her 5th zoo, in 1993. Surrogate mother to Luna, Elok, and Indah.

Rudi Valentino
Hybrid male, born December 9, 1977 in Brownsville, TX, and moved to the Houston Zoo when he was 6 months old.

Kelly
Bornean female, born September 22, 1980 in San Diego, CA, and joined the Houston Zoo in 1981. Mother of Luna and Solaris.

Doc
Bornean male, born December 25, 1984 in Dallas, TX, and arrived at the Houston Zoo at age 3. Father of Solaris.

Luna bela
Bornean female, born September 18, 1997 to Kelly and Bubba (now deceased). Hand raised for 2 years and then adopted by Cheyenne. Now resides at Busch Gardens in Tampa Bay, FL.

Elok
Sumatran male, born November 1, 2000 in Memphis, TN, and brought to the Houston Zoo one year later to be raised by Cheyenne. Moved to Oklahoma City Zoo in November, 2007.

Indah
Sumatran female, Elok's sister, born January 25, 2004 in Memphis, TN. Arrived at the Houston Zoo in October, 2005, to be raised, along with her brother, by Cheyenne.

Solaris
Bornean male, son of Doc and Kelly, born June 22, 2003.

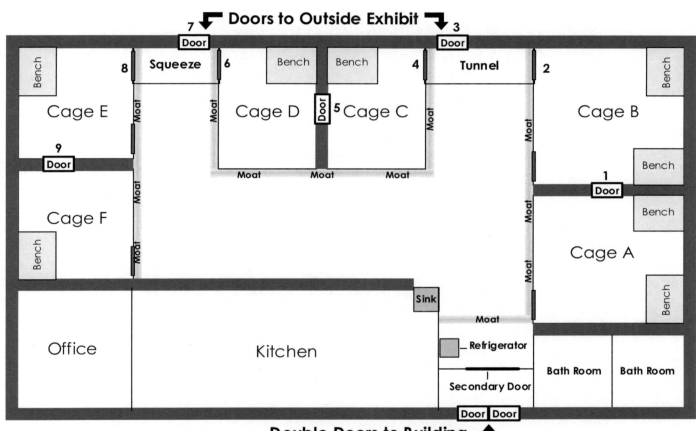

Squeeze cage
A small cage in which the orangutans station to go outside, and where they recover after being sedated for examinations.

Tunnel
An area where the orangutans station before going outside, and where they station to receive a sedation injection.

Bench
A four foot high platform for play and toys.

June 30, 1998

At last, today arrived! Last night I could hardly sleep. I felt like I did as a kid, the night before the first day of school; excited, somewhat anxious, anticipating the next day.

Why? Today I began my training to be a human caregiver to Luna Bela, the baby orangutan.

Luna is 9 ½ months old, weighs 11 pounds at this time, and is the cutest little thing you can imagine. I so wanted to be a part of her nurturing. I've been very happy the last two weeks since I was notified I was one of the ones selected to be a caregiver.

I'll back up and start at the beginning................

Luna Bela was born September 18, 1997, weighing 3 pounds. She was born the week of the full moon – hence the name Luna. (Bela means "beautiful.") Kelly is her mother and Bubba is her father. (Bubba died in April, 1998.) Luna is Kelly's first baby. She was 16 when the zoo was given permission by the Species Survival Plan program to breed her. (The mission of that program is to manage and conserve a select and typically threatened or endangered *ex situ* species population.) Kelly had been hand raised herself, and had never been around other orangutans with offspring to observe, and learn parenting. She needed parenting lessons. She is very smart, and the hope was she'd learn her lessons well, and her instincts would take over when the baby was born. When Luna was born, Kelly cleaned her, cuddled her, and the keepers were hopeful she would nurse her as she had been taught. She was given 72 hours for the instincts to kick in. After 48 hours, and nursing had not been observed, Kelly was sedated, and Luna nursed without difficulty. The next day Luna whimpered, Kelly held her up to her lips, and she quieted. Kelly seemed to think she was parenting, but of course Luna could not nurse there. Once again she was sedated, and Luna was pulled for hand rearing. (The orangutans are trained to present their arms for sedation, along with other behaviors. This helps in assisting to assess them.) Kelly was noted to be sad for a few days after Luna was taken from her, retreating to the corner of her cage and staring into it.

Luna required 24 hour care and the keepers provided it. She thrived. On nice days she was carried about the zoo for visual stimulation, and to teach her to "hang on" as the keeper walked with her. Baby orangutans cling to their moms for their first year, and the keepers were Luna's moms. During the walks about the zoo, Luna seemed to especially like visiting the giraffe exhibit and watching them. Her trips about the zoo were stopped, however, when it became apparent that the zoo sightseeing was much more exciting than her fellow orangutans. The goal was to immerse her into the orangutan community, so she needed to remain there.

In March, 1998, I received a letter sent to zoo volunteers. More Luna caregivers were needed. I'd only been working in animal areas (large mammals) for four months. I didn't think I had a chance, but decided I needed to pursue this dream. As required, I wrote a letter of application stating how I viewed the orangutan program, why I wanted to do this, and my qualifications; a nurse, a mom, and a grandmother. Then we were to be called for an interview. I sent my letter and waited, and waited, and waited some more. I finally phoned and was told the process was moving slowly, but all applicants would be interviewed. After my interview I continued to wait. On June 15, I was notified that I'd been one of the ones selected. I cannot describe the feeling I had when I got that phone call. It was almost like winning the lottery. I never have won, but I imagine that is what it might be like. I was told to go for training on June 30. Those two weeks dragged by. I told everyone who would listen all about it. I could hardly wait to get my hands on that baby. June 30 finally arrived!

Before entering the orangutan night house we (two of us who were training that day) were given extensive verbal and written instructions by Barbara, the curator, who was with us. There Luna was, with the volunteer caregiver of the day. Kelly was in the next cage, watching us as we all trooped into Luna's cage. Kelly picked up one of her toys, a traffic cone, and put it on her head to get our attention. It worked! We all laughed. The next six hours were spent watching the caregiver work with Luna in front of the other orangutans. They could see her, and she could see and hear them too. As she is so active, we were advised we must never let her out of our sight. When Luna was fed her rice cereal, Kelly rolled up a paper towel and pushed it out to the keeper. The keeper put a bit of Luna's cereal on the towel, and gave it back to her. Later in the day, Luna was playing passively in her crib (a big plastic bin), and we were sitting nearby on the floor. Luna came to the edge, put her hand on my leg, and pushed her head against my knee. This first day we were instructed not to touch her, so of course I didn't. But did I just melt? Oh, yes! What a sweetie!

Also, while I was sitting there, Kelly spit at me. She doused me good with a whole mouthful of water. That got my attention, but wasn't as funny as the earlier cone head gesture. Luna also untied my shoes two or three times, putting the laces into her mouth. She's at the age where everything goes there.

We also watched the caregiver exhibit her to the public during what I will refer to as the Luna Show. She slept through it with her thumb firmly planted in her mouth.

Next week I'll be "HANDS ON" caring for her! Yea!

July 7, 1998

Last night, and this morning, I read and re-read the protocols for caring for Luna, but was quite nervous. I thought a keeper would be with me to make sure I did the right thing. SURPRISE! Barbara, the curator, came by, told me to go into the night house, get a report from the morning caregiver, and carry on. She said she'd be right outside if I had questions. Talk about apprehensive!

Luna was receptive to me, and only whined a bit when the caregiver left. I watched her play on her bamboo jungle gym, and with her bin of toys. We went into the aisle area so she could play in front of Kelly. I learned how to feed her small bites of steamed veggies, and give her yogurt in a syringe. I went with the primate supervisor, Lynn, to the education building for the Luna Show. While Lynn talked about her to the crowd, Luna was active on the jungle gym on the stage. She hadn't napped all day, and fell asleep in the cart on the way back to the night house. I pulled a chair up in front of Kelly's cage and let her sleep.

What a Kodak moment; Luna all snuggled up on my chest, sleeping for nearly two hours, and no one coming into the building with a camera. However, that wonderful memory will always be with me. While sitting there, I watched Kelly eat her afternoon snacks and play with a package of latex gloves. That was interesting. She pulled one onto her face, put another on her hand, and filled several with water, getting drinks and spitting them into the gloves. She'd then suck the water out.

After Luna woke up and had her formula, she played with her toys in front of Kelly's cage. Kelly was very attentive, sitting high up in her cage, watching us with a paper bag on her head. At first, she climbed up there with a glove full of water in her mouth and spit it at us. She missed.

Luna kept finding bits of things to put into her mouth, including pieces of bamboo from her jungle gym. I'd swipe them out and say, "Good girl." I would also offer a trade such as a drink of juice from her Sippy cup. She did try to bite me once and I scolded her with a firm "No," as I'd been instructed.

It was a great afternoon, even better than I imagined it would be. She is so cute and so sweet. I loved being with her, and can hardly wait until next week. This is the best job I ever had for no pay.

July 14, 1998

Today Doc and Cheyenne were in the night house. It was the first time I'd seen them. They are good buddies, and it was fun watching them throughout the day, wrestling and being silly.

Luna has not been very interested in eating her cereal lately, and it takes much patience and encouragement. Meanwhile, Doc was very interested in it. He pushed a piece of cardboard out as a plate, hoping for some. He was given the leftovers. Luna was a sleepy girl. After her cereal, she sprawled on her small hairy mama (a stuffed orangutan) in the aisle, and took a short nap. Afterwards, she ate her steamed carrot and yogurt while playing on her jungle gym. She then played in the aisle before the Luna Show, during which she was very active. She was a bit clingy today with no independent play until late in my shift. She'd play but had a hold on my hand. She was fascinated with a liter coke bottle, trying to drink from it. Lynn said she hadn't seen her do that before. After the bottle was washed and filled with water, she did drink quite a bit from it.

Lynn sprayed Doc and Chey (Cheyenne's nickname) with a hose which they seemed to enjoy a lot. She then hooked the hose over a ladder sending a fine mist toward their cage. They thought that was neat. Luna climbed the ladder and got her little face into the spray too. However, when I played with her, squirting her with the water spray bottle or sprinkling her with water from her Sippy cup, she acted like it was not fun and hid her face.

It was another great day with the Great Apes.

A few words about the four adult orangutans..........

This morning one of the vets was outside the night house, waiting for assistance from Lynn to draw blood from a diabetic lemur. Chey was very curious when she saw him, and sat with a very disturbed look on her face. Doc sat beside her and worried with her. Lynn says the vet is not their favorite person.

A caregiver shared a cute story about Doc and Chey. Awhile back Doc found a stick in his cage. The keeper didn't know how it got there, but wanted to get it. She offered Doc a handful of raisins to make a trade. He wasn't interested, put the stick under him, and pretended he hadn't a clue what the keeper wanted. Chey watched with great interest. She finally sighed a big sigh, went over to Doc, pulled the stick out, handed it to the keeper, and held out her hand for the raisins. Orangutans are very smart!

Lynn brought Kelly and Rudi in early today. A storm was threatening and she was afraid a power failure might disable the hydraulic door. Rudi Valentino is a huge, long haired, distinguished looking orangutan. He came in carrying a big branch, and had to work a bit to get it through the door. Then Kelly was playing with it, and pushing it through the cage mesh. Lynn traded a handful of raisins for it. Lynn needed Kelly to go into a cage, but needed her to go outside because Chey was being a toot and not going into the cage she was supposed to. Lynn told Kelly to go to the other door and she did. Lynn said she'd never done that before. She also told me that she'd taught Kelly to pee into a cup on demand about 8 years ago.

When the evening keeper came, she gave the orangutans their juice. She told Kelly to get a bucket, which she did. The keeper poured juice into Kelly's mouth which she spit into the bucket, saving it for later.

It is amazing how smart these animals are. I still can't believe I'm getting to do this. I love it!

July 21, 1998

Luna was napping when I arrived. She woke about 30 minutes later and was her usual sweet self. Doc and Chey were the ones inside. Luna climbed and climbed on the portable jungle gym in front of them. She also played with her basket of toys. Doc was very attentive, watching her play. Chey showed some interest, coming to take a look when Luna was banging a plastic rod on the cement floor, and seemed quite proud of the noise it made. Doc extended his hand under the mesh, hoping someone or something would "grease his palm." He and Chey were wrestling a lot early in my shift, and Luna showed interest in that. Also, when Doc would move about his cage or go into another one, she would stop in her play and watch.

She was such a sleepy wee soul when she had her 4 p.m. bottle. I was sure she'd take a nap, but "Oh, no." She kept on playing but was a bit more subdued.

Rudi pounded on the door when it was getting close to the time for him and Kelly to come inside. Luna was playing on the chair and she jumped into my arms, frightened by the noise. Then there was some thunder and she immediately looked up to the skylight. What a smart little thing!

She found a bruise on my leg very interesting, occasionally picking at it. All in all, she was quite independent in her play today, not clingy like last week.

July 26, 1998

Today I attended the Luna caregiver meeting. We discussed ways to handle her when she wants to bite us, and ways to distract her when she rubs her genitals on us, her toys etc. It's normal that she's discovered herself, but during the Luna Show it invites questions that might be uncomfortable for some. We also talked about feeding her; the new foods, and how to get her to eat the things she really doesn't like. We will also share some of her foods and beverages with the other orangutans, preventing jealousy.

July 28, 1998

WILD CHILD! That pretty much describes Miss Luna today. The caregiver said she napped a bit in the morning, but this afternoon her only nap was during the Luna Show. She would not get on the jungle gym for the crowd, just wanted to cling, and then she fell asleep.

In the night house she climbed and climbed on her jungle gym in the aisle, and in cage B. She also climbed on the equipment in B. That was a good thing because she could leave her scent there for the others. Her climbing was swift, not slow and deliberate like some other times. She was definitely more animated. Late in the shift she quieted, and briefly snuggled on hairy mama. She did try to bite me a few times, but I gave her a firm "No," and distracted her. I also aimed that little hand toward her own mouth a couple of times, as suggested, but she was too smart to bite herself.

Pears were on the menu today and a big hit. She spit out the small bites I offered her like I had before. She wanted the whole chunk to hold in her mouth and chew on.

Rudi and Kelly were inside today. Rudi doesn't pay much attention to Luna, but Kelly was attentive all day. I gave them the peel from Luna's pear and sweet potato. I also squirted water and juice from Luna's bottle to Kelly. One time I missed her mouth. The next time I aimed the bottle her way, she covered her eyes and opened her mouth. What a clown!

A couple of times today Rudi went nuts, pounded on the steel doors and threw things around his cage. He is so strong and can put on great displays. The first time he did it, he threw his buckets of water into the tunnel between cages B and C. Kelly stayed out of the way of course. After the chaos, she moved the buckets back where they belonged; picking up after him I guess. Luna leapt into my arms. She always does that when Rudi displays.

I watched Lynn do training of Rudi and Kelly, asking them to present their arms, ears, show their tongues etc. She also had Kelly retrieve something. Luna watched closely. She seemed especially interested in the baby food pudding which was given as the reward for the behaviors.

Luna's Gatorade must have been sweeter today. She drank a lot! She pulled the nipple off the bottle when she drank her formula. We both had formula all over us.

I washed her with a cloth. Between the formula and the spilled juice (being sloppy with her Sippy cup), she was one sticky baby.

It was a fun day!

August 4, 1998

As usual, I was anxious to get to the zoo. The outside temperature has been 100 degrees the last few days, and 90 in the night house. With the fans going it hasn't been too bad, however. Kelly was in today and very attentive to all Luna activity. The morning caregiver said Luna and Kelly had touched lips through the mesh this morning, and then Luna offered Kelly a drink from her Sippy cup. "Give mommy a drink." I wonder if Kelly has a sense of Luna being her baby. During the Luna Show the keeper told the crowd that Chey seems quite interested in Luna, but perhaps it's because she dislikes Kelly and simply wants her baby.

Luna was really sweet today. She didn't get upset and try to bite me, but she playfully put her mouth on my hand a couple of times. She played quietly with her toys most of the day in the aisle. She had a long piece of very stretchy material that she loved. She would also go toward the carts, and then turn around and look at me. She knew she wasn't supposed to do that. She had a lot of fun with a roll of industrial strength brown paper towels too.

She napped for an hour on big hairy momma in the aisle. Another Kodak moment not recorded. I did get a new camera yesterday. Hopefully I'll know how to work it by next week. She is used to having her picture taken and poses quite well. She was cute when she woke up. She looked around and seemed kind of startled because she was not asleep in her kennel.

A few times today, I'd swing her around and let her ride on my back. Of course she untied my lower mask strings. Right after her nap, I picked her up and put her on my back. That was a big mistake. Why? Because she peed and wet MY pants. She saturated the back of my shorts, my legs, and my socks. Oh well, live and learn.

I tickled her under her arms and she is ticklish. She wiggled and got a silly grin on her face.

The keeper opened the door from the yard and set up a "mister" hose. Chey parked right in front of it, and sat there for almost an hour. She loves water. After her front was thoroughly soaked, she turned around, scratched her back on the mesh, and sat there to get her back wet. Silly woman.

Again today, I just sat there watching Luna sleep, watching Kelly eat her fruit, Chey playing in the water, and thinking what a wonderful non-paying job this is. I absolutely love it!

August 10, 1998

As I'm going to be gone for two weeks, I worked with Luna today instead of tomorrow. Poor little tyke has the "sniffles." She sneezed three times, had to have her nose wiped, and she did not like that. The drainage was clear however. She was stuffy and breathing through her mouth most of the day. The vet came about noon to listen to her chest; no problem there. Kelly was inside today. When the vet came she pitched a small fit, throwing things about in her cage, which was next to Luna's. She watched closely as Luna was being examined. The keeper said that was significant. She has been quite indifferent to

Luna, but showed concern today when something was being done to her. Luna was very active in spite of the sniffles. I tried to get her to play in front of Kelly when Kelly was moved down to the end cage. But oh no! Luna kept taking my hand and leading me back to her own cage so she could climb on her jungle gym. She did a lot of swinging on her hanging plastic bin, and then would fall into her crib full of hay. Once she banged her head on the edge of the crib, but that didn't faze her. She tried to untie my shoes several times, but was unsuccessful. I'd double tied them. She fell asleep on big hairy mama for about 45 minutes after her 4 p.m. bottle.

Kelly tried to bait Luna through the introduction door. She pushed a cardboard roll, and the foil box it was from, through the mesh. She also tore a cardboard box and used it as a tool to push the cardboard roll completely past the red line into cage A. I let Luna play with it briefly, but took it away when she started chewing on it.

The adults had their afternoon snacks in containers today. Doc and Chey's were in boxes, and Kelly's were in a large plastic jug with about a 3" opening. Her fruit and vegetables had been chopped. However, she was not patient, and proceeded to chew into the bottom of the jug to make a bigger opening. She also had a bag of popcorn.

I had my new camera and snapped away, hoping some of the photos turn out. Right before I left I went to Doc's cage, called his name, and he looked up from his snack. I aimed my camera at him, and he turned his back to me. Oh well, I'll try another day.

I'll miss Luna while I'm gone, but hope she's all well by the time I return.

August 25, 1998

Back with Luna today. Yea! While I was gone, I told my family and friends all about the orangutans. Someday people will hate to see me coming. I do go on and on when I get a chance. Of course I had photos too.

When I got to the zoo, they were making handprints of Luna's on large sheets of paper. Apparently National Geographic had contacted them. They wanted a baby orangutan's handprint. She was fairly cooperative, especially when distracted with drinks of juice that I offered.

Rudi and Kelly were in today, and Kelly was quite interested in Luna. I shared Luna's water with her. I didn't offer juice with the squirt bottle. That way she didn't have to cover her eyes in case I missed her mouth. I also gave the peelings from Luna's potato and pear to Rudi and Kelly. As usual, when the morning caregiver gave Luna the rice cereal, she didn't want it. So the caregiver set the dish on the floor. Luna tasted it, dumped it out onto the floor, and covered it with a paper bag as if to say, "It's all gone." Silly little girl.

Today the keeper had me take Luna into cage C after it was cleaned. This is one of the adult cages. As soon as we went into the cage, Luna started whining, grabbed the door, and wanted out. We returned to her cage and got her snack. I hoped she'd eat that in cage C, but she still wanted out. I then got her stuffed bear, which she cuddled, and we went into C again. She snuggled and slept for about 45 minutes on her bear in the hammock in C. I took photos; she looked so cute.

THE ORANG GANG ET AL - LOVED, HUGGED AND PEED ON

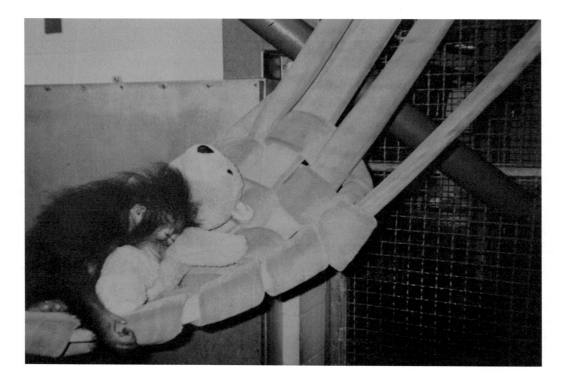

She spent a lot of time playing with toys and straws in her aisle play bin. She then initiated a game with me. She came to the end where I was sitting on a stool. She took my hands, stood on the edge of the bin, rocked back and forth, laid back, and I then lowered her into the bin. She positioned herself again, but before starting to rock, she buried her face on my thigh for a few seconds, kind of like a love. I then scratched her back before lowering her into the bin. She did this over and over for about 30 minutes.

When Chey and Doc came in at 6, Luna and I went to greet them. Doc was busy eating his dinner. Chey was looking for hers. She pulled the hay out of her big black tub, and looked behind her buckets. I noticed the bag with her dinner outside of her cage, with just the edge of the bag pushed into the cage. I got her attention and pointed to where it was.

Also today, Luna would not take her potato and pear from me, so I put them in her tire swing. She then climbed onto the tire, picked them up with her mouth, and ate all quickly.

She is now 11 months and 1 week old, and weighs 13 lbs.

September 1, 1998

I received a letter stating volunteers were needed in primates, so today I went in at 7 a.m. to help clean monkey cages and trim shrubs. After taking a shower and changing all of my clothes, I ate lunch and then went to care for Luna, or "Girley Girl" as I sometimes call her, or "Toonses" as one keeper calls her, or "Looney Toons" as a vet called her today. The vet came to check Kelly who was the only one staying inside. They thought she might have a cold. She seemed rather listless early on my shift, but seemed to perk up after the vet left. She was very cooperative during the vet's exam which was done through the cage mesh of course. I kept Luna away from her as instructed, but while Luna was climbing on her jungle gym, I gave Kelly a few sips of water from Luna's squirt bottle.

The caregiver said Luna kept diving into her bin of hay this morning, not even wanting to stop for her yogurt. She said Kelly watched and clapped her hands, seemingly in approval.

Luna is getting so independent, no longer needing to hang onto me for reassurance. She climbs, swings, acts silly, and every now and again comes and takes hold of my hand. I guess that is for reassurance, but also to use to climb, swing, and act silly.

We ride to the Luna Show in a cart called the Fetchasauras. On the way back to the night house today, I thought she was going to fall asleep during the ride, but not so. She got right back onto her jungle gym. At 3:45 she came to me and wanted to be held. The thumb went in the mouth, and she had her sleepy face. I decided I'd better try to get her to take her 4 p.m. bottle. I put it in to heat, but she was long gone at the end of the 4 minutes. I could not get her awake to drink, so I just settled on the lounge chair and held her little sweet self. I did wake her at 4:35 so she could get her formula, and be ready to go to bed on time for the next caregiver. The rest of my shift she played quietly. One thing she kept doing today was climbing up the pole of the bench; the platform at back of the cage on which we store supplies. She'd look over her shoulder to see if I was watching. She knows she is not supposed to mess with the things on there. She would grab whatever she could if I didn't get there fast enough.

When the others came inside I greeted each. Rudi came to the intro door in Luna's cage when I called out to him.

They are all so neat!

September 8, 1998

Luna fell asleep on my lap, on her bear, the first hour I was there today. I knew when that little thumb went into the mouth it was naptime. At least she was awake and cute during the Luna Show. There was a small crowd now that school has started.

I read in the notes today that Chey had presented her nipple to Luna this past week. "Good girl" was the reply to that. We are all hoping like crazy she'll be accepted and raised by THIS orang gang.

Luna was very lovable today; such a sweetie. However, when she climbed the pole of the caregiver's bench and I reached for her, she threatened to bite me. She has that response when she's stopped in misbehavior. She continues to be more and more independent, spending most of my shift climbing on her jungle gym. We did play in the aisle in front of the adults, but she held onto my hand during that time.

I had a slight crisis right before I left today. My relief was going to be a few minutes late. I decided to go ahead and give Luna her 6 p.m. sweet potato and pear. After she ate, I stepped to the faucet to rinse my sticky hands and didn't lock her cage. When I turned around, she was out and climbing up the outside of the cage. I was so afraid she'd go "next door" to where Chey was. I grabbed her syringe of yogurt and the ladder. Fortunately, the caregiver came in at that time and went into Luna's cage. Luna followed her as she is one of her favorite caregivers. I'll be sure to lock it from now on.

Some notes about the adults................
Today I offered Kelly some water from Luna's squirt bottle, and she took it like always. Later, when I offered it again, she grabbed one of her large buckets and pushed it close so I could squirt the water into it. Then she took her drink. She seemed to be feeling better today. Her cold is gone.

When the rain started today, the keeper opened the door to the yard so the gang, Rudi, Doc, and Chey, could come into the tunnel if they wanted. Chey was given a raisin, just out of reach, and it was fun watching her try to get it using a twig as a tool. Later I heard a rattle. She was using her twig to fiddle with the padlock. Then she was poking at the lights with it. When one of Luna's toys rolled close to her, she tried to retrieve it with a branch. She only succeeded in moving it farther away, however.

Rudi and Doc were wrestling; then Rudi was grooming Doc. At least it appeared that way. He was picking through his hair, examining his head, his hand, his neck etc. Chey watched closely. At one point I saw her pull his hair. Then Doc was just hassled by Rudi. He wouldn't let him go, and appeared to be trying to "make whoopee" with Doc. The keeper bribed Rudi to separate them, and they ended up in separate cages.

September 14, 1998

A bonus day today. Lynn phoned last night to see if I could fill in for an absent caregiver this afternoon. Of course I jumped at the chance and arrived about 1:30 p.m. I had to work at my paying job in the morning.

When I arrived, Luna reached out for me, took my hand, and pressed that sweet little face against my leg, giving me a love. She was so active today and very independent in her play. She would play for awhile in her cage, then lead me out into the aisle to play on the portable jungle gym and the rolling cart, and then go back into her cage. She spent some time diving into the hay in her crib. Part of the time, I locked her in her cage and stayed close outside. She didn't fret and wouldn't even come to take a drink. "Little Miss Independence." She did some wrestling with her bear and her small hairy mama, and dragged them around her cage too. No nap today, although she did seem sleepy at times.

Chey and Doc were in today. That old phrase, Wild Man of Borneo, suited Doc. He raced from cage to cage, swinging, dragging things about, and just having the best time. The hose was set up to spray into the cage, and he had a great time playing in the water too. At one point he just stood there getting his butt sprayed. He was busy masturbating after his afternoon snack. He's such a teenager!

Chey was quiet. She is just such a sweetheart. The keeper had put honey, birdseed, and Rice Krispies inside a cardboard tube. She loved that! Her snacks were in a box under shredded paper. She first took a few bits of paper out, then decided to dump it all out. Later she took the box apart and sat under it. She then got into her black tub, arranged the box around her, and made a nest. After awhile she left the box in the tub, and continued to play quietly with stuff in her cage. Both she and Doc watched Luna occasionally, and I did give them sips of Luna's water and juice. Doc did spit a mouthful of water at me.

September 15, 1998

When I woke up this morning I had a sore throat so I left a message for Barbara. I called again at 10:30 (she'd been out of town and hadn't checked her messages) and told her the problem. She thought it would be okay for me to still work with Luna. She is so independent now, and doesn't require long, close encounters. She told me to wash my hands frequently. I told her I'd wear a cone shaped mask which seemed less porous. Actually, I wore two and changed masks when I sneezed.

Chey and Doc were inside the night house again today. The keeper put streamers of toilet paper, paper towels, and lots of shredded paper into their cage. The caregiver got the video camera ready to film Doc's actions when they transferred into the cage. We thought Doc would go nuts with all the streamers, but because we were expecting him to perform, he didn't. After they left I watched him playing in a cardboard box. He was completely inside of it, looking out through a flap. Then Chey took it away from him, put it on herself, and walked away in it, all the way from cage C to cage F. Doc followed in a few minutes and tried to climb in too. Needless to say, they both didn't fit.

Today, Luna's favorite activity was standing on the edge of the crib of hay, and falling in backwards while still holding on with her feet. She kept going to the same corner. At one point she did this about 20 times in a row. She also somersaulted into the crib, and later held my hands and fell backwards into it.

I sat outside her cage several times, allowing her some independence. During one 20 minute session, she came to the door and tried to open it three times. After the third time, she went directly to the supply bench and started to climb the pole, looking at me before she did. Naturally I zipped into the cage. She grabbed my note paper, but gave it to me as soon as I asked for it. Later she did the same thing, going toward the pole after trying the door just once. She looked directly at me before climbing up the pole, and got down as soon as I headed toward the cage. What a little stinker! Just like a toddler. She also wrestled with her toys a few times today.

Luna on new jungle gym

It was raining and the keeper opened the outside door so Rudi and Kelly could come into the tunnel. Kelly brought in some small branches to use as tools to try to pull things into the tunnel. She pulled all the leaves off of one to make a stick tool. At one point she was waving a branch at Rudi. He took it from her and wrapped it around his neck.

I gave the adults some ice cubes. Kelly put her stick through the mesh when I asked her if she wanted some ice. I told her that wouldn't work, and put it on the floor so she could pull it inside. When I gave Chey a second one, and went to Doc's cage to give him one, I didn't see that she'd picked hers up. I asked her if she'd gotten her ice cube, and she opened her mouth and showed me she had the ice. She is such a sweetie! I think she's my favorite of the adults. When I left today, she'd made a bed with hay in the black tub, and was curled up in it.

When it was time to shift Rudi and Kelly into their respective cages for the night, Kelly was sitting in front of the door HE was to go through. The keeper tried to bribe him but he wouldn't budge. She thought he'd just shove Kelly aside. He's generally been going into another cage, so going into this one wasn't that familiar. The keeper kept trying; he kept refusing. He got angry and pounded on the metal door of the cage he thought he should go into, roaring or growling, whatever you call the sounds orangutans make. Needless to say, Kelly fairly raced outside and that cleared the obstacle. Luna doesn't panic anymore when Rudi does this. She just sat and stared, and didn't even come to cling on me. When he got into the cage, he gathered his snacks and went back into the tunnel to eat them. Making a point I guess.

It's really nice to see Luna doing the things that orangutans do. We don't want her to take on human traits. As much as we love her, we do want her to be back in the orangutan community.

September 18, 1998

Luna is one year old. Visitors to the zoo signed a huge card for her.

September 22, 1998

Luna's cage was full of brown paper toweling today. She'd been having a great time with it before I arrived, but the caregiver was holding her when I walked in. She reached out, took my hand, pressed her mouth against it, and gave me a love.

Our supplies have been moved from the bench to the aisle, and put on a rolling cart. Now Luna's cage is an official orangutan cage; no outside equipment. A large black tub full of hay is now on the bench. In reading back through the notes, she was apparently very interested in exploring that area after the supplies were removed. She always had much curiosity about that shelf.

I sat out in the aisle as much as possible today, allowing her to play independently in her cage. I gave her sips of water, snacks, and a drink from a cup without the "sippy" top through the mesh. She ate on the run at her 1 p.m. snack time. Part was eaten as we strolled down the aisle with Kelly following along though all the other cages. She was the only one inside today. We shared a few small bites and some peelings with her.

One time today, Kelly came to the intro door between cage A and B. She had a monkey biscuit which fell through the mesh. She got a newspaper, rolled it up to make a tool, and pulled the biscuit back to her. She is such a clever girl. I gave her sips of juice today too. She was trying to hold a liter coke bottle in such a manner that I could pour the juice into it, but I just poured it into her mouth. Later, when she was eating corn on the cob, she spit little bits through the mesh as Luna and I stood there. I wondered if she was trying to share, but maybe that was wishful thinking. I also gave her an ice cube, and she pushed a kale leaf through the mesh as a trade.

Luna and I spent the better part of an hour exploring cages C through F. She spent an extended time climbing in the squeeze cage. She loved it! She would reach for my hand, but only to use as a prop. In the other cages she held onto my hand probably 90% of the time. Hopefully, she left her scent here and there to help her ease into the orang gang.

The keeper did simultaneous training with Luna and Kelly today. Naturally Luna is a beginner, but she does respond well to "show me your tongue." That is what we say to her when she puts something into her mouth that we need to retrieve. She loved the pudding reward after each command.

The plan remains that Luna be returned to the group at age 18 to 24 months. The keepers seem pleased with her progress.

And, just like the last two or three times I've been there, that little thumb went into the mouth before the 4 p.m. bottle. She was whining loudly when I took the bottle from the warmer, and walked to her cage. I've never heard her carry on so.

September 29, 1998

Today, when I arrived, Luna took my hand and gave me a love as she has done the last several times. She was a bit unhappy about the other caregiver leaving, but she didn't whine.

New arrangement today; spending time in cage B. The plan is to get her used to other cages. We have been encouraged to climb up on the equipment to show her the process. After all, we are mama orangutans. After the Luna Show she seemed like a sleepy girl. I took her with me, and climbed onto the bench at the back of cage B. There was a black tub on the bench with hay, the small hairy mama, and a few toys in it. She sat quietly and played, but "in this new place," held onto me with one hand. I then gave her the hairy mama. She hugged it and fell asleep. I placed her in the tub of hay, crept out of the cage, and sat in the aisle while she had a 20 minute nap. I was concerned she might be anxious when she woke up. However, when I saw her sitting up, she was just looking at me with sleepy eyes. I was planning to climb on the hammock and up to the large props, in my best orangutan form. However, the keeper needed to set up B for the night, so we moved back to A. Next week I hope to climb with her to the top of cage B.

A new PVC jungle gym, thought up by a volunteer and constructed by a high school shop class, was delivered today. Luna loves it! It was out in the service court and she had a blast! She even smiled. I hope the pictures I took turn out.

Today when the evening keeper caregiver came to take over, Luna ran into her kennel and shut the door. ????

October 6, 1998

It was a rainy day and the whole orang gang was inside. I knew there would be no Luna Show as there were no people at the zoo. Therefore, I was in for a fun afternoon interacting with everyone. Since all the cages were occupied, I also knew we would be confined to cage A and the aisle. Her new jungle gym was in the aisle by B and C.

When I first arrived, the caregiver was sitting with Luna on the bench in A. After she left (no separation anxiety today) I took Luna into the aisle to play on the jungle gym. Well, Chey was chasing Doc from B to C and back again. They were also grunting and slapping at each other. Luna kept jumping and holding onto me. She did watch them, but the noise and commotion seemed to frighten her. Therefore, we went back to A, and climbed up on the bench with the stuffed bear. She had her thumb in her mouth so I figured she was sleepy. She grabbed her bear and promptly fell asleep. I eased her down into her crib full of hay. She slept for over an hour, clutching her bear. She slept through the 1 p.m. feeding so it was delayed until 2. She loved the pear and banana, but the sweet potato was shared with Doc and Chey because Luna spit it out.

As she's been doing the last few days about 3:50 p.m., the thumb went into the mouth as she waited for the 4 p.m. bottle. She drank it eagerly while on the new jungle gym in the aisle. Other liquids weren't taken so readily today. The night house was cooler; maybe that was why. She also preferred drinking from an open bottle today, not through the sipper straw. We shared some drinks with the rest of the gang.

I also gave everyone ice cubes today. As she did before, (I'd wondered if it was just a coincidence) Chey opened her mouth and showed me her cube when I asked her if she'd gotten it. I'd put it where she could pull it into the cage. I dropped Doc's directly into his mouth. When I offered Kelly one, she pushed some paper through the mesh for a trade, and opened her mouth. I told her to hold out her hand, which she did, and I dropped one into it. They're all just so smart. I checked with Chey three times, and she always opened her mouth to show me she had her cube.

The BIG EVENT today was I crawled up and sat on the large prop in the center of Luna's cage. She had been climbing wildly at the top of her cage; swinging, dangling upside down etc. I had been sitting on a prop above the bench. Well, I moved to the center prop, mainly to retrieve her 15" long plastic rod which had been up there several weeks. She had pushed it through the mesh covering the skylight, and couldn't figure out how to get it back. When she saw me on the prop, she immediately came over and gave me a love. She did this two or three more times while I was up there. When I gave her the rod, she smelled it from one end to the other, then took it down to the floor and played with it for awhile. I also put the large hairy mama up on a prop in the corner. Luna went right over to it and gave it a love. So all of us orangutans, real and imagined, were up on the props today.

Chey was in the cage next to us. She pulled the black tub over to the intro door, climbed in, lay on her back, just "chilled," and watched the entire goings on. She is so funny; so likeable.

When Luna saw the evening keeper caregiver come into the night house, she Velcroed herself to me. For some reason she doesn't like her. The keeper even said, "She doesn't like me," so this is common knowledge. I'd gone ahead and given Luna her 6 p.m. fruit and vegetable before the keeper came into A. Like last week, she ran into her kennel and peeked out the window. Such a silly girl!

October 13, 1998

As usual, a wonderful day at the zoo. Doc and Chey were inside when I arrived. She was having a nap in cage F. He was in the squeeze cage playing with hay. I moved the PVC jungle gym down to where they were, and Luna began climbing and swinging. She did lead me back to A for awhile. She seemed sleepy, but I didn't encourage that. It was nearly time for her snack and the Luna Show.

Chey woke up and proceeded to "read" a small phone book, carefully turning the pages, staring at each. I told Lynn maybe she was looking for a pizza place number. Lynn said she was probably looking for a date.

I took Luna into B before Lynn cleaned it. There was a bunch of orange paper, appropriate for the Halloween season. I put a piece on my head in my best Kelly impersonation, and sat with Luna while she played. Lynn came in, noticed me, said she wished she had a camera, and expressed her appreciation for my orangutan impersonation. After all, we <u>are</u> trying to remind Luna she is an orangutan.

I shared the peels of her sweet potato and pear with Doc and Chey. When I got the syringe of yogurt, Chey pushed a bamboo branch through the mesh for a handout. I put a dollop of yogurt on it. Doc noticed this, immediately grabbed a branch, and offered it for a dollop too. They are wonderful creatures!

The Luna Show was on an outside stage. Luna was a bit of a sleepy girl and was clingy during the show. There was also the strangeness of the different stage. She sat on the jungle gym, but kept a hand, and sometimes a foot, on me. It was a small crowd, but I always enjoy watching the faces. They are faces of wonderment about this little girl.

After the show, the sleepy girl stuck her thumb in her mouth and fell asleep on my lap, snuggled up with a small surrogate. I laid her in her crib and she slept about 30 minutes. After her nap, I spent an hour with her on the high prop in A. We had some brown paper toweling to play with. I kept putting it on my head, and she would interrupt her climbing to come take it away. She did give me a love when I got up there, just like last week. She went down to the floor and retrieved a piece of kale, brought it up and sat on the prop next to me, munching away. So I got some hay and pretended to be eating it through my mask. Two orangutans having a snack. She took the hay away from me with <u>her</u> mouth from <u>my</u> mouth.

She drank her bottle while climbing on the PVC jungle gym, leaving 10cc which I gave to Doc. I also gave Doc and Chey ice cubes again today. They love those!

Late this afternoon, Chey was building her nest in a black tub as usual. She had hay in it and was sitting in it, slowly tearing pages from a large phone book, and squishing them into the tub.

Meanwhile Doc had two black tubs, and was playing a game all by himself. He was sitting in one with the other one on his head, holding onto the one he was sitting in and rolling about. Then he stacked them together, and was rolling about the floor, while wearing them on his head.

October 20, 1998

Today Kelly was the adult inside. It was a bit of a nasty day, weather-wise, and I was hoping they'd <u>all</u> be inside. I took some National Geographic magazines for Chey to "read," but gave one to Luna, one to Kelly, and put the others in for Doc and Chey to enjoy later. Kelly and Luna had fun with them. They sniffed the pages, Kelly turning hers slowly like she WAS reading, but also tearing pages to roll up and use as tools to beg for handouts.

Luna and I spent a lot of time in cages B, C, and D. She did NOT want to be alone in those cages, whining loudly if I tried to leave her, so we stayed together. I climbed up onto the props in B and C. Not too much to climb on in D. Luna came to give me a love when I got to the high prop in B. She played a little game in that cage. She would slide down the hammock, looking back over her head at me. She did this several times. She's not too sure about grasping those four inch props. Her little hands are not quite big enough.

She didn't play too much on the PVC jungle gym, mostly wanting to play in her cage. She played independently in there. She had a great time free falling into the crib of hay. She also pulled her chair into the crib, right on top of her, of course.

The Luna Show was on the outdoor stage. She was clingy like last week, but let go of me towards the end. Right after the show, the thumb was in the mouth, the sleepy face came on, and she snuggled with a surrogate for a 20 minute power nap. In reading the notes, I noticed the daytime naps are almost non-existent now. However, she's going to bed about 7:30 each night.

Some new forage foods have been added. Today I tried to give her corn flakes, but NO WAY. So I gave them to Kelly. They were soggy with milk when I gave them to Kelly. She passed me a saltine wrapper to put them in before handing them back to her. Some slipped into a space in the cage door, but clever Kelly used her two index fingers to pull them out.

When Luna and I were sitting on the floor playing with magazines in front of Kelly, she kept pushing a large piece of cardboard out wanting a treat. I tried giving her a page of a magazine, but she quickly tossed that aside. I just kept giving her ice cubes.

There were two birds in the night house late this afternoon, enjoying snacking on the gang's snacks. They worried Luna so much. She really seemed frightened by them. They'd hop about, and she'd hop onto my lap, grab my hand, and get a frown on that sweet face. What a wimp!

Again, at 3:45 p.m., the thumb was in the mouth anticipating the 4 p.m. formula.

Another great day in the world of primates. Oh, how I love this job.

By the way, Luna now weighs 15 pounds.

October 27, 1998

All of the orang gang was in today due to a power outage earlier, disabling the hydraulic doors. I chatted with all of them, and gave ice to Chey and Doc. I also gave Chey an American Express catalog to browse through so she could select something for Christmas. She seemed to enjoy it, staring thoughtfully at the different pages, especially the jewelry. I also gave a catalog to Doc; he wasn't interested. After all, men don't like to shop. Luna and Kelly looked at theirs. Kelly rolled her pages up and stuck them in the mesh.

Luna was very independent, playing on her own in cage A most of the day. I gave her a medium size paper bag. She put it on her head and played with it quite a long time. She's on a new feeding schedule since the time change. Now I get to think of innovative ways to get her to eat rice cereal. When it was time to give her cereal this afternoon, I put dollops of cereal on a scrap of the bag. She licked them off. We were in the aisle in front of Kelly. Of course she was going nuts passing out cardboard pieces for me to put cereal on. Luna tired of eating and headed back to A. Therefore, I decided to roll up scraps of the bag, in my best Kelly fashion, and hand them through the mesh with a dollop of cereal on the end. Luna ate two servings that way; then was full. But at least she ate half her cereal.

The sweet potato was not cooked enough and she refused it. The others were only too happy to have it.

There were two Luna Shows today, at 2 and 4 p.m. She was very active during both, and there was quite a good crowd. We rode to the shows in an open cart, attracting lots of attention.

I got arboreal only once today. Luna was too busy playing with a cardboard box on the floor of her cage. It was lonely at the top.

At 5 p.m., the whining began, the thumb went into the mouth, and it was time to heat the bottle. She drank it immediately.

I checked on my other orang buddies before leaving. Chey was in the black tub with a few papers on the bottom, and a brown bag on her head. Guess it was bedtime. The others were still finishing their dinners. The time changed three days ago, so they are now probably getting ready to settle in earlier at night.

Luna now weighs 16 pounds.

November 3, 1998

Today Chey and Doc were the adults inside; my favorites. Luna was a bit of a "cling-on." She did have a great time in the squeeze cage. I tied a stretchy rag to the top of it and she had a ball, swinging wildly, climbing up the rag etc. For awhile she went back to cage A. She played quietly on the floor with some activity on her PVC jungle gym. Her bamboo jungle gym was dismantled. The PVC one was put into Cage A. She can swing with much more abandon on this one. She did a cute thing today. She was sitting on the floor, back to the wall. She would stand up with her arms going straight up the wall. Then she would slide back down to a sitting position. She repeated this several times. I think she was just scratching her back.

Once again the yam was not taken with any enthusiasm; she only ate half. The pear was not a problem. I gave Chey and Doc the yam. It fell into the space between the mesh screens on the intro door between A and B. Doc and Chey had to work diligently to get the pieces out. Chey made a paper tool; that didn't work. I gave her a bamboo twig, but that wasn't too effective either. Then I gave her a cardboard tube and that helped. They got all but one piece out. We went to the Luna Show and didn't see how they did it.

Right after the show Luna seemed sleepy, sucking her thumb while sitting on my lap. The moment passed and she carried on. However, she was clingy the rest of the day, and I could not leave her alone in cage A. She would whine loudly if I started to leave. She also wanted to have a hold on me with a foot or hand most of the time.

Since I was quite successful with the rice cereal last week, I thought I could be innovative today. Ha! She was not at all interested. She probably took in just one tablespoon of cereal mixed with all of the milk from a glass. I put cereal on paper, in a plastic container she'd been playing with, and around the neck of a milk jug she'd also played with. By the time the "meal" was over, it looked like we'd had a food fight. It was all over the floor, on her face, head, and some on her legs. Well at least she was hungry for the 5 p.m. bottle. Chey and Doc were quite happy she didn't want her cereal. Doc grabbed a sack and shoved it out for me to put cereal on, but Chey just made raspberry noises and opened her mouth.

Today Lynn brought in a little paper fan with bright animal pictures on it. It absolutely terrified Luna. She would literally run when I showed it to her. Doc loved being fanned with it, as did Chey. Luna is still quite a little wimp.

I gave Chey a limo magazine today. She climbed into the hammock in B and browsed through it. When she was shifted to E and F, she took it with her. After her snack, she was looking through it one page at a time. She laid it on the threshold between E and F, sat in E, and thumbed through it. She is so funny! Another thing about her was the way she ate a piece of raw pumpkin. She took mouthfuls of the stringy pulp with the seeds, ate the good "stuff" from the seeds, and proceeded to spit them out, one at a time, into a pile in front of the cage. She went to bed at 4 p.m. She put hay into her black tub and climbed in. When the keeper passed out bananas, she just reached for hers and ate it in bed. She got up for a small sip of juice, and jumped back into the hay. She continues to amaze me.

Doc made his bed from hay and a phone book. When he was shifted to D, he grabbed the hay from C, Rudi's cage, and took it with him. I guess Rudi's long hair will be padding enough.

As Luna was snuggling on my lap today, and later in my arms, I couldn't help but think this will end all too soon. It'll be so good when she is able to join the community, but we are going to miss taking care of her.

It was quite dark when I left the zoo. I'd better start taking a flashlight. It was rather scary walking to my car.

November 10, 1998

Well. Luna has an injury. The rolling cart flipped over on November 7, and pinned her left arm underneath it. Nothing is broken; it's a soft tissue injury. She is favoring it only slightly; using it but not putting her full weight on it. She's taking grape flavored liquid Tylenol with no problem. She thinks it's yummy.

According to the notes, Doc was very concerned when it happened. The caregiver said he was trying to open his door, and fiddling with the padlocks. I guess Luna let out quite a scream and kept whining. After she was quieted, the caregiver took her to Doc's cage to show him she was okay. Chey didn't pay much attention to the commotion. She was in a "nest" in the squeeze cage. However, the adults outside banged on the metal door when they heard the scream.

Today I was arboreal with Luna for awhile in cage A. We now put all of the pieces of fruit and vegetables out at once. That way she can pick and choose. She quickly chose the pear, but had just a tiny bite of the sweet potato. Naturally, she gobbled the yogurt when that was offered.

We played in cage B for about an hour. I sat up on the prop. I'd draped a sheet over it which served two purposes. It was a toy, and I sat under it avoiding the cold air from the vent. Then I stretched out in the hammock in B, and just watched Luna as she played with the sheet and climbed. At one point she came down and sat on my lap for about 10 minutes, chewing a piece of hay. These are the moments I realize how much I will miss the cuddles when she is back in with the gang, and we are no longer her mommies. She is so sweet! She let me give her a long hug today, just snuggled up to me. She also had lots of smiles.

When it was time for the cereal I tried several methods; a dollop on a rolled up paper (Kelly style), a smear of cereal on the neck of a bottle, and a dollop on the floor mixed with apple juice, which she loves. With that one she managed to lick up the apple juice and leave the cereal. I even put some on a syringe that I use to give her yogurt. Before her cereal she had been drinking from Kelly's cup. So I liquefied the cereal and put it in the cup. The first swallow also had some apple juice in it. She consumed about half the cereal that way. Then she was full, and kept turning her head from side to side as I offered it, just like a human kid.

Luna had some Gatorade popsicles today. The keeper brought us four and Luna had about 1 ½. Kelly gladly had the rest. Luna's mostly melted and was licked off the floor. She was a bit of a sticky baby after that.

When I offered Kelly the sweet potato skin, she put a piece of hay through the mesh. I took it, thanked her, and asked her to hold out her hand. Later, when I gave her the sweet potato pieces, she rolled up a page from a book and presented it through the mesh as a dish.

The keeper said she was telling Lynn, in Kelly's presence, there was no hay for their cages. Then, when Kelly was shifted to C from B, she took her tub full of hay with her. Hmmmm........taking no chances I guess. She made her nest in the tub, and was in it by 5 p.m. I took photos and hope they turn out.

Luna was settled in her kennel by 6 p.m. Kelly and Chey were also down for the night. Doc and Rudi were still finishing their snacks when the zookeeper and I left at the same time.

November 17, 1998

Well, the injury from 10 days ago is history. Luna seemed 100%. She is getting more and more independent, and that's the way it's supposed to be. When I first got there today, cages B, C, and the tunnel between them, were open for our exploring pleasure. We stayed mostly in C. I sat on the hammock while Luna climbed. I tried to get her to eat in there, creating a buffet of two pieces of yam and two pieces of pear on the bench. She suddenly became a cling-on, and would have no part of it, other than a sniff. So it became a moveable feast relocated to the bench in A, and she ate everything. I did get her to take her yogurt through the mesh while in cage B.

Oh, great! The feeding schedule has changed, and Luna now gets 6 tablespoons of rice cereal on my shift. It was a big enough challenge to get her to eat 4 tablespoons. Well, I tried all the tricks to get her to eat it. She finally drank some of it from a glass, after I mixed it with juice. I'd tried that before, giving it to her in a glass of juice, but she'd refused it, moving her head back and forth. She also took bites from a spoon while I held her. She probably ended up eating about half of it. Of course Doc and Chey, the adults inside today, were making all kinds of gestures and sounds while I was trying to get Luna to eat. They were letting me know they liked rice cereal; just bring it on!

I gave Chey a Target catalog to browse through, and she really seemed to enjoy it. At first she turned each page with her mouth. She actually worked on making sure it was one page at a time. If two stuck together, she would deliberately work to get the pages apart. She also put it on the threshold between the cages, and thumbed through it, spending about 30 to 45 minutes with it. When she was given her monkey biscuits, she put them in her water bowl. In other words, she dunked them to soften them up. Amazing! She made her bed at 4:30 with a cardboard box and some catalog pages squished into her black tub. Before I left, she moved her bed from one cage to another, rearranged the cardboard, and went to bed.

Doc made his bed with hay in a black tub. He had a paper bag and put it over his head.

When I left, Luna was climbing on her jungle gym, in the dark. I'd tried to get her to stay in her kennel, but she wasn't yet ready to go to sleep.

November 24, 1998

Another big step in Luna's trip towards independence today. Tonight her kennel is to be left open, and she can choose to sleep in there or somewhere else in cage A.

Kelly was the only adult inside today. The keeper felt sorry for her because she had no one to play with. So she played tug-o-war with her using a magazine. Kelly is so strong she was barely holding it, and the keeper was pulling like crazy. She also did some training with her. Kelly liked that, especially because baby food was the reward. She had her go through the exam routine; presenting her tummy, her chest, her nipple, and peeing into a cup. It's amazing. The keeper put Rice Krispies in bark shavings in a cage, and when Kelly shifted to that cage, she was busy foraging for a long time.

There were a lot of people at the Luna Show today. We had to ride there in an open golf cart, and Luna seemed to like that with so many things to look at. Of course everyone noticed her and made remarks. I'm always so proud to be the one sitting there holding her.

She was very active on her jungle gym today. She even took some of it apart, and it was a challenge figuring out how it went back together. I was only arboreal with her a couple of times, and I did take some pictures up there. I also had to untie a shirt from up high so we could remove it for the night.

I stayed out of her cage most of the shift. About 4 p.m., after I fixed her jungle gym, she whined when I tried to leave the cage. She'd whine, cling to me, and then go to the door. I finally figured out she wanted to go into the aisle. She had fun climbing on the metal shelves, and especially wanted to get up to the one that holds things she can't have.

I worried about how I was going to convince her to eat her cereal today. No problem! She was hungry and cereal was just what she wanted. In fact she was pulling my hand with the spoon to her mouth, and ate all but one bite.

At 5 p.m. she had her bottle. As instructed, I removed the bottles and locked her in cage A. I sat in the dark watching her. She climbed, took the soft blankets out of her kennel, took big hairy mama out of the crib of hay etc. At 5:45 she went into her kennel and closed the door; I think. As it was dark, it was hard to see. There was not a peep after that, and I left the night house at 5:50.

Kelly was already asleep in a tub of hay on the bench. Chey was sitting in her black tub, piling in hay to make her bed, and Doc and Rudi were still munching.

I'll be with Luna again in 3 days. I'm filling in for someone.

November 27, 1998

Well, today was my bonus day. Apparently, she was very distressed last night when the caregiver tried to lock her in her cage, so today we have a new plan. I kept her out of A except for about 30 minutes; the idea being to have A be a "new place" when it was time to lock her up. She played in the aisle in front of Doc and Chey on the bamboo jungle gym we brought inside. We also explored B, C, and the tunnel.

She ate everything in sight today. I figured that would help her go to bed more easily too. She even licked her bowl clean after the cereal was gone.

At 5 p.m. I put her in her cage and locked the bolts. She whined so I gave her two cheerios while I warmed her bottle. I then put her formula in a Sippy cup as they don't want her to have a bottle with a nipple (hazard) in with her at night. I gave her two sips through the mesh before going in and giving her the cup. She immediately became clingy, and wanted to leave the cage with me. I distracted her onto the jungle gym and left the cage. She whined but not frantically. She went to the back of the cage, threw the cup down, and proceeded to pull all of the bedding out of the kennel. She put it into the crib of hay. The whining had stopped. The keeper came in to bring Rudi and Kelly in from outside. Luna came to the front of her cage, and the keeper gave her some juice. I gave her a piece of banana and then locked her cage. She went back to the rear of the cage, removed the bone shaped pillow from her kennel, and snuggled into the crib of hay with all of her bedding. Not another peep out of her and I left the building.

I had a magazine for Chey and, as usual, she enjoyed it. Lynn gave her and Doc monkey biscuits. Chey gathered as many as she could, and poor Doc missed out. Lynn gave him a few more in another cage. Chey is a greedy gut. They were given clothes to play with today. First Chey stuffed a pair of sweatpants with hay. Later she threw an apron around her shoulders. Then when she was making her bed (today she just piled hay in the tunnel between B and C) she kept trying on a purple skirt. She is so funny! Doc ripped his clothes and material. He kept threading bits through the mesh. He also had a rubber toy with slots, and threaded material through that too. He was put into cage B for the night; a first for him. He likes Luna, and Lynn thought it would be a good idea to put him there.

December 1, 1998

Luna was a wild child today. I kept her out of her cage until 4:30 p.m. except for a few minutes. She made a nest today with paper toweling, newspapers, and PVC pieces. She wadded the paper, and arranged things very much like the adult orangutans. She also kept trying to climb to the top of the metal shelves to grab things she shouldn't. She played wildly on the portable jungle gym in the aisle. Several times she took off on her own when it was time to change activities. She didn't want to be in her cage at all. Cereal time was not easy. She ate on the run. I put cereal on toys, the floor, and also just spoon fed her. After about 2/3 was gone she took off for the jungle gym, and would not eat any more. Then about 10 minutes later, she let me feed it to her while she was climbing. Only about a tablespoon was left.

She's back to having a bottle at 5 p.m., so I took it into her cage, gave it to her, and sat down quietly. She guzzled it while hanging on a piece of bamboo. As soon as she finished she took hold of me like, "I know you're going to lock me in here and I don't like it." So I took her with me to get a piece of banana. We then went back into A. I placed the banana on a shelf and left the cage. She focused on that and no whining. I locked her in, pushed in another piece of banana, and threw cheerios in for forage food. After she ate the banana, she climbed into the crib of hay with the bedding from the kennel, and not another peep out of her.

When the keeper let Rudi and Kelly in, Rudi made his usual grand entrance, vocalizing and throwing things about his cage, but Luna didn't budge. All the lights were turned out, and the only sounds were Rudi and Kelly munching on their veggies.

Chey went to bed at 3:30 p.m., lining her tub with newspapers after "reading" them.

Chey and Doc had a big box to play with today. Chey wore it for awhile, walking around in it. Doc's game involved sitting in the box, under and hanging onto a dangling piece of fire hose, and spinning around in it.

The orangutans have active libidos. Chey and Rudi are hybrids, with both Bornean and Sumatran genes) and have been sterilized. The keeper said Rudi likes having his nipple touched, sometimes inserting a piece of straw into it, and wanting someone to pull it out. She also said Chey loves Rudi. One day she let Chey and Doc out through the door at one end of the night house. She then opened the door at the other end of the night house so Rudi could go out. However, as Rudi was walking toward the door, Chey rushed in, pushed him down, and proceed to perform oral sex. Doc was behind her, and he left when he saw what was happening. The keeper also left the building, allowing them some privacy, and returned 30 minutes later. She then showed me what Doc does when given a plastic glove. He bit the fingers off and put them on, one at a time, as a condom. He seemed to be thoroughly enjoying himself.

It's a silly, silly group but so much fun. I'm learning a lot.

December 8, 1998

It was a cold day today, only 50 degrees. I wore a sweatshirt and jeans. All of the adults were inside when I got there because the moat in the exhibit was being fixed. Rudi and Kelly were let out about 1:30 p.m. Before she went out Kelly peed into a cup for Lynn. She is so smart!

When I first got to the zoo Chey and Doc were separate. Chey was busy playing with a box and looking at a phone book. (She's still trying to find a date.) Actually, Doc was playing with a phone book too. He was leafing through it, but then just started acting silly, wadding it up and throwing it about. After he and Chey were put together they wrestled a lot. Later, Chey was leafing through an energy magazine, probably from the world energy conference held recently in Houston. It was fun watching her. Every little bit, as she was thumbing through it, she would touch her head, like she was scratching it. Maybe she just couldn't figure it out. I did notice she paused to look at the pictures in the book.

Luna and I played a lot in the squeeze cage. It was blanketed with hay and I sat in there with her. She'd climb and swing from the top, then jump down and charge into my leg, trying to bite through my jeans at times. I'd roll her over and wrestle with her. She repeated this over and over with her play face on. Had a little game going!

She was a bit clingy in that she was constantly reaching for my hand to lead her to the next activity, only venturing on her own a few times.

Cereal time went well. She was hungry and ate every bite.

She seems to know the last bottle means we're going to leave her alone soon. When I took the bottle from the cooler she became a cling-on. I put her in the crib of hay with her bottle, and she got out and sat near me. Then she climbed awhile, sat near me, climbed again, sat near me again, but did not drink her formula. She finally drank it at 5:40 p.m., but when I reached for the empty bottle, she Velcro-ed herself to me. So we fetched pieces of banana together. I put one piece in her cage where she had to let go and go get it. I left and locked the door. She looked so pitiful sitting there by a tubful of surrogates, hanging onto one. I pointed out where I put the other piece and her cheerios, and turned out the lights. I left the night house at 5:55 p.m. as instructed.

I didn't hear a sound and couldn't see her anywhere. (I was peeking with my flashlight.) She may have gone into her kennel.

Today Lynn did "Luna one on ones" with Chey and Doc. Of course Miss Libido Chey wanted to check out Luna's genitals. Doc just poked her here and there with his fingers. He had his play face on. I'd never seen that. He seems to be very interested in Luna. Luna nibbled on his fingers.

I also observed Lynn teaching Chey and Doc a new behavior; brushing their teeth.

It was another fun day at the zoo.

December 15, 1998

Luna was a bit clingy today, wanting to hold my hand a lot. I think she was cold during the Luna Show. It was 62 degrees and sunny, but the stage was shaded. She spent the whole show huddled on the stage floor in the jungle gym. Toward the end of the show, her thumb was in her mouth. I kept her out of her cage all day except for brief moments when I needed to do something without her help. She played a lot on the shelves, and built a good nest next to them. Doc demonstrated sitting in a box. I gave Luna a box her size in front of Doc, but she didn't learn the lesson.

She absolutely would not eat her cereal for me. I tried every trick in the book. She tried to enter cage A during cereal time. When she's in her cage and doesn't want her cereal, she heads to the skylight so we can't reach her. She didn't eat the cereal this morning either.

When it was time for her 5 p.m. formula, I placed her with the bottle in her crib of hay. However, she promptly came with the bottle to where I was seated on the floor, sat on my feet, and leaned against my shins. When she was finished, she let me take the bottle, but squealed loudly and Velcro-ed to me. So I took her with me to get her banana slices. When I placed one in her cage where she'd have to get off of me to get it, she raced to it, grabbed it, and then wrapped herself around my leg. I took it away from her and threw it farther away. I retreated and locked her in the cage. She didn't cry. Victory! I then tossed in the other piece of banana and the cheerios for foraging. She roamed around her cage, went in and out of her kennel, but was not unhappy. She'd almost fallen asleep after the Luna Show, so I knew she was a tired wee soul. She finally got into the crib of hay with her bone pillow and blanket, and settled down for the night.

Doc and Chey were the adults inside today. I gave Chey a new magazine to enjoy, which she did. I hope my photos of her looking at magazines turn out.

The adults had packing straw for bedding today. At first they carried all of it to the tunnel. The keeper had to redistribute it when it was time to separate everyone into his/her cage for the night. Doc carried a clump of it around all day. Maybe he was afraid there wouldn't be any for his bed. At one point he was tossing hay up in the air in the tunnel. Of course Chey used her packing straw to make a bed in the black tub, and was in it by 4:30 p.m. Doc went to great lengths fixing his bed with hay, straw, and paper toweling. The keeper said Doc was macho today. He kept poking Chey when she was sitting on the bench under a blanket.

When the keeper did training today, she did Chey first. Then when it was time for Doc, Chey raced to sit right beside him, hoping to do more training and get the baby food reward. Chey always dominates but Doc didn't force the issue. The keeper just enticed Doc to go elsewhere for his training.

Today I brought the calendar of Luna that I had ordered and some Christmas goodies for the primate party tomorrow. I hope they like it.

I'm going to work again Saturday morning, and also in the morning on January 1. Working mornings will be a new experience, and I'm looking forward to it.

December 19, 1998

A new experience; working the morning shift. I learned it was my job to mix the formula, draw up the yogurt, gather stuff into the cooler etc.

Luna was awake, climbing on the jungle gym, when I went in. She drained her bottle of formula right away. We went out on the exhibit, but the grass and equipment were wet. So FORGET IT! After 20 minutes of her being a cling-on, we went back inside.

Kelly and Rudi were sent outside. Kelly was asked to pee in a cup before she left. That just amazes me; not only being able to produce a specimen on demand, but also her accuracy in a 2 inch cup.

Mornings are busy with lots of food to squeeze in: fruits, veggies, cereal, monkey biscuit, juice, formula, kale....... She didn't eat her cereal, but ate the banana bits I mashed into it. She actually managed to eat the banana and spit out any cereal attached to it. As usual, Doc and Chey were glad to finish the cereal.

I wore a sweatshirt with an armadillo on the front which frightened Luna at first. She then took swipes at it.

They did training. Doc is very apprehensive about the "show me your arm" test. He doesn't like those shots. Chey let the keeper touch her tummy which she doesn't usually do.

Chey had a bed sheet she was trying to fill with paper. She did quite well, but the shredded paper fell out easily. I gave her a T-shirt which worked much better.

Doc was doing his usual bit of threading strips of material through the mesh and pulling on it. Then at one point, he stacked all the red pails together, took them to a corner, and constructed a fort around himself.

December 22, 1998

It was a cold day today so all of the orangs were inside. Just as I arrived the keeper had separated Doc and Chey because their play was getting rough. They were attempting to amuse themselves. Chey had some material and a knitted blanket. For a brief while she just rested in her black tub with the blanket lining it. Doc was contemplating his body parts. Both of them watched Luna when she was close by, and Chey made sounds at her.

Kelly had a bright chartreuse blanket to amuse her. She put it into a tub of hay, and had a nap up on the bench. Then she threw the tub down, and just sat there under the blanket. When I called her name, she'd peek out. There was a hole in the blanket, and for awhile, she just sat there looking out through it.

Shortly after I arrived, Rudi came to the front of his cage as I was standing nearby. When I turned to acknowledge him, he opened his mouth, showing me he had coins. I'd forgotten they said he brings in coins that people toss into the exhibit. I realized he wanted to make a trade so I offered him a monkey biscuit. He spit a quarter out at me. Then he produced a dime when I gave him a second biscuit. The keeper said he'd given her a quarter earlier. Another keeper came in and said he gave her $1.35 yesterday after she gave him a Popsicle. Later he put a sheet over his head and shoulders, and looked like a sheik sitting there.

They all wanted Luna's leftover cereal. Kelly shoved a box out, Rudi rolled up a brown bag and gave it to me, Doc slid his vegetable bag out, and Chey just opened her mouth.

They said wee Luna had diarrhea this morning. This afternoon she had several stools, but they weren't loose. We were pushing fluids. She didn't want water, but did drink 18 ounces of Gatorade. She ate half her cereal after I added Gatorade to it. She was also somewhat subdued today. She played here, there, and everywhere, but it was generally quiet play. She was also a bit clingy. When we played near Rudi, she'd grab me if he moved, and watched him very closely.

When it was time for the 5 p.m. bottle, she did not drink it. She played with it for 30 minutes while hanging onto me. She didn't even eat the "separation" banana. When I left at 5:45 p.m. she was in her kennel, but not asleep.

Chey was in a tub of hay, Doc was still constructing his bed, Kelly was in a tub of hay covered with her blanket, and Rudi was lying on his back just staring at the ceiling.

December 29, 1998

Well, I really scored at Christmas. I got the book on primates I wanted, a video about orangutans, an album for my Luna photos, a wildlife calendar with an orangutan mom and baby on the cover and inside, and a stuffed orangutan. My friends and family know how much I love this non-paying job.

Today Luna and I spent most of our time in the squeeze cage and cages D, E, and F. She actually played on the tires in E and F. I've tried to get her to play on them in the past, but no luck. She ate most of her cereal while hanging upside down in the squeeze cage. How can she do that?

The keeper said they are going to have a meeting about keeping her out of the aisle. She is so quick, plus she is getting into things she shouldn't. We'd be able to take items into the adult cages for her to play with. I am glad this may come about. She has to be watched so closely in the aisle.

There was a huge crowd at the Luna Show; the biggest I've seen. Luna climbed and mugged for the crowd. It was a beautiful sunny day and about 70 degrees; a perfect day to go to the zoo.

Luna would not drink water today. When I gave it to her in a cup, she'd fill her mouth and then spit it out. Kelly's daughter for sure. She took a few sips from a large plastic soda bottle. I then saturated a rag like we did in the summer, and she sucked on it. She rewarded my efforts by peeing on my sock while sitting on my foot.

She was great about her p.m. bottle. As the bottle was warming, I was in A with her. She was swatting at a bug on the floor. She then picked it up and put it into her mouth. She started squealing like crazy and climbing wildly. The bug must have been bitter or something. We went together to get her bottle. I placed her in the crib of hay, and she drank it right away. Then I was able to leave her cage - ALONE- to get her banana. I went back inside, took her bottle, and placed the banana on the edge of the crib. I left, locked her in, and not a peep out of her. She stayed in the crib awhile, then climbed into her kennel and went to sleep. Not a sound out of her by 5:45 p.m.

Chey and Doc were inside today. Doc's birthday was Christmas day. He was 14. According to the Luna notes, all of the orangs got Christmas stockings with goodies. I would have loved to have been there for that.

Chey had some magazines and catalogues she was enjoying today. I think she's trying to find something in her size. Doc was playing with a strip of material as usual, weaving it through the mesh and pulling on it. I took a couple of pictures of him sitting in a hammock. He even put on his play face.

When it was bedtime today, Chey took the hay out of her tub, and made her bed with a big woolly blanket. The keeper said they hadn't been using much hay for bedding since they've been giving them blankets.

January 1, 1999

Happy New Year!

Today I took another caregiver's place on the Friday morning shift. Luna was just coming out of her kennel when we entered the night house at 7:40 a.m. She squeaked when she saw the bottle, grabbed it, and drank it quickly. After she was finished she gave me a sniff and a kiss. Interesting priorities today.

All of the orang gang stayed inside until 11 a.m. There were intermittent showers; well actually downpours at times. I took Luna outside during one break, but the exhibit was so wet she Velcro-ed herself to me. She played in the tunnel for a couple of hours. The door to the outside was open. She had a long bamboo branch, a surrogate, a sheet, and a wet rag to suck on, so she was a happy camper. She played ghost with the sheet. Chey and Doc were in the cages adjoining the tunnel. I'd given Chey a new AAA tour book, and she was busy with that for awhile. However, when Luna managed to poke the branch through the mesh where Chey could see it, she became interested in what Luna was doing. She pushed an unraveled wrapping paper tube towards us. When we were playing with the sheet, Doc came over to watch too. I fed Luna her rice cereal in front of them. I hoped the fact they were both pushing cardboard out under the mesh for handouts would inspire her to eat her cereal just because they couldn't. Luna is generally pleased when the adults want her cereal. I made a big production of having her watch me pour apple juice into the cereal. That worked. She ate ¾ of it.

When all adults but Kelly went out, we had cages D, E, F, and the squeeze cage to play in. She had a blast! Lynn put all of the blankets, buckets, traffic cones, and clean cardboard from the 3 cages into the squeeze cage. I tied a sheet from the top of the squeeze to the tire chain in cage E. I also tied a cloth to the top of the squeeze so she could swing from that. And I tied a knotted sheet between the mesh and the tire in cage F. She played and played in the squeeze. Then I got her into F. She started playing on the mesh, and I managed to leave, shut her in, and NO WHINING! I watched from out front. When my relief came she fed her some soaked monkey biscuits for lunch, and I exited.

I didn't see it, but Lynn said Kelly was standing on her head in cage C while she was on the phone nearby. Good attention getter.

January 5, 1999

A cold day today so no Luna Shows. The tunnel door was open to the outside so Doc, Chey, and Rudi could go in and out. Kelly was in cages E and F. Rudi held court most of the day in the tunnel, but Doc and Chey wandered in and out. Kelly had a long rest in a tub of hay, and then spent a great deal of time organizing, reorganizing, and disorganizing her cage. What a mess!

Luna was a bit clingy. I tried to leave her alone in cage B with a bunch of enrichment articles that I brought from home. In my pre-orangutan days, these items were known as trash; cereal boxes, mouthwash bottles, orange juice cartons, and such. She played with them a bit, but needed one hand on me. At one point I did back out of the cage, and she whined halfheartedly. Chey plastered herself to the tunnel mesh to observe. Then Luna started sucking her thumb, which she does at stress times, so I went back in. I climbed upon the bench, but she was not happy about that either. She whined and came toward me, reaching for my hand. At this point we went back to the squeeze cage where we'd been earlier. She played independently in there while I sat just outside. I'd tied a silky cloth to the top and she really seemed to enjoy swinging on that. She did stop briefly to watch Kelly rearranging her things. Earlier, when we were in the squeeze together, she tried to get me involved in her games; had her play face on. She ate her lunch in the squeeze. She fed herself her yogurt, pushing the plunger of the syringe. She also ate her cereal eagerly today. We no longer put any monkey biscuit powder in it. She licked the bowl clean.

Bedtime was easy. She drank her bottle in the crib. Then I took the bottle, gave her the banana, and left. Not a peep out of her. When I left the night house 30 minutes later, she was in her kennel with the door closed. She was a tired girl.

It was fun watching the interaction of Doc, Chey, and Rudi today. Doc and Rudi wrestled some, but Doc was outside a lot. Rudi, as stated earlier, held court most of the day in the tunnel. At one point he was examining his chin, or throat pouch, or something, and Chey was in his face watching. Then Doc came in to have a look too. I went to offer a snack, planning to give it to Chey, but she deferred to Rudi. After all, he is the dominant one. He ate the snack off the paper (monkey biscuit mixed with formula) and then Chey licked the paper. I wasn't able to give any just to her. Doc wanted a treat, but knew he was out of luck. Later I did give him Luna's leftover soggy monkey biscuit, but he looked at Rudi anxiously before he took it. Then when I went to give Chey the skin from Luna's bedtime banana, she looked around to see if Rudi was there. It seems she's only dominant when she's determined to have a sexual encounter with him.

Some idiot zoo visitor threw a lipstick into the exhibit. Chey was in the tunnel when I noticed she had it. She gave it up for a cracker. Later she had what appeared to be foil in her mouth. When the last bit was spit out, I noticed it was a dime wrapped in foil. She spit it through the mesh, and then worked hard to retrieve it with a paper tool. She also worked diligently to get some cereal she saw on the floor, using a twig.

January 12, 1999

I wore a sweatshirt with Dalmatians on it today. When Luna greeted me she gave them a good sniff.

Cages B and C, connected by the tunnel, were open to us through half the shift. In C, I got on the second highest prop, hoping Luna would climb up there with me. She did use my legs and arms to climb, finally wanting me to give her a pull up. Then of course when she got up there, she wanted down. She's so small she's probably not secure on the large props and the fire hose ropes.

We also played tag. She would follow me through the cages or the tunnel, OR come find me and grab my legs. She had lots of play faces on while doing all of this activity. When she did a poop in C, I needed to go back through the tunnel and B to get a paper towel. (C and the tunnel door were padlocked). I was afraid she'd really whine when I left her, and saw I was completely out of the cages, but she didn't. I talked to her the whole time, got her juice, and gave her a drink through the mesh of the tunnel. I was pleased she was able to be shut away in those less familiar cages for awhile, and not protest. At other times in our play today, she did have one hand gripping my shirt or my hand.

I gave her the cereal with banana through the mesh of A. She ate it eagerly, taking a bite then swinging away, and taking another bite and swinging away. The American way – eat on the run!

Chey and Doc were inside today. I gave them a shirt and a pair of trousers to play with. I thought Chey might stuff the clothing with hay, but she didn't. They did have fun tearing it to pieces. I also gave Chey the hockey team media guide. I thought she might like to pick a hockey player to swoon over. The keeper gave her a blanket for her bed. By 4 p.m. she'd arranged it in her black tub, along with remnants of a cardboard box, and was sitting in it "reading" the guide. It looked very funny and I took a photo. Meanwhile Doc was in the remains of a box in the tunnel.

I also noticed Chey sitting on a hard hat tinkling. (She always uses the moat or a basin or the water bowl. She is such a tidy lady.) Afterwards, she appeared to take a sip. YIKES! There's that 3% of the DNA we don't share. Oh well, in the wild if there is no water, they do drink their urine.

The keeper locked all of the cages at 3 p.m. so I returned Luna to A, and she played there without complaints the rest of the afternoon. I joined her for a short while, but she is very good about amusing herself in A.

She pulled all the bedding out of her kennel at 4 p.m., so I had to get all of that set up again. She would not drink her bottle tonight, only taking about 20 cc. She discovered the nipple was great for stimulating her genitals, however. She squeaked a little after she was locked in, but went into her kennel at 5:50 p.m. She did check the cage padlock first to see if she could pick the lock.

Luna has her very own stainless steel cup now, just like the big orangutans. She also has her own little hook to hang it on in the kitchen.

January 19. 1999

Well, Luna is now 16 months old.

Kelly was inside today. I didn't interact with her much. At one point she was in a tub of hay up on the bench, covered with a cloth of some sort. I spoke to her, she peered out at me, and then covered her face again. Later on, I did give her a banana peel and a left over cracker. She made her bed and was in it by 4 p.m.

Luna and I spent a great deal of time in cages E, F, and the squeeze cage. She played wildly in the squeeze while I sat nearby in E. She is still not comfortable in E and F, or cage D for that matter. I tied a sheet between the mesh and the tire in F, and she played briefly on that. I put her lunch in a box on the bench. She downed the yogurt immediately, and then took a piece of pear and headed to the squeeze cage. So I moved the buffet to just outside the squeeze, hoping she'd come graze, but no. I ended up hand feeding her, or placing bits on the bars of the squeeze, and on some of the items in there.

Before the Luna Show I got 6 small plastic water bottles and a cardboard beer carton, and placed them on the floor in E. I sat down there with her, and she played wildly, pulling the bottles out of the carton over and over. However, she kept one hand on me about 80% of the time.

The Luna Show was outside plus we rode there in an open cart. She always seems to enjoy that as she can look at everything, feel the wind in her hair etc.

After the show we returned to cage E, and she played on the floor for awhile. Then I remembered how she'd been apprehensive in cage B a few months ago, and ended up napping in a black tub of hay in there. So I put some hay in a tub, placed the bottles and a couple of other things in it, and put it up on the bench in E. I climbed up on the bench as she was clinging to me. I took her hands and we played the "fall backward in the tub of hay" game. She got the idea that the tub was a fun place, and sat down in it. She played with the bottles until we had to leave that cage.

We played in B and C and the tunnel for awhile. She ate her cereal in the tunnel. She then took her bowl into C, climbed high up in the cage, licked the bowl, placed it on her head, and ended up with bits of cereal in her hair.

At bedtime she sat by me, leaning on my leg as she drank her formula. She handed me the empty bottle, but grabbed onto me immediately so she could go with me to get the banana. When I put her down in the crib of hay, I placed the banana on the edge. She took it, and I left the cage and locked it. She didn't let out a peep, but did come to check the lock. She was in the kennel when I left the night house.

Lynn told me she felt like a waitress this past weekend. When she gave the orangs their morning juice, they spit out money. We were talking about how they put things in their mouths but don't swallow them. She also said on Friday, when they were given their worm medicine, they all took it except Chey. She wouldn't swallow it. Lynn kept giving her bites of sweet pudding, and she still wouldn't swallow it. Lynn left the night house to get more banana pudding. Luna's caregiver told Lynn that Chey swallowed the medicine as soon as Lynn left the building. She'd just figured a way to keep getting more sweets. What a con artist!

This continues to be so much fun. I hate for the end to come.

January 26, 1999

It was really an uneventful day in the orangutan night house today. Kelly was the adult inside, and she didn't do anything too interesting. When she was shifted to E and F for the night, she was determined to get the sheet untied from the skylight in E. She didn't undo the knot; just ripped it. What was unusual (not for her I understand) was her holding onto the skylight with her feet, using her hands to work on the sheet. She was spread-eagled, suspended by her feet. It looked really strange and made me hurt just to look at her. These orangutans would be great yoga instructors.

Luna's old portable bamboo jungle gym was "refurbished." We are putting it into empty adult cages for her to play on. That way she'll be more comfortable in the cages. She loves it! She wanted me in the cage with her, however. I'd sneak out of sight and the whining would begin. There is also now a thick rope, with knots, that can be hooked on the skylight in two separate cages for her to climb and swing on. She loves that too! She would not tolerate being alone in E or F, but was more at ease playing in them, and managed to play without one hand on me. She did come to me every once in awhile, take my hand, walk me toward the jungle gym, and then jump back on it.

She drank her bedtime bottle sitting next to me, clutching my shirt, but did not whine when I locked her in.

Another thing she had a blast with today was the crisp plastic bag that held the enrichment articles (AKA trash) I'd brought. She loved crushing it into a ball which made a lot of loud noise. Then she'd put it on her whole body, take it off, and wad it up again. Great fun!

February 2, 1999

Well, most of the day was spent in all of the adult cages. At first her jungle gym was in C, and I also hooked "The Rope" from the mesh on the front of C to the mesh in the tunnel. She played like a wild child. I served her lunch in that cage too, putting it all in a carry out dish. After the Luna Show I tried to sit outside of C, but she started whining. So I just parked on a bucket at the back of the cage.

Chey and Doc were inside. When Lynn wanted to shift them into B and C, we transferred the jungle gym into D. Luna made a brief stop in F, walked through E, but played wildly in the squeeze cage between D and E. There were bits of material suspended from the top. She'd swing like crazy on them, and then spin round and round. She ate her cereal on the "fly by" upside down. Lynn put a pile of beta chips (finely ground wood) in D. Luna would race through, fling chips, go into the squeeze, swing a bit, back into D through the chips, fling a handful on her and me, then up on the jungle gym, climb like a nut, back down through the chips, throwing them over and over. I was covered – in my shoes, socks, and hair. She was covered. What fun!

Rudi, who was outside, started banging like crazy on the metal door at one point. Maybe he thought it was time to come in. Fortunately, Luna was not in the squeeze, where the door is. She was in D, but climbed high upon a prop in the farthest corner and froze during his display.

Lynn did an intro with Luna and Chey. Chey poked and poked and Luna didn't seem to mind. Of course Chey poked Luna's genitals which was fine with Luna (saved her touching herself.) Then Luna solicited the genital touching, positioning herself where Chey could lick her. Then Luna kissed Chey's face or sniffed it; couldn't tell which. It's not unusual to see Luna rub her genitals on something, then sniff the something. Lynn was encouraged by the interaction. However, when Luna put her arm in Chey's cage and pulled the hair on her head, Lynn was nervous. Chey is unpredictable, and she was afraid she would hurt Luna.

Lynn also did training of Doc and Chey. That's always fun to watch. Poor Doc; he gets so nervous when asked to present his arm. Lynn said he had a bad sedation experience when Bubba died, and he's been this way since. He did fairly well today. He hesitated, but finally let her stick him. She praised him like crazy.

At bedtime, Luna again held my shirt while she drank her bottle, but allowed me to lock her up without a peep. As usual, she did check the lock, just to see if escape was possible.

February 9, 1999

Perpetual motion pretty much describes Luna today. She did spend time in all the cages. I was able to leave her in F. She whined, but I kept talking to her while I went to get her a treat. I fed her monkey biscuit powder mixed with formula through the mesh. I encouraged her to go into E, which she did, to have more of the treat. After about 20 minutes I had to go back in with her as the whining got worse. She played independently pretty much all day. In B, I was showing her there were monkey biscuits in the bark chips, and encouraged her to forage. I'd hold one up; she'd reach towards me, but wouldn't come get it. Lazy little girl.

She tried to bite me a lot today. I think it was just playful stuff for the most part. She did pull my hair a couple of times as she swung by. She also grabbed my mask, leaving a small scratch near my nose. Another time, as she was swinging by, she slugged me in the cheek.

Hard day at the zoo. One thing I noticed today; she initiated wrestling with her surrogates, one small one and one Luna size.

Tonight after I locked Luna in her cage and was writing my notes, I heard a plink on her cage floor. It sounded like a coin dropping. Well, she had a bolt about 2 inches long. I coaxed her to the front of the cage with a raisin. She held the bolt with her foot, then shifted it to her hand, and got close enough for me to grab it and give her the raisin. Who knows where it came from?

Doc and Chey were inside today, but I didn't have a chance to chat with them much.

I was told about something very interesting that happened with Kelly last week. There are fluorescent lights in the aisle fixtures, covered with plastic covers. The cage mesh usually goes all the way to the ceiling. HOWEVER, there is a space about 3 inches at the top of cage F. It seems Kelly, using a piece of bamboo as a tool, unscrewed the light cover, and opened it. She was able to unscrew a bulb about 4 feet long, and pull it into her cage. She was holding it, sitting up high by her skylight, when Lynn came in after being alerted by Luna's caregiver. When she saw Lynn she broke it against the skylight as if to say, "I don't have anything I shouldn't." Lynn had to lure her into another cage with a bagel so they could clean up the mess. Kelly is so smart!

Then there's Luna, her daughter, who is also smart, but who had a memory lapse today. She was climbing up and down the prop above the tire swing in E. Suddenly she couldn't remember how to get down. She started whining and I had to rescue her.

February 19, 1999

It was a fairly uneventful day at the zoo. We spent most of the day out of cage A. In cage B she kept sliding down the hammock. There was no Luna Show today. Lynn was swamped with work and a meeting that lasted all morning.

We moved into the squeeze and E and F. I tied a sheet from the mesh to the tire swing, and she sat on the swing for the longest time, playing with the chain. There was also a sheet in the squeeze, and she had a blast every time she went in there. She got whiny every time I was out of sight, so I just sat on the cage threshold and watched her.

We moved to D when Kelly was shifted to E and F. I draped the rope from the skylight, and around a prop. She was one wild baby. I left the cage, talking to her as I left. She whined, but stopped when I gave her water through the mesh. She played alone in the cage for 40 minutes while I stood outside. Then the whining started; nonstop. As I stood up to go in with her, she screeched loudly. So I knew it was definitely time to go in. I did, and sat in a corner and watched her play. We did make trips to the laundry room during this time.

As I held her while her bottle finished heating, I hugged her tightly, and she snuggled as I rocked her back and forth. Oh, how I will miss this one on one, hands on, care.

Kelly has learned a new behavior. She lets Lynn brush her hair, and presents whatever body part is requested for a brushing. She is so smart. I wonder what goes through her mind as she watches all of us holding her baby.

February 23, 1999

I'm getting a bonus this week. I'll be caring for Luna tomorrow morning also. Goody, goody! As I told Lynn, when she called me at work Saturday morning to ask if I could work, "I know our time is winding down, and I welcome a chance to spend more time with her."

Chey and Doc were in today. I gave Chey a AAA tour book to peruse. Doc came to see what she had, and I gave him a hockey media guide. Chey just stared and stared when I gave it to him, like he didn't deserve it or something. He took it into the squeeze cage to tear up for his nest. Chey "read" hers thoroughly before tearing it up. At one point, she placed it on an upside down bucket, and sat there looking through it, just like at a table. She's so funny!

Luna and I spent most of our time together in cage C. I'd strung the rope up for her to climb and explore. I left her alone for a good portion of the first half of our shift. She was alone for 15 minutes before the Luna Show. There was a very small crowd, only a handful, so it was a short show. After the show, I was able to leave her in C for an hour while I sat in front. I gave her some crackers and monkey biscuit powder to munch on. I then went into C through B, and made her follow me, the leader, back and forth between the two cages a few times. I then sat on the bench in C while she climbed about. Every once in awhile she'd come over to me, take my hand, and sit by me. She even snuggled against my leg a couple of times.

There was a short intro with Chey. Chey was eating her carrot during it. Luna touched Chey's face (that's new) but Chey was passive, poked a little, and kept eating. Doc was too busy eating to come to the mesh for an intro.

All in all it was a rather quiet day.

February 24, 1999

Well, it was too cool this morning to take Luna out on the exhibit, so I had to come up with some fun stuff to do inside.

The funniest thing happened; maybe just strange. The keeper had two Band-Aids on her leg, and Rudi noticed them right away. He started making gutteral sounds, love sounds. She said she wondered if he would do that. She'd heard this is what he does when he sees a Band-Aid on someone. THEN he presented his nipple through the mesh, wanting her to touch it. Dirty old man! She touched him, told him that was enough, and gave him the Band-Aids. A little love token, I guess. He would NOT go outside, and just sat in the squeeze cage. Maybe he didn't want to leave the keeper. He finally went out about 10 a.m., but until then Luna was confined to her cage. Even though he only had access to one cage besides the squeeze, they are uneasy about us being next door to him with only a metal door between.

Luna found plenty to do in cage A. It seems the morning shift is non-stop grazing. She refused her bottle at 7:30, ended up pulling the nipple out and spilling all of it. However, she ate her fruit and veggie, 2 monkey biscuits soaked in juice, yogurt, peas, and greens. She was a wild child in A for an hour, swinging about wildly. I used a surrogate to wrestle with her too.

At 10 a.m. we had access to E, F, and the squeeze. I constructed a playground in F, using the big rope and a couple of sheets. She actually allowed me to leave the cage for a few minutes to get the second sheet, but after that there was no way I could leave. The whining began immediately. So I just sat on the floor and let her play. We left for 30 minutes for the Luna Show. During that she was active and cute, mugging for the audience. She tried to leave the jungle gym a few times to explore the stage, but didn't protest when I lifted her and put her back on the gym. After the show she continued to play in F. A couple of times she took her surrogate, and went alone into E. However, she returned quickly.

I had to give her a chewable vitamin this morning as they're out of liquid vitamin. I crushed one up in case I had to disguise it in something. But when I gave her the whole piece, she ate it without complaint. It was a cherry flavored one. I understand another caregiver tried to give her a purple one. NO WAY! She also refused to drink formula from a purple bottle one afternoon. Hmmm……..

Today, when we were in the aisle, the phone rang and she reached for my hand like, "Come on, let's go." Later we were in cage F. The phone rang again and she did the same thing. Silly little girl.

Its fun to do the mornings sometimes because it's a different routine.

March 2, 1999

My goodness – I'm starting my second journal. When I bought the two blank books way back when, I didn't think I'd use both, BUT I'm very happy it has come to that.

When I got to the zoo today, all of the orangs were still inside. There was some work being done on the exhibit. However, Rudi and Kelly went out shortly after my arrival. Doc and Chey had access to cages C through F. Right after Kelly left B, Lynn cleaned it so I could set up a playground in there. While I waited, I swept cage A. After cleaning the hay out of the crib, I noticed a little mouse racing out of the cage. Ah yes, the night house is inhabited by some NOT listed in the directory.

I hung ropes in B. We had some new climbing ropes so I was able to hang ropes everywhere. She climbed and climbed immediately. I left the cage, and she played alone for at least 30 minutes before the serious whining started. I'd given her the yogurt through the mesh, and placed her orange slices (new fruit for Tuesdays – yea!), and sweet potato in a small box on the beta chips. There were also crackers in the chips for forage. She really wasn't too interested in the food. Why? Because when she went down to get the box and held it upside down as she headed back up the ropes, all of the food fell out. She did eat all but half the sweet potato later.

When the whining started, I re-entered and sat in the back of the cage. However, she came immediately to where I was sitting, Velcro-ed to my leg, and played with a box I'd brought. Then she spent about 20 minutes playing with my shoes and laces, while sitting in the box turned on its side. When I'd pull my feet away, she'd pull them back to where she could continue playing with them while sitting in the box.

Doc and Chey came to the side of C every now and again to watch the "goings on." I gave them a few treats trying to keep them close by, but they wandered off to pursue other activities.

At one point I sat in the aisle making a few notes, and Luna played alone. Chey spit a mouthful of water at me to get my attention. That worked. When there was no more water, she just worked up saliva to spit at me. Doc was amusing himself with a bed sheet. Luna took her bear surrogate to the back of the cage, and acted like she might actually fall asleep, but didn't.

The keeper came in to play with Luna when I took a break. She gave her a small terry cloth ball, and Luna really liked playing with that. Earlier, the keeper tried unsuccessfully to get a splinter from Luna's hand, and she'd left with Luna not liking her much. Therefore, she wanted to play with her and make it up to her. It worked!

Between 2:00 and 3:30 p.m. Luna actually played alone in cage B for 75 of the 90 minutes. Then Chey and Doc started wrestling, and making a lot of noise vocally. Luna was in the tunnel and it scared her. She started whining loudly, almost screeching, So I re-entered cage B, and stayed there until 5 p.m. We sat on the floor while she ate her cereal. Then I sat in the hammock while she climbed about. Every now and again she'd go by, make a play face, grab at me, or give my leg a love. I almost dozed off. At 5:20 Lynn hadn't returned with fresh hay for her crib. Therefore, I filled it with surrogates and a couple of blankets. She had her bottle at 5:25 p.m. while lying in her little hammock stretched across a prop. She then went with me to get the banana slice, as usual. I put her in the crib and locked the cage. Lynn came and wanted me to give her the hay. I re-entered the cage quickly, didn't say a word, put the hay in the crib, rearranged the surrogates and the blankets, threw some dry rice cereal about, left, and relocked the cage. No whining!! A major milestone! What a sweetie!

March 9, 1999

A fun day at the zoo, as usual. Kelly was the adult in today. When I first got there, Luna was playing in the aisle by the cart. Kelly was in cage D, sitting up high and watching. However, when I would look at her, she'd look away like "Who—me? I'm not watching." We made a quick pass through C while Lynn was getting ready to transfer Kelly to B and C. When she opened the door for Kelly to move, she wouldn't leave D until she got the sheet untied from the hammock to take with her. Never mind that there were sheets and blankets in B and C; she wanted to take the one from D. She spent part of the afternoon napping in a tub of hay, and then on the bench in C, covered with a sheet, but of course not the one she took from D. When I called her name, she'd lift the sheet and peek at me.

After the Luna Show I constructed a rope playground in F. Someone had attached a bicycle tire to the rope, and that was a new fun toy. She played like crazy; swinging, then climbing up and down, and swinging from the tire to the bench. I'd stretched one part of the rope into cage E, and she even went in there, hand over hand on the rope. By this time Kelly was in B only, so Luna and I played tag, racing from F all the way into the tunnel through the cages. I let her catch me, but she never let me catch her. She only let me leave her alone in F for about 12 minutes, whining quietly the whole time. I finally went into the cage, and sat quietly in the corner while she played.

We had interesting interactions when we returned to A, and Kelly was in B. She was at the intro door watching Luna, so I got some cracker pieces to share with her. I made a point of giving Luna a piece so she'd know we were sharing Luna's crackers. The first two pieces fell. She could reach one using her two index fingers, but she used a piece of straw to reach the second one. The next two pieces also landed with one close enough to get with her fingers, and the other slightly out of reach. I couldn't believe what she did. She picked up an orange peel lying nearby, sort of folded like a bowl. She first tried to pull it with the bowl facing up. That didn't work! She realized quickly she needed to turn it over, and use it like a scoop to pull the piece to her. Amazing! She then tore her paper snack bag, rolled a piece up, and handed it through to us. Later we were in the aisle, and Kelly mashed a plastic water bottle enough to push it out under the mesh to me. I put some juice in it, and put it down so she could pull it back in. I filled it again for Kelly, but because I had Luna on my hip, she grabbed it and guzzled it. Looked like a little wino. So I gave Kelly more later. We observed Lynn training Kelly also. That's always fun because she's so smart. When she asked her to present her arm for a shot, Kelly didn't. She made a face instead; a kind of "grit the teeth" face.

Earlier today I gave Luna water in a well cleaned Nyquil bottle with a lid. I'm always trying to think of new ways to offer her water because she doesn't readily drink it. When it was empty she attempted to put the lid back on. Clever girl.

I'll be working an extra morning shift later this week. Goody, goody!

March 12, 1999

Bonus day! I entered the night house at 7:35 a.m., and Luna was at the front of her cage, climbing about. She came to the door and fiddled with the padlock. She urinated about a gallon while trying the lock. I let her out (noticed all her bedding was dry) and she led me down the aisle. We said "good morning" to all of the adults, and she then settled by the shelves to guzzle her bottle. Afterwards, she proceeded to build a nest by the shelves with the stuff from the bottom shelf; paper, PVC pieces, ropes, plastic pieces, and T-shirts. Kelly was in cage F, and came to the front to check out all the activity. When she made a sound Luna looked that way, and then moved toward her. She started climbing on the ladder that hangs by cage F. Kelly sat and watched all of her activity closely. By that time I'd given Luna two face masks to play with. Well actually, when I turned my back for a split second, she climbed up and grabbed the box of masks off the shelf, and had pulled two out. Anyway we gave one to Kelly.

Breakfast was late and they only sent her fruit. However, she gobbled her two pieces of papaya quickly.

At 9 a.m. we went out on the exhibit. I hooked some ropes to the slanted poles, but she took hold for only a moment. She then led me through the wet grass (surprise, she didn't mind getting her feet wet for a change) to the large wooden structure. She quietly explored and I quietly watched. I did snap a photo. Lynn came out to leave monkey biscuits and greens for Rudi and Kelly. They would be going out first. She placed five monkey biscuits by Luna, and she tried to gather all five. She did manage to get two into her mouth at once, in her best "stuff mouth like Chey mode." She then took them out and nibbled a bit.

I fixed her cereal after we went in, but she really wasn't interested. She ate about a fourth of it with much coaxing.

After Rudi and Kelly departed we moved to D through F. She played exuberantly in the squeeze cage. She ate about a tablespoon of Rice Krispies as forage, but only foraging from my hand. I made a production of showing where I was sprinkling them, but no go.

When Lynn and a volunteer came in to clean those cages, we moved back to A. Chey and Doc were playing in B, C, and the tunnel. Lynn suggested I move Luna's crib into the aisle by their cages. The crib had leaves in it. Chey was acting silly with butcher paper; wrapping it around herself and putting it over her head. Therefore, we pulled a length of the same paper out of A, and tried to imitate Chey's antics. Hers was on her head, ours was over our heads. She laid down in hers; we laid down. At that point Luna seemed kind of quiet, and snuggled up next to me. When Chey moved to another activity, I wrestled with Luna in the paper, and with her surrogate for a few minutes before leaving for the Luna Show.

It's the first week of Spring Break. It was a long show with a fair crowd asking lots of questions. Luna was very active on the jungle gym during the show. I'd taken a long, skinny bamboo branch, a monkey biscuit, a leaf of romaine, and paper toweling. She kept busy.

After the show, I constructed a playground in B. Chey and Doc had been shifted to D, E, and F. Suddenly it was noon and time for me to leave. The morning shift goes really fast.

Yet another fun day in Primates.

March 16, 1999

I phoned the night house early to remind Lynn my daughter, Daiquiri, and granddaughter, Sterling, would be visiting, and we'd be there as early visitors. The morning caregiver said Chey had done a clever thing earlier. She and Doc were the adults inside, and the caregiver fixed some cereal for them. Doc pushed a book out as a plate for her to use. Chey looked around her cage, but all she had was a piece of paper. She picked up a piece of bowl shaped onion skin, and gave it to the caregiver. I can't believe how smart these orangs are.

Since its Spring Break week there was a huge crowd at the zoo. When Daiquiri and Sterling arrived, we first went around to view Rudi and Kelly on exhibit. We then went to the night house. The caregiver brought Luna to the door so Sterling could see her up close. She's too young to go into the night house. (She is only 6 and children under 12 are not allowed inside.) Daiquiri remarked how adorable she is; even cuter "in person" than in pictures. Lynn was doing an intro with Chey in cage C. Since that cage is visible from the door Sterling was able to see that too. I then took Daiquiri inside. I brought two AAA tour books. Doc put his hand out to get one, and I pushed one through to Chey. Of course she immediately started "planning her trip" with page to page browsing. Doc was busy making spitting sounds at Daiquiri. Not sure why. Maybe because he didn't know her. Luna and her caregiver were in cage A by this time. At one point Luna reached her little hands out towards Daiquiri, but of course she couldn't touch her.

After Daiquiri and Sterling left I started the afternoon activities. I set up ropes in B so she could climb. I went ahead and swept out last night's mess too. I like to help the keepers if I can. I served Luna's lunch in B. She would not eat her sweet potato and pear because they were quite hard. I KNOW she can eat raw fruit and veggies because she has swiped leftovers from the grownups. I took some of the peel off the pear. She watched, tried some, noticed how juicy and tasty it was, and ate it. She didn't eat the sweet potato at that point, however. (Ate it after the Luna show.) I told Luna "In the jungle you would NOT find steamed vegetables and fruit so get a grip, Baby Girl, and eat them as served."

Daiquiri and Sterling were front and center at the Luna Show. Luna was very active on the jungle gym during the show. Toward the end of the show she was sucking her thumb. That's always cute.

After the show we had to dismantle the rope play yard in B because Lynn wanted to move Doc into there. She likes to rotate the adults through B. That way a different one spends the night next to Luna. We set up a new rope play yard in F with a sheet rope strung through to E. She went nuts; climbing and swinging like a crazy girl. I fixed her cereal and stood by the bench in the cage. She literally grabbed bites on the "fly by." However, she carefully checked each bite to see if a bit of banana was in it, and spit out the few bites that were banana free. Spoiled? Not much!

She would not let me leave her alone in the cage, but I did move to E when she was in F. When she realized I was gone she came into E via the sheet rope, and played in there awhile. She invented a game. She held both of my hands, and I lifted her up to the bench. She jumped off while still holding onto me, of course. She wanted to be launched back to the bench to jump again. We did this over and over. As I currently have some weird, painful problem with a muscle in my right neck and shoulder, it was truly a labor of love.

About 4:45 Lynn did another intro with Chey and Doc. Chey was in the tunnel and Doc was in B. At first there was touching but then Luna didn't want to be on the mesh. She wanted to roll around on the floor in front of the tunnel, dive into the two surrogates we'd put there, or into Lynn's lap. It was a play activity but with the mesh there. Chey was very attentive. Doc was busy tearing up a phone book to put into his nest, but then he shoved a big handful of hay out to Luna. She grabbed it and threw it about. She did bite on Chey's fingers, and they touched lips and tongues. Doc stuck his tongue out, and also extended his hand under the mesh. Luna touched his tongue with her lips and bit on his fingers. She had her play face on for some of this intro.

Bedtime was uneventful. She guzzled her formula and wolfed her banana. After I padlocked her cage, she came over to check the lock, of course.

The phone in the night house rang a lot today. Luna always looked at me, reached out her hand like, "Come on, we've got to answer the phone." She is so used to the caregivers taking her with them to answer the phone; Pavlov's response. When Luna is about 10 years old and hears a phone ring, I wonder if she'll automatically reach out with that hand. Hmmmm……

March 23, 1999

I went in at 10:30 a.m. today because the morning caregiver needed to leave early. Therefore, I was involved with two Luna Shows. She was very active on her jungle gym during both shows.

Chey and Doc were inside. I gave them each a road map after I demonstrated unfolding it. Chey did hers just like she was supposed to, but Doc wasn't interested. Lynn asked if I gave Chey a map of Borneo. ☺

After the second Luna Show, I constructed an elaborate rope playground in F, with one rope going into E. Luna played like crazy. I sat with her in F, tried backing out once, but OH, NO – the whining began. I sat in E for awhile and she'd peek in at me. We also played tag. She always catches me, but when I'm it and chase <u>her</u>, she climbs up the side of the cage, and that's that! I played a couple of games of hide and seek with her too. I raced from D into F and hid in the corner. She came into F but didn't look to the right where I was hidden. She got up on her ropes and then saw me. A short time later I repeated the game, and she came into F, didn't see me, and sat there very quiet and still. She then ran back into E, the squeeze, and D. Well, the whining began because she couldn't find me. I was really hoping she'd let me leave her alone for a bit in these cages today.

There was a great intro with Chey and Doc. At one point she was using Doc's hands to pull up, and then fall back into a crib of hay. He tried to share an onion with her, extending his hand and his arm, but she just nibbled his fingers. He had his play face on. Chey was very gentle with her too. Slowly, but surely, this all will be okay, and someday she'll be back in her community.

March 30, 1999

A great day at the zoo! When I first arrived, Luna was playing alone in A while the morning caregiver was writing her notes. I went into A, she sniffed my hand, leaned over, and gave me a love. She did not want to leave A no matter how much I coaxed her. At 1 p.m. I spread the lunch buffet out in the aisle in front of A, making sure she noticed the syringes of yogurt. Well, that did it! She wanted that yogurt. She gobbled it, and I moved the rest of the lunch into B. She sat on the hammock and ate, but kept one hand on me. She would not climb up the hammock to the mesh like she usually does in B. I carried her through the tunnel into C. She would not disengage from me at all. Lynn thought it might be because of the huge blue barrel in B. Someone had brought it in for the orangs. I bent down close to it, and Luna touched it very quickly and that was all.

Apparently Kelly and Rudi played with the barrel yesterday, and today it was there for Chey and Doc. The other caregiver said Chey tried to put the barrel on, but her round tummy prevented her from wearing it.

There was no Luna Show due to the rain, so at 1:30 p.m. I placed some ropes here and there in F. Doc had been moved into B with the barrel, and Chey was in C and the tunnel. The squeeze cage was open to the outside so Rudi and Kelly could get in out of the rain. We caregivers have been given permission to do some intros by the tunnel. The adults cannot get hold of Luna there. However, Lynn did caution us about letting Luna climb too high on the mesh by the tunnel. She also said I could do intros with her and Chey, and if Luna made the first moves, praise her by saying "Good girl."

As we walked down the aisle to F, hand in hand, Luna wanted to stop by the cart. I kept going and she threw a tantrum. She started screaming and wrapped herself around my leg. Then she was screeching like crazy, but would not let me pick her up. What a mess! She finally let me hold her. I reassured Lynn, who was walking by to a meeting, that all was well, and we headed to F. She played wildly in F as I sat on the floor at the back of the cage. We stayed in F for 2 hours, but did go to the tunnel twice for intros with Chey. It was so neat! During the first one, Luna put her back against the mesh, and Chey poked and touched her gently. Then Luna touched Chey's lips with her lips, and touched Chey's face with her fingers. I quickly and gently stroked Chey's fingers, and told her what a good girl SHE was too. When we headed back to F, Kelly was in the squeeze. She put her fingers out to Luna, and Luna started to reach. Kelly barely touched Luna's fingers, and Luna jerked her hand away. She does seem afraid of Kelly.

Meanwhile, I looked in cage B and didn't see the blue barrel. Doc had put it up on a bench, and covered it with a blanket. Hiding it? Who knows? Then he sat on the floor and gently pulled on the blanket, looking rather frightened at what might happen, and sure enough – it did! He pulled the barrel off the bench. It came crashing down, and he "flew" up to a high prop. The barrel was upright. A few minutes later he started to get down into the barrel, but stopped. Maybe he realized he'd disappear as the barrel is very deep. Later, he was just sitting on it by the intro door between A and B.

When I made Luna's cereal at 3:30 p.m., I made extra to share with Chey. I sat down by the tunnel, and fed Luna as she was hanging on the mesh. Chey kept sticking her tongue out, and I'd drop bites of cereal on it. Then I gave Luna the bowl to lick out. She was still on the mesh. Chey took hold of the bowl with both index fingers. Luna was licking the bowl, and Chey would lick one of her own fingers that had a bit of cereal on it. It was somewhat difficult getting the bowl from Chey. It's amazing what a grip she has with just two fingers. But it was a really neat moment; sharing the cereal.

There was the second intro between 4 and 4:15. Luna put on her play face when Chey poked her around her neck in her tickle spots. Meanwhile, Doc so wanted to have an intro with Luna. However, he was in B and would be able to grab her with his hand, and I didn't have permission to put her that close to him. He even had his play face on. I tried to give him a few extra treats.

The bedtime bottle was consumed while she lay in her little hammock. She sucked the bottle almost flat.

April 6, 1999

An interesting day at the zoo, but aren't they all? When I got there, the morning caregiver was holding Luna. Luna reached out to take my hand and give it a sniff. Then she went into A so the caregiver could do her charting, and I could get organized. It was easier to extract her from A today. However, I did let her play in there for about 30 minutes while I just sat up on a prop and watched her.

She was a hungry baby today. I took her lunch to the aisle in front of Doc and Chey. Chey made all kinds of kiss squeaks, so we shared the sweet potato peel with her. Luna sat right next to my leg, and ate everything.

There was no Luna Show as there was no driver to take us there. Therefore, at 1:30 p.m. we headed to D, E, F, and the squeeze for fun and games. I hung a few ropes in F, and in doing so managed to knock the ladder over. Yes, while I was on it with one foot, and placing the other foot on the bench. It went crashing down, and I tried my best orangutan move, trying to grab the prop. However, I didn't get a grip, so I hit the floor with my right knee, and scraped the back of my left leg on the ladder. I got some ice from Luna's cooler, and held it to the back of my leg to ease the pain, and prevent too much bruising and swelling. I really was glad I was the only person in the night house at the time. However, had I knocked myself out or broken a leg, it might have been helpful to _not_ be alone. I gimped around the rest of the day.

We played in all the cages, mostly in F, but I moved from cage to cage, and she followed along. She played alone very briefly in D and F. I wanted to exit, but every time I even _headed_ toward the door, she was right there. As long as I was inside with her, she was fine. I put monkey biscuit powder in the cages for her to forage, and she did.

She had a great intro with Chey. First, however, Lynn tried with Doc. Luna was on the mesh and he poked her a bit. She bit his finger and he jerked it away. Her crib was right there, loaded with beta chips, and she kept playing with those, and was covered with them. Doc lost interest quickly, and went to play in a large cardboard box. Luna did watch him with interest.

Chey was in the squeeze cage. She'd made a bed of hay, and had a couple of magazines with her. Lynn put Luna on the squeeze cage and Chey tried to touch her, but there were too many bars. So we went to the front of cage D, and Lynn called Chey over. She was very gentle with Luna. They touched lips. Then Chey touched Luna's genitals with her lips and fingers, but very gently. (This is normal orangutan behavior.) Luna put her finger in Chey's mouth; no problem. Luna touched Chey's face, her arm, and her chest. Chey took hold of Luna's little arm but was very gentle. It was great! It would be so wonderful if she'd take care of this baby, but she is so unpredictable and could hurt her so quickly.

The 5:30 p.m. bottle routine did not go smoothly today. First Luna sucked the nipple flat. I fixed it, but she then pulled the nipple off the bottle, spilling milk everywhere. (I did manage to get her to drink some from the lip of the bottle through the mesh.) In reading the caregiver notes, I see this is happening occasionally. Maybe it's time to give the last 150cc of formula in a Sippy cup. On the other hand, she gets whiny and starts sucking her thumb when its bottle time, so perhaps it is too soon to give up the bottle of formula.

Two funny things – one about Chey and one about Doc. When I was ready to put Luna to bed, I went back to check on Chey. She was in the squeeze cage on her tummy, thumbing through her magazines. She rather looked like a person.

I put Luna's favorite surrogate, the bear, in a gunny sack today. It was in the crib by Doc's cage when we had Luna on the squeeze cage with Chey. We turned around and saw Doc pulling the gunny sack into his cage, bear and all. Lynn and I both pulled like crazy, but he is much stronger than we are, so we just let it go. It kept him busy for the next 30-40 minutes. He did finally get it all pulled into his cage, and he removed all of the stuffing from the bear. I went over to him and commented about it, and he shoved the now empty bear under the mesh towards me. I took hold, thinking he was giving it to me but, OH NO. He then pulled it back. He pushed it out again but wouldn't let me take it. Yes, he was playing a game of tug-o-war with me. Silly boy!

April 10, 1999

Tonight at the hockey game I saw another Luna caregiver. She said the Thursday morning slot is open because that caregiver quit. I left messages on Lynn and Barbara's machines saying I want that slot in addition to Tuesday afternoons.

April 12, 1999

Barbara called me this morning. The Thursday morning slot is mine! Yea! On the 18th there is a caregiver meeting. We'll discuss the introductions of Luna with Chey and Doc that we will be doing.

April 13, 1999

Luna got her polio and tetanus shots today. The morning caregiver said, after the vet left, it took her awhile to like people again. I could not get her out of cage A for the longest time. I showed her I had syringes with yogurt, and her food in Girl Scout cookie boxes in the aisle. She didn't care! After about 10 minutes I gave up and moved the buffet into A. Of course the yogurt was consumed eagerly. However, the pear was eaten slowly, and the sweet potato was totally uninviting. I exited the cage, sat in front of it, and read the notes of the last week.

Finally about 1:45 p.m., after I made a major production of having her watch me pour apple juice into a small plastic bottle, she decided she'd come out. Juice is just too good to pass up.

We went into B. I tried to put her on the hammock, but she kept one hand on me while she drank the juice. I got the ladder, a few ropes, and proceeded to climb the ladder and attach the ropes with a baby glued to my hip. Hey, if mother orangutans can carry their babies attached to them for a year as they climb and swing through trees, I can climb a ladder with one attached to me. However, Luna is almost 19 months old and weighs nearly 20 pounds. Hmmm.......

Once I attached the ropes, she finally climbed off of me. I sat on the hammock and watched her play. She mostly climbed on the front of the cage. I'd also draped a sheet over one of the props, making a tent of sorts, and that fascinated her. I climbed onto the prop at the front of B, and sat there awhile. I was hoping to get her to stay alone in B, but every time I even acted like I might leave, the whining began. FINALLY, after I moved the ladder over by the bench, she climbed up, holding onto me, and started investigating the tire and black tub that were on the bench. I waited – patiently. As soon as she let go of my hand, I raced to the door and shut her in. I also raced to get her crackers to feed her through the mesh, because the whining had started. She whined quietly, but did eat the cracker pieces. Then I zipped into A to get the forgotten sweet potato, and fed her that through the mesh too. It was 3:30 p.m. and I decided to fix her cereal and banana, and also fed her that and a monkey biscuit. The whining had stopped. After she ate, she untied the sheet from the prop, and played with it while hanging on the cage mesh. She wrapped it around herself and acted quite silly. When she started to get bored, I got the "bear skin" (remember Doc took her bear apart last week) and poked it through the mesh. She grabbed it and pulled it on through. She then put it on her head, and wrapped it around her neck. She seemed to be so glad to have her bear again, even torn apart.

Kelly was across the aisle in cage C, but I'd been told to ignore her and totally leave her alone. This was because she'd refused to shift into another cage, even though her food was there. Naturally, when Luna's food was being served, Kelly went nuts trying to get me to give her something.

Luna played alone in B for a total of 90 minutes. What a good little girl! Lynn came into the night house, and Luna's thumb went into her mouth. Anyway, it was time to clear out of B. Lynn needed to set up for the night.

I cleaned all the food particles off the floor, and readied cage A for the night. It was time for her bottle. Time was short, and I was afraid she'd pull the nipple off. Therefore, I took it off and let her drink it from the open bottle. She had a little milk mustache and looked like that commercial, "Got milk?"

I told Lynn I'd seen Luna pulling a strand of her hair through her mouth, while she was reclining in her hammock. Lynn said that was self grooming and to make a note of it.

Lynn also remarked that Luna is very calm with me. She said she'd noticed that sometimes she was clingy with me, other times playful, but generally calm. She said that was all positive. I told her I'd raised my kids to be independent, and she said maybe Luna feels the confidence I have. It made me feel really good. Yesterday, Barbara told me that Luna really liked me, and that was one reason she was glad I'd be doing another shift. Is my head swollen? Well, yes. I so love taking care of this baby, and really appreciate their confidence in me.

April 18. 1999

Today we had a Luna caregiver meeting to go over some new procedures, review old protocols, and be briefed on the introductions we'll be doing with Luna. If one thinks a room full of moms bragging about their children, or a room full of grandmothers bragging about their grandchildren is bad, just get a room full of Luna caregivers, all wanting to talk about their very special little lady. Three hours later we adjourned! We received some very useful information, however; not only regarding the introductions, but also just sharing information about what we've done, not done, things that worked, didn't work, and so forth. All in all, Barbara is extremely pleased with everything. There are now just nine caregivers, including Barbara, who will be doing two of another one's three shifts. That caregiver is going to be caring for her twin grandsons. My goodness, what's wrong with her priorities? ☺

It is really exciting that we're going to be doing the introductions with Chey and Doc. And we'll be doing them when they are in regular cages, not just the tunnel. Therefore, it will be very important to be watchful that neither of them grabs us.

A side note……. Today, for the meeting, Barbara brought sandwiches and strawberries for our lunch. However, the neat thing was she put portions of trail mix in paper towels, and into assorted containers for us to choose. In other words, we had enrichment articles. Cute!

We also learned today this is only the third time that volunteers have helped hand raise a great ape at a zoo. We will be the first to have volunteers do the introductions with the adults. The reasoning behind this is the fact that we volunteers spend hours with Luna, and have more time to do the introductions. How very exciting!

Barbara said they are looking for a "kid" orangutan to be Luna's cage mate. She is working with the Species Survival Plan people, hoping to obtain a "kid" 4 to 7 years old. She was sent a list of 12, and eliminated 7 as they were too old. They are hoping for her to be introduced to a young cage mate, and then the two of them will be introduced to Chey and Doc. We do know we will at least be with Luna through her second birthday.

Embarrassing moment! Last week I mixed Luna's formula before ending the afternoon shift, as per protocol. Well, dumb me; I put her bottles in her little cooler and then put the cooler into the freezer. Duh……. Needless to say, the next morning there was a problem. Lynn said they microwaved it to thaw. We all had a good laugh.

Never a dull moment in the World of Primates!

April 20, 1999

It was a beautiful sunny day at the zoo. There was a Luna Show (first I've done for at least 2 or 3 weeks), but the crowd was small and non inquisitive.

Kelly and Rudi were inside so no intros were to be done. I noticed in the notes there had been earlier intros done with Doc and Chey, before they went outside. It's unusual for Rudi to stay in, but the keeper that he loves came in to train Luna, and he wouldn't leave. With Rudi and Kelly inside it was very quiet in the night house. Chey and Doc usually wrestle with each other, and Doc plays with his toys in a very noisy fashion. Therefore, when <u>they</u> are inside, it's not quiet.

Kelly was in B and I'd given her a magazine. Before the Luna Show, she was stretched out on her back in a sunbeam, playing and slapping the floor with it. Luna went to the intro door for a quick peek. That was the extent of any interaction. Of course when it was Luna's cereal time, both Kelly and Rudi begged for some. Kelly shoved a plastic container out, making sure it sailed across the red line boundary. Rudi pushed out a paper bag. Naturally, I gave some to both of them.

When I arrived this morning I gave Luna a pair of socks which she played with for awhile. Later in the day, when I was tidying her cage for the night, I decided to give them to Kelly. (I'd given Luna another pair in C.) Anyway, Kelly sniffed each carefully, stretched them out, and then threw them out over the red line. I tossed one back to her, but she threw it out again. Hmmm….. Rejection of Luna??

After the Luna Show I set up a playground in C and D with ropes. One stretched all the way from a high corner of C, through the door between cages, across D, and was attached to the squeeze cage. I put her bear skin on it for comfort, scattered a few crackers on the bench for forage, and exited. She played so well by herself in both cages. I sat in the aisle in front of them so she could see I hadn't deserted her. At one point she whined a bit, and put her thumb in her mouth. I tossed her new blue stuffed bear in, and she quieted right away. She gave a few minor squeaks when I walked to A to tidy it for the night, but quieted the moment I sat back down in front of her. She foraged for the crackers and sunflower seeds that were in the hammock in C. It was really neat seeing her play so independently. The bear skin is still very popular. She totes it around, wears it, and wraps it around her. She moved freely, without apprehension, from C to D and back again. She played in all areas of both cages. I fed her cereal through the far side of D in front of Rudi. She stayed alone for two hours! At 4:40 p.m., when she saw me put water into the bottle warmer, the thumb went into the mouth. I went into the cages to clear out the stuff I'd put in them. After we left C and D, I put her back in A to play while I got her bottle ready. When I gave her the bottle, she was pulling on the nipple. I took it off so she could drink from the open bottle. She started screeching so I put the nipple back on the bottle. She then guzzled it down quickly. Sometimes she wants to suck her bottle, sometimes not. I just have to play it by ear.

Thursday morning I start working the a.m. shift in addition to what I'm doing. I am really looking forward to being her "mom" twice a week.

April 22, 1999

It was a busy morning with Luna. It seems it's a nonstop buffet in the mornings. However, this morning, the girl's appetite seemed decreased. For starters, she only took 110 cc of her 150 cc bottle. About 8 a.m. we went out on the exhibit. I took Rice Krispies for forage and her breakfast of avocado, sweet potato, and yogurt. WELL, a new zookeeper was cleaning the outside exhibit, and Luna seemed very suspicious of a "stranger." I put the Rice Krispies along the platform, but she only ate those she could reach while keeping one extremity attached to my person. We got down on the grass, and she headed for the night house. I took her inside to get the bear skin for security, and a couple of ropes to hang. She only wanted to use the rope to access a good falling down place in the grass, and then would race towards the door of the night house. I'd head her off at the pass, pick her up, and we'd go back to the ropes. The whole process would start again, and I realized she had a new game going. Therefore, I took her back up on the structure. She then played with bird poop she could reach while attached to me. I was trying very hard to push it off the structure with my foot.

Luna with her "bearskin"

Luna being pouty

When we went back inside, we spent 30 minutes playing in the aisle on ropes strung between cages B, C, and the tunnel. Chey was in the tunnel and Doc was in B. We were there for introductions. However, the new zookeeper was cleaning A, so Doc stayed by the intro door checking out <u>her</u> actions. Chey had her worried face, sort of like the one she has when the vet comes by. Luna pressed against the mesh of B, and Doc didn't care. She also pressed against the tunnel mesh, and Chey poked her a few times and kissed her ear. That was it!

When they went outside, Luna played in the aisle in front of Kelly. Kelly showed some interest. When she was shifted to B and C, she took the blue barrel with her. I guess she's claimed it for herself.

Before I knew it – it was time to go home.

April 27, 1999

Today Chey and Doc were inside. The secondary mesh on the intro door was off, and Luna was just one mesh away from the occupant of B. When I first got there, she was swinging on her fire hose from the jungle gym to the intro door mesh. Doc and Chey were wrestling in the tunnel, and paying no attention. I took Luna's lunch to F, but she was not interested in eating it there. She seemed uneasy in that cage. After I gave her the yogurt, while holding her, we returned to A so she'd finish her food.

We started for the Luna Show but the cart wouldn't start. Therefore, due to "unforeseen technical difficulties," the show was cancelled.

Lynn set up some ropes from B and C to the tunnel, and Luna had a great time. Chey was in B and Doc was in the tunnel. They were quite interested in her, but she was too busy swinging and climbing to want their attention. Chey did manage a few gentle touches. There was a huge hard ball in the moat track. Chey would reach out under the mesh and give it a shove down the track toward A. I'd push it back and so the game went. The morning caregiver said she'd been playing the same game earlier. Luna joined in too, giving the ball a push with her feet as she hung on a rope.

We interspersed the intros with some play in F, but Luna was really whiny. She was actually screaming at times about being in F. Needless to say, I was unable to leave her alone anywhere but A.

The secondary mesh screen was left off between A and B tonight since Chey was going to stay in B. I anchored the large surrogates with dog collars so Luna couldn't drag them where Chey could reach them.

She'll probably be okay, but Lynn was fretting a bit when I left. This is something new; only one mesh between Luna and Chey.

April 29, 1999

Well, Luna did fine Tuesday night with the secondary mesh off.

I'm kind of pondering what's going on with this baby. Today was my second morning with her, and she wasn't as independent out on the exhibit as I read she is with other caregivers. I'm wondering if she senses I don't belong in this routine yet. After all, I'm the afternoon mom. I remember the first morning I ever worked with her, she wanted to go back to A like it was bedtime. Anyway, last week she played only while holding onto me while we were outside, and today she was only slightly less clingy. First, she did not want to come out of cage A at all. I tried enticing her with the bear skin, a piece of romaine, and then got the magic yogurt. That did it! I loaded up a crate with ropes, corn flakes for forage, her breakfast, the bear skin, and my camera. Away we went! I placed some corn flakes on the structure. That way she could forage close by as I hooked some ropes from the structure to nearby poles. She really didn't want to use the ropes except to get to me to be picked up. Then the sprinkler system came on and those huge drops raining down on us were very scary. The only time she seemed at ease was sitting on an area of the structure where she was surrounded by wood. She was clutching her bear skin the whole time. I was able to stand away from her as long as I was on, or near, the structure. However, if I walked away, the whining began. One time there was a screech followed by her wrapping herself around my legs. I picked her up and she just needed a long cuddle. I love doing that!

After we went inside, I put her in A while I fixed her cereal. I let her eat from a shallow dish. After all, orangutans don't need spoons.

We then went down by D, E, and F to do intros with Chey and Doc. Lynn turned on a water source by F. That was great fun. Chey was trying to get a drink from it. Both she and Doc put their hands out to catch the water. Luna, the baby who was very frightened of the sprinkler system, stuck her face in the water. Hmmm.......The big ball was in the track, and Chey and I played ball a bit. At one point, Chey jumped quickly up on the mesh which scared Luna. Luna flew to me but then got right back on the mesh. Chey did some gentle touching and they touched lips. Doc put his fingers through the mesh but Luna ignored him. When Luna had a piece of bamboo and Chey tried to take it, Luna pulled it back quickly. That's probably good; that she didn't let her take it.

After about an hour, Luna started sucking her thumb, reached for me, got down, and led me back to A. I left her there while I wrote my notes.

I'm wondering if Luna is struggling with this independence we're trying to enforce. She has gotten clingier the last couple of weeks, except when in A. I think she's fighting growing up. Poor little tyke.

May 4, 1999

Barbara was the morning caregiver today. She was with Luna in cage A when I arrived and joined them. She was able to exit without complaint from Luna. Luna continued wild play in A while Kelly sat by the intro door watching. All of the other orangutans were outside, so I knew I wouldn't be doing any intros today.

Cages E and F were open. I left Luna playing in A while I hung ropes in both cages, and spread the lunch buffet, some monkey biscuit powder, and crackers on the bench in F. Luna did not want to leave A. I put yogurt on my fingers. She'd lick it off and wouldn't let me grab her. She kept trying to bite me. Finally, I put the yogurt on the silver tray she's had for a couple of weeks, and put it out in the aisle. THAT was just too tempting and she came out of the cage. I picked her up and off we went to F. She was a hungry wee soul and ate everything immediately, but would not let go of my hand. When I'd try to "escape" her grasp, she'd grab my other hand. After she ate, she led me to the door two or three times but we did not leave. I tried to get her to go into E with me, but she did not want to go there. I finally took her to get her bear skin and the bag of small boxes I'd brought. We went back to F. She whined very loudly and let out a few screeches too. However, I showed her the boxes, and it just looked like too much fun not to play. I put some monkey biscuit powder in a box for forage. She proceeded to play like a crazy wild child throughout F, and also into E on the ropes. I just sat quietly on the floor observing her. Every once in awhile she'd stop by for a quick touch. When Lynn came in to set up cages, she suggested I hang the new canvas hammocks up for her to play on. I hung them in E.

I left the cage to get a piece of banana to feed her through the mesh so she wouldn't whine, and that worked nicely. After she ate, she retreated to the bench with her bear skin, and sucked her thumb. I couldn't tell if she was just taking a rest from her wild play or stressing. I poked some paper toweling into the mesh, and she proceeded to play. I guess she'd been taking a breather. She played between both cages, including being out of my sight, for 85 minutes. I fed her cereal through the mesh of both E and F. I then gave her the dish which she took to the hammock. We only left when we did because the adults came inside early. I took her back to A, and she played alone for the remaining hour and a half I was there. She can now unscrew the nipple of her bottle, so she drank half from the open bottle and the floor.

Kelly was still in B and did a lot of Luna watching through the intro door.

May 6, 1999

An interesting morning at the zoo! Luna tried to unscrew her a.m. bottle so I went ahead and poured it into a Sippy cup. She promptly poured the milk out so she only got about an ounce. (Incidentally she does now weigh 20 pounds.) Lynn said she needs to be weaned as the formula supply runs out, and asked my opinion. I suggested they could decrease by one ounce every day or two. I also said they could mix her cereal with the yogurt.

Chey and Doc were going out today, so Luna and I stayed inside for intros before they left. I hung two ropes between B and the tunnel. I also hung one of the new canvas hammocks between B and C with one hook on the tunnel. Luna and Chey interacted so well. There was a lot of gentle touching, kissing etc. Luna would put her head against the mesh for Chey to kiss her head. Chey also handed Luna bamboo twigs. Later she would push a bamboo twig through to Luna, and when Luna would reach for it, she'd pull it back. Then

Luna would be on the mesh. I think that was actually her plan. Earlier, before the intros, Chey was using the bamboo to try and unscrew the light cover in the aisle. During the intros she also kept trying to get Luna's toys, cup, etc. with the bamboo. They were in the crib in front of the tunnel. She deliberately put the bamboo through the cup handle to try and pick it up. Doc was watching, busy eating an onion, but watching. Luna went to the mesh of his cage once, but he wasn't interested. He then went over to the intro door, and I took Luna back into A to interact with him. I fixed cereal for both of them. Luna ate about two bites on the "fly by" as I sat by the door. Doc ate all of his, however, pushing paper through for me to use as a plate. He also spit a bite of sweet potato through for Luna, but she didn't take it.

Meanwhile, unnoticed by me, Chey was busy unclamping one of the hammock cords. Then she had the cord in the tunnel, tightly gripped. Therefore, the hammock and remaining cords were slack. Doc noticed that and started pulling the hammock into B. Well, I had to do something. Chey was not giving up the cord, and Doc wanted the hammock. I decided I'd unhook a rope, wrap it around the hammock, and pull it tight. When I reached for the rope clamp, Doc acted like he was going to grab it. I finally unhooked the rope, wrapped it around the hammock, and using all of my orangutan mom strength, pulled it as tight as I could, and hooked it on the side of cage C. Whew! Chey was finally distracted and I yanked the rope from her. Then those two went outside.

After I returned from a quick break, during which a keeper watched her, Luna was playing in the aisle by the shelves with the assorted boxes I'd brought. One was a huge cardboard box. Luna was also playing with some of the ropes. Kelly was in D right in front of us. Luna gave a push, and boxes, two ropes, and the bear skin fell into the moat. Kelly grabbed a rope with a piece of PVC on it. She was more animated than I've ever seen her, fooling with her "prize" and trying to decide what mischief she could get into. She tried very hard to get the PVC off the rope, but the knots prevented that. She mostly used it to push the skylight completely open. She finally tired of her treasure and shoved it toward me. I took it, praised her, and rewarded her with corn flakes and a pair of panty hose.

We then returned to A. Luna was shoving her surrogate around on the floor, and fell asleep on it by her cage door right before I left. All tuckered out. Me too!

May 11, 1999

Rudi was in today, in addition to Chey and Doc. Why? Well, Lynn wasn't there and he wouldn't go out. And why not? He loves the keeper who filled in for Lynn, and Barbara who was caring for Luna. He simply refused to go. The keeper said he wanted her to touch his nipple. What a guy!

Ropes were strung between A, B, and the tunnel. I also brought a large cardboard box, and other assorted boxes for enrichment. Chey and Luna had some great interactions. Doc was sitting on the blue barrel in B, near the mesh. Luna was on the mesh, and Chey displaced Doc and sat there herself. There was a lot of "kissy face" with lips and tongues. Luna also took Chey's finger, and guided it to her genitals for stimulation. She turned upside down so Chey could lick her genitals. This is all very normal, appropriate behavior for orangutans. Chey also turned her shoulder, pressed it to the mesh, and Luna groomed her by pulling on the hair with her mouth. Chey just seems so gentle with her. One wonders how it will go if Luna is in a cage with her. Will her possessiveness take over? Luna better learn food foraging on her own, or Chey will take it all. The keeper said she wonders if Chey watched a baby orangutan with her mother at some point in her zoo life. Chey makes the appropriate mama sounds, but the keeper said she doesn't think she's ever had a baby, however. (I learned Chey was raised by her mother and probably observed her mother with another baby.)

Chey was funny earlier in the day. She had a shallow blue plastic bucket with handles. She kept putting it on her head etc. At one point she stuffed it full of papers and then stood on her head in it. Silly woman. Doc had a large, oblong, shallow, plastic bin that he was wearing, bending, shoving, banging, scooting; you name it. I gave them road maps. Chey unfolded hers and put it on her head. Doc checked his over quickly and then laid it down. I also gave each of them a pair of panty hose. Doc loves to loop stuff through the mesh and pull on it. Chey wasn't too interested past the initial checking the panty hose out, and looping them through her cage mesh. After all, this is the book worm, and I've not given her any new reading material for a couple of weeks.

Right before Luna's 5:15 p.m. formula, I did a brief intro session with both Doc, in cage D, and Chey, in cage C,. I put Luna on the short side of those cages. There was more gentle touching with Chey, and Luna put her finger in Chey's mouth but didn't get bitten. Luna nibbled Doc's fingers but he didn't pull away.

Luna started to pull the nipple out of her bottle, so I just poured the formula into the bottle cap and she drank it all that way.

May 13, 1999

A great day at the zoo. We started the day with Luna guzzling her bottle as I held her. I'd just taken it out of the warmer, and she wasn't going to wait 'til she was out of my arms.

Lynn opened the door to the exhibit, and we were in and out three times in the next hour and a half. We had cheerios for foraging. I scattered them along the structure, and she promptly scattered them off the structure. The birds foraged very well, however. I also strung a rope from the structure to the upright poles, and she played on that. I could get 10 to 15 feet away, but any further and she came over and sat beside me. She still needs that closeness, like little orangutans in the wild.

We went inside twice for brief intros with Chey. All intros today went very well. Chey was so gentle touching her. I think she is gentler than she used to be. The poking used to be so deliberate, but now she is gentle and sweet. Luna also had positive intros with Doc. At one point she rubbed her genitals on his fingers. He didn't budge. He also had his play face on during another intro. When he moved away quickly, Luna didn't Velcro to me. Instead, she stayed on the mesh, but just reached out to take hold of me.

One of her former caregivers came to visit. She hadn't seen Luna since last September. Luna sniffed her fingers and squeaked in recognition. Amazing!

We'd also strung a rope, and Luna was holding onto it, jumping up and down like she was in a "Johnny Jump Up." Silly baby!

Not much else today. Just a very positive day.

May 18, 1999

Luna is 20 months old today. Wow! She is growing up so fast. I don't suppose orangutan moms think that.

When Barbara left she had a little screaming tantrum. I went into A with her, tried to distract her, but screaming was more fun. When she quieted, I picked her up and we went into B. I strung some ropes across the cage. I also put one on the trapeze, and left one hanging from the skylight. I also took her lunch in there with us, and she ate it without much hesitation. I backed out of B, leaving her alone about 1:30 p.m., and not a peep. She dragged her bearskin and a sheet around, and then went to the corner, laid down on them, and fell asleep. I had to wake her for the Luna Show. It was a small, but inquisitive group, and we were there about 30 minutes.

When we got back I strung ropes from C into D, and some crisscrossed in D. I left the ones hanging from the skylight and the trapeze in B.

Kelly had been in C, D, and the tunnel, and she did not want to shift into E and F, where she'd be all night. I had to carry Luna down the aisle in front of those cages so she'd move. Lynn said she thinks she just didn't want to go away from Luna.

Anyway, Lynn went off to a meeting so Luna and I were left to play. D was locked, but B and C just latched. (By the way, Luna now knows how to undo the latches from the inside, and we cannot leave her unattended at all.) After the "playground" was set up, I exited through the door of cage C. Luna screamed bloody murder; so loud the keeper came in to see. I said she was okay, just a little tantrum. She realized what was going on and quickly left, shutting the outside night house door also. The screaming stopped in about 15 seconds. I then gave her some crackers, and a bite of banana through the mesh. She continued independent play in B, the tunnel, C, D, and the squeeze cage for the next 2 hours. It was terrific! I was so proud of her. No whining, just playing. She mostly played in B. The suspended rope was just too much fun, spinning one way; then the other. I enticed her all the way to D for her cereal. I gave her a couple of bites through the mesh of B, then the tunnel, then showed her I also had a banana, and she followed me to D. We shared a bit with Kelly who was offering applause. (Today, when we walked into the night house after the Luna Show, Kelly applauded. It's so funny; sometimes her actions are very appropriate.)

It was great having Luna be so independent today. She's been such a whiny butt, and a cling-on the last few weeks. Lynn says I'm the most successful of the caregivers getting her to play alone. However, this is the first she's done so well in several weeks.

I gave her formula in a Sippy cup. That way she wouldn't bite the nipple or pull it out of her bottle. She did fine, drinking it all immediately.

There were no intros today as Kelly was the resident orangutan. Earlier I gave Kelly a clean, empty Nyquil bottle to play with. She pushed it out under the mesh for juice, and I gave her some. Then she tried to mash the bottle enough so it would fit through the 2 inch square of the mesh for more. Silly woman.

As I was getting ready to leave, Luna came to the front of the cage and spit a piece of poop out, offering a trade. (Another example of the 3% of DNA we don't share.) I gave her a piece of banana.

May 20, 1999

Miss Luna was at the cage front when I entered this morning. She opened the bottom latch of the cage, and then started working on the padlock. I heated her bottle, unlocked the cage, and she led me down the aisle to the shelves. She sat and guzzled her formula; only releasing it long enough to let the nipple re-inflate as she finished it off. Kelly was in D, by the shelves, so we sat there awhile for Luna to play. Chey was in B, and Doc was in the tunnel and C. I strung some ropes so we could have intros until they went outside. It was Kelly's turn to be inside. For the next hour or so we alternated between the shelves and the ropes. When she climbed onto the tunnel mesh, Doc came out of C, pulled up a red bucket as a chair, sat down, and wanted to interact. There was brief touching of her genitals with his toes. Chey tried to kiss Luna, and also touched her gently here and there. Luna was only mildly interested in the intros as it was more fun to play in the aisle.

Before we went outside, she was playing on the shelves and there was some tapping on the roof. Some workmen were doing something. She made a leap into my arms, and clung like she hadn't in months. What a wimp! But I enjoyed the snuggles. She then got down, grabbed her gray blanket, marched into A, and retreated to the far corner.

We were outside only briefly while Lynn cleaned the yard and put food out. I sat on the end of the structure, and Luna did a quick exploration of it.

When we went in, I fixed her cereal, making extra for Kelly, and served it in a shallow dish. She eventually ate it while playing near the shelves. Kelly was very happy to get some, and pushed another dish out for Luna's leftover soaked monkey biscuits.

Before Kelly was shifted to the clean cages, baby food was put on the pages of a phone book. That kept her busy for quite awhile, looking through the book, licking the baby food from the pages. Lynn is always looking for enrichment activities for her. Before she moved her, Lynn told her to take the blue barrel with her, which she did. She loves that thing! She also gave her the big hard ball, but she hadn't started any action with it before I left.

After D, E, and F were cleaned, I set up ropes in E and F. I was able to leave her alone in there. She whined a little but I fed her corn flakes through the mesh. She'd been alone for about 10 minutes when my relief came and I left the zoo.

May 25, 1999

Today I took two 10 inch plastic balls for Luna. She seemed to really like something new, and played with them at intervals throughout the day, generally acting quite silly. She rolled them with her feet, batted them, and rolled on them.

She played briefly in A. I then took her to E and F. I'd constructed a playground of ropes, the hammock, boxes, her new balls, and her lunch placed in boxes, with crackers for forage. She did a medium loud cry when I exited, but she played alone for an hour. Then it was time for the Luna Show, during which she was very active.

After the show, Chey was shifted to B and Doc was in C. (They were the two inside today, together in B and C.) During the setting up of their cages, as they were being split up for the night, Luna played for a short time in A. Chey's food, plus alfalfa, was in a black tub by the intro door. Luna grabbed a few stems of alfalfa through the mesh, and kept swinging to the door as Chey sat there eating. Strawberries were on the menu, and she thoroughly enjoyed those. I was hoping she'd offer to share some with Luna, but such generosity never crossed her mind. I then took Luna back into the aisle to play on the ropes set up in the aisle between B and C. Doc was busy eating, and when Luna went to the mesh of C, he made no attempt to visit. Therefore, we headed back to E and F to play until we were evicted. I stayed in there with her for about 10 minutes and then exited. She whined quietly for a moment, and when she quieted, I gave her some juice. Lynn threw about 10 monkey biscuits on the cart for her, and she sampled each. The way she chewed on them today was almost like she was teething. When cereal time came I fed her through the mesh, and she was a hungry wee soul. Then I pushed the bowl in for her to lick it clean. She then grabbed a sheet and played with that for the longest time. She rolled up in it, put it on her head, and swung with it on her head over to the cart from the bench and back again. She was so silly. I wondered if she could see through it because she would just sit there with it over her head. I'd put a lot of her "stuff" from the aisle shelves on the cart. Barbara had suggested this, wanting her to quit playing on the shelves. I'd anchored the cart tightly to the cage front, remembering how she'd tipped a cart over a few months earlier and injured her arm. At one point she was sitting on the cart with her back to me. I scratched her back saying, "scratch your back" over and over. After that, when I'd say, "scratch your back," she'd press her back against the mesh. What a smart baby! Actually, one of her training behaviors is "show me your back" so…… but it was cute anyway. She played alone for an hour, and then it was time to head to the aisle for intros.

The intros were brief but positive. Chey touched her gently with her fingers, tongue, and mouth. At one point Luna put her finger in Chey's mouth, but Chey didn't bite her. Luna then took her finger out and licked her own fingers. Chey vocalized a lot to her, and offered her an orange peel. Even though I pointed this gesture out to Luna, she didn't get the hint.

When I called Doc's name, he came to the mesh when he saw Luna there. Luna rubbed her genitals on his knuckles, and licked water from his fingers. He didn't poke at her.

When bottle time came she guzzled it, only stopping to let the nipple re-inflate. She's being weaned. This week she's down to 125cc in each bottle. She insisted on going with me to get the banana slice, but got right off when we went back into A and I put the slice on the bench. I locked her in; no complaints. Whenever we leave her alone now, we have to lock whatever cage she's in. Why? Because she watches closely, and as soon as we turn our backs, she opens the cage.

May 27, 1999

What a great job! After working 15 hours yesterday at my paying job, I felt like I was running on empty when I got up this morning. However, a morning with the orang gang revitalized me. They are so funny and so much fun!

Luna was playing quietly in her cage when I arrived. She didn't seem eager to come out, not trying the latch or padlock as usual. I heated her bottle and then went in to get her. We walked down the aisle to greet everyone as she drank her bottle. Rudi was in B, Kelly in C, Doc in D, and Chey had the suite, E and F. As we passed by C, we noticed Kelly had a pair of panty hose on her head. (I really think the police would recognize her, however.) Luna wanted to get on the mesh of Chey's cage so I let her. Chey did some gentle touching, but was really hoping Luna would share the bottle. No such luck!

I placed ropes between D, E, and F so she could play before we went outside. We did go out for about an hour. She climbed some about the structure, but was not too excited about exploring. I'd strung a rope over to the poles that she could use to get to me, if according to her standards, I strayed too far away. She didn't forage for the Rice Krispies I'd strewn about the structure, but the birds did. At one point a bird landed too close, and Luna made a flying leap onto me. Because she had a mouthful of avocado and some on her hands, I looked really nice when I set her back down. Twice she wanted to return to the night house, so we made a quick pass through. One time she walked by herself, through the big door and all. When we made our final entry, Lynn used the hydraulics to open and close the door, so Luna can get used to the sound.

Kelly and Rudi went outside. While their cages were being cleaned for Chey and Doc to shift to, Luna played in the aisle by D, E, and F. I'd anchored a rolling cart there, and that was great fun too. She tried to bite Doc's fingers but he pulled them back. She did rub her head on his fingers.

After Chey and Doc were shifted to B and C, I strung ropes and anchored the cart to the tunnel mesh. I also attached a rope so she could spin. Lynn pulled the crib into the aisle too.

We made a trip into A, and I fixed ropes so Luna could spin in front of the intro door. As I did this, I thought I heard Chey messing with the rope clamps in the aisle. Meanwhile, Doc was sitting by the intro door with a piece of paper between him and the mesh. He then poked his tongue through the paper and Luna kissed him, "French" style. We then went back into the aisle, and I saw what Chey had been messing with. She'd pulled the hammock cord from the box on the cart shelf where the hammock was stored. She was trying very hard to pull the hammock into the tunnel. She wasn't about to let me have it. Well, Luna's cereal bowl was sitting there, needing to be licked out. Knowing how Chey loves food, I took the bowl and walked around to the front of C, showed her I had the bowl, and asked her to come get the cereal. She couldn't resist and came immediately. HOWEVER, she's so smart she realized what I was up to, and it was a race to the tunnel to grab the cord. I won! But only by a nose.

Luna was also rolling about the aisle today with her bear skin, just like the adults roll about. I'm so glad she shows such good signs of typical orangutan behavior.

Yet another great day at the zoo!

June 2, 1999

It's Wednesday. I switched days with another caregiver as I had a meeting yesterday.

Apparently Doc has had a couple of bad days. It was storming on Sunday afternoon, and the keeper was hurrying to get all of the gang inside. She was afraid the power might go out. Doc came in last. She then closed the hydraulic door to the outside, and the power did go out. He was trapped in the tunnel for the night. He was so scared because he thought he was in the small space to be sedated. They gave him a blanket but it didn't help. He developed stress diarrhea. Poor baby. Anyway, he's better now.

Doc and Chey were inside today, and they had access to all the cages. There were ropes strung at both ends of the night house. I also put a spinning rope by the intro door in A. Luna played in A and in the aisle. Chey was the resident in B for the night, and Lynn locked her in there after the Luna Show. When she was setting the cage up, Luna reached through the mesh of the intro door and grabbed Chey's apple, managing to get a few bites. Chey pretty much parked at the intro door while Luna was in A, and Luna kept going there, taking "stuff" with her. She gave Chey a toothbrush she'd been playing with. Chey tried to give it back but Luna wouldn't take it. Then Chey brought it to me, and traded it for a monkey biscuit. ("Will work for food.") Later, when I put Luna in her cage, I put soaked monkey biscuits and a drink of juice on the threshold of the intro door. Luna offered Chey a drink of juice, and Chey also had one of the biscuits.

The other cute thing Luna did today was jumping up and down in a puddle of water on the top shelf of the rolling cart. Just like a little human kid. She was stomping and splashing away. 97% of our DNA---definitely!

June 3, 1999

Kind of an uneventful morning at the zoo. I didn't let Luna out right away. I heated her bottle, strung some ropes between B and C, and gave her vitamin to her through the mesh. I shoved her bottle into the cage, as per the new protocol. She promptly unscrewed the top, and drank from the open bottle. She did spill quite a bit on the bench, but she licked that up. When I did take her out we greeted all of the others, and then she started playing on the ropes. There was no interaction with Doc or Chey.

I needed to take a potty break, so I took her back into A and put her down. She screamed and managed to get to the door so I couldn't close it. I got some bread cubes, put them on the intro door threshold, and raced out. Apparently she knew I meant business because she didn't complain. When I returned, I praised her and gave her a treat for being a "good girl." I told Lynn I thought the problem (screaming when left in a cage) might be due to the fact she prefers playing in the aisle, and suggested that if she isn't interacting with Chey or Doc, maybe she should be in a cage. After all, that is her future except for going into the yard. Lynn agreed and said she plans to write a protocol.

There's also a new thing we're now doing. One of the hydraulic doors to the squeeze cage is opened just enough for her to fit through. Her big hairy mama is latched to a pole in D or E, and the caregiver sits in the squeeze cage so Luna can go in and out of the "creep door" as it is called. She needs to see we haven't deserted her. I think eventually, when she is in with Chey, a creep door will be available for her to go through and get away from Chey. Today she did have a few moments of intro with gentle touching, but she mostly played in A.

Doc still has a touch of diarrhea so he's not his silly self yet.

June 8, 1999

Today I worked the whole day. Doc is on medication and is better. He was active and silly before he went outside. He was on his back on a big piece of cardboard, and spinning around. However, Kelly has diarrhea now. This gang must have caught some sort of little bug.

As Chey and Doc were going out, along with Rudi of course, I had to do intros early. I was a little late, and it was 7:40 when I arrived in the night house. Anyway, I heated Luna's bottle, slipped it into her cage, and she promptly guzzled it down. I tried to get her to trade the empty bottle for a monkey biscuit, but of course she couldn't get the bottle through the mesh. She tried. I couldn't get her to understand she needed to bring it down to the space that we slip the bottle through.

I took her to the aisle and put her on the mesh of B. Chey came immediately from the intro door. Luna presented her genitals for a touch. She also briefly took hold of Chey's finger. Doc wasn't interested in interacting, but Luna did try to bite his finger at one point.

I set up ropes in D, E, and F, and Lynn made a creep door between the squeeze and D. Luna played on her own before and after the Luna Show for a total of about 3 hours. What a good little girl! She played like a wild child, swinging and racing from cage to cage. It was a sight to see.

She had a big appetite today except she didn't want bananas. She ate 6 soaked monkey biscuits. At one point she traded me a dry biscuit for one that had soaked in juice. Smart!

When I took breaks she was really good. There was minimal complaining; just some thumb sucking when I returned.

Twice today I had to have her unlatch the lower latch on her door when we were in the cage, and I'd accidentally latched it. She reached right through to open it as her hands are small enough.

June 10, 1999

Luna was quite independent today. She drank her bottle right down, and tried again to slip it through the mesh to the keeper instead of pushing it under the cage at the slot we use. When she did drop it, the keeper praised her and gave her a treat. She's still not wanting bananas, but ate other things.

Kelly was the one to stay in so we did quick intros early. Doc was not at all interested. He lay on the floor, covered his head with shredded paper, and didn't even look at her. Chey came to the cage front immediately. Did a brief touch and that was all.

The zoo was short staffed, so I decided to help the keeper clean cages. They'd all had shredded paper and hay for nest building, and the place was a mess. It looked like they'd had a wild frat party, minus the togas. I wanted to have Luna go with me to the different cages, but she was quite happy to stay in A and play. Without thinking, I set my broom against the mesh of C where Kelly was, and of course she pulled it in. Well, sunflower seeds and monkey biscuits weren't adequate trade items. After I lost a brief tug-of-war, she had the handle and I had the bristles. The keeper got some baby food to make the trade more appealing. Kelly then broke the handle into little pieces, giving the keeper one piece at a time, receiving baby food after each trade. She is so smart.

Earlier, I was shocked when I was making cereal, and Rudi offered me a piece of paper to get some. He usually ignores us. I soaked a biscuit in formula, and the keeper let me give it to him after he stationed to go outside. She also let me spoon feed Kelly the extra cereal. That was neat.

The keeper put a big box in A for Luna. She got under it and moved about the floor. She also gave Kelly one and she put it on. She thinks box wear is fashionable anytime.

Before I left, I set up ropes in D and Luna had access to D, E, and F. I'm glad she was happy to play independently today. I was operating on 3 hours sleep. I worked 'til 2 a.m. (a 19 hour day) at my paying job. We're doing the transportation for the George Bush birthday gala at the Astrodome, and it took us that long to get the finishing touches on the schedule. As we're transporting some very important people it's a big deal. Anyway, it was a lazy day at the zoo.

June 15, 1999

I arrived at the zoo with arms full of enrichment articles, mostly soft drink boxes and a few "carry out" containers. My son, Derek, his girlfriend, and two others were at the zoo today. Lynn said they could tour the back area. I didn't ask; she offered. However, they left after the Luna Show because it was raining so hard. Derek said they'd come back another time.

The a.m. caregiver had ropes strung in D, E, and F with a creep door between D and the squeeze. Luna played independently, mostly in D, until the Luna Show. I'd given her an empty plastic bottle, but I was worried about her having the sharp plastic pieces when she broke it. Therefore, I went into D, traded a soaked monkey biscuit for the bottle, and left with no whining from the girl. In fact, I even left the night house for a potty break, and she didn't complain. When I returned, she did have big hairy mama in tow, and her thumb in her mouth, but no whining.

There was a large crowd at the Luna Show. She was wild on the jungle gym, and then went to the floor in front of it. When I started for her she moved to the other end. A little game of tag with me losing. She was watching me the whole time, making a "monkey" out of me in front of everyone. Lynn told me to stand in front so the tag game would at least keep her away from the crowd. I wonder how much longer we can do the Luna Shows. She's becoming a bit unmanageable.

It was raining so hard when we got back to the night house, Lynn had me take the "playground" down so she could bring Doc and Chey inside. She hated to banish Luna to A for the rest of the afternoon, so we constructed a play area between D and E. Lynn opened the front of the squeeze cage, and the door to the outside, so she could play in the squeeze. We made a blanket "roof" to keep her off the top of the squeeze. As I was tying one end of it, she climbed up the other side. I had to get the ladder and the rake to retrieve her. She then responded to a firm "no" the next time she started up there. When Lynn came back I told her about it, and of course she started up there again. I said, "No" and she stopped, but then looked at Lynn to see if she'd let her do it. She is so bad!

We returned to A at 5 p.m. She drank her 50cc of formula, and traded me the empty for a piece of banana and a monkey biscuit.

Kelly and Rudi were inside today. Kelly kept giving me things for treats. Lynn shared Luna's cereal with all of them. I also gave them leftover formula.

June 17, 1999

Interesting morning at the zoo. First off, the keeper gave the gang juice. It was orange juice. Doc licked the cup, and made his "orange juice is really too sour" face. Kelly took sips and spit them into a plastic glove, filling it half full. She then walked to the back of the cage and laid it down gently so as not to spill. She ate her hardboiled egg (Thursday fare), picked the glove up, bit a tiny bit from the end of each glove finger, and sucked her juice out. Well, that's one way to get a drink.

Rudi, Doc, and Chey were scheduled to go outside so I tried quick intros with the latter two. When I put Luna onto the mesh, Chey came immediately to the front of her cage, and touched Luna ever so briefly. Luna wasn't at all interested. I took her to Doc's cage, put her on the mesh, and he totally ignored her. Oh well.

I took her outside with her breakfast of avocado and sweet potato plus sunflower seeds and peanuts for forage. She explored just a few feet away from me. Clingy was the operative word as she sat right beside me, on me, or held onto me. When I got off the platform she whined, and when I started to step away she made a flying leap onto me. At that point we went inside, and I locked her in her cage. I needed to take a potty break. She didn't say a word. When I came back she had a grip on her bone pillow for security, but her thumb was not in her mouth.

We went back outside while the keeper cleaned the exhibit. She was slightly more courageous, even taking off once across the wet grass toward the keeper. She did enter the night house alone. I was right there, but she climbed off of me to go through the door. The keeper awarded her with an egg (she only ate the yolk) and her vitamin.

We swept cages. Well I swept; she played. Did C, D, E, and F. Kelly had been shifted to B and was a happy camper. She had the big ball and the blue barrel. Luna was quite happy as long as I was inside a cage. I decided to exit out of C. She screamed and parked in the door so I couldn't close it. I picked her up, carried her back inside the cage, placed her on the hammock, and left quickly. She screamed like crazy. I felt bad but knew I could not "rescue" as it would reinforce her badness. I talked softly to her as I went to get her juice. The keeper left to get more peanuts. When she quieted, I gave her the juice and some peanuts. She whined quietly for awhile, but eventually settled down. Meanwhile, Kelly had come into the tunnel so she could get a close up of what I was doing to her baby. I gave her some peanuts, and reassured her Luna was fine.

After the cages were all scrubbed, I constructed an elaborate playground with ropes, toys, and paper toweling in C, D, E, and F. When I left, locking her in F, she didn't cry. However, she was lying prone on big hairy mama looking like a dejected, rejected baby.

The caregiver, the one who follows me on Thursdays, says Luna doesn't like her, and the separations are hard. Poor little darlin'.

When all of this is over, I'm going to have separation anxiety.

Wednesday, June 23, 1999

I switched afternoons this week as I had a meeting at church yesterday, right in the middle of my work day. I'm getting ready to go on vacation for two weeks, so this afternoon and tomorrow morning are my last times with Luna for awhile.

I went to the zoo armed with enrichment articles as usual. I had assorted boxes, a milk jug, a juice carton, and a large piece of foam I'd purchased at some point for some reason. I also had a broom to give to Lynn. I felt so bad about Kelly taking and breaking the broom two weeks ago.

Lynn suggested I give the foam to Kelly, the adult inside today. I'd had Doc in mind, but Lynn said Kelly had been bored all morning. There were two workers inside the building working on the hydraulic doors, and Luna had been pretty much confined to A. Kelly had spent the morning applauding, hoping for someone to play with. She promptly dipped the corner of the foam into her water bowl and sucked on it. How did she know it would soak the water up? Hmmm...... She found it a boring item, laid it down, and didn't pick it up again after the drink. When she didn't take it with her when she shifted to B, I knew it was a nothing toy.

Luna played in D until the workers came back from lunch. She screamed when I left her alone a few minutes after I arrived, but the screaming only lasted about 10 seconds.

After the Luna Show, I set her up in E and F, in addition to D. The workers were done. She had absolutely no complaint when I left her alone. She foraged in all three cages for sunflower seeds. The creep door was between D and the squeeze, and big hairy mama was in D. She wrestled with it, rolling all over the floor. Lynn commented she would have a rude awakening when she tried to wrestle with a live orangutan. She tried to pull big hairy mama through the creep door, but of course that didn't work. The opening was so narrow she had to suck her tummy in when she went through. She played alone for an hour and a half before it was time to take down the playground and move her to A.

Kelly was in B and parked at the intro door when Luna was back in A. She got a bamboo stem about 2 feet long, and poked Luna through the mesh. She actually poked her quite firmly; in the side, the back, and the head. Luna just sat there, but had a rather strange look on her face. She said nothing so I guess it didn't hurt. A few times she tried to grab the bamboo, but of course Kelly grabbed it back. Lynn gave me some baby food pudding to place about A for Luna to have, and to share with Kelly. Kelly passed her bamboo through the intro door for me to give her some pudding. She pulled it back ever so carefully so as not to spill it off her stem.

Smart little Luna tried to hand me her bowl for another soaked monkey biscuit this afternoon. She tried to push it through the mesh, but of course that didn't work. When I put my hand down on the floor under the mesh, she dropped it there for me to get. She's learning! When she was drinking her bottle, she placed it upside down in a glass, and was pounding the bottom of it. I opened it, poured the formula into a glass, and let her drink it that way.

Watching her being so independent today makes me realize this is all going to end very soon. I will definitely continue to volunteer in Primates to keep up with the gang.

New world record - Luna ate 11 monkey biscuits today.

June 24, 1999

This morning I entered the night house about 7:40. Luna was on the mesh. She started sucking her thumb when she saw me heat her bottle, but didn't drink it when I gave it to her. She kept pressing the nipple against something to make the milk come out. She finally unscrewed the top and poured it out. Oh well! After the monkey biscuit pig-out yesterday, it was famine today. Refused every one I gave her. Maybe the fact they were soaked in grape juice yesterday made the difference.

She was in no hurry to come out of her cage. Finally about 8:30 I got her to come to me. We tried brief intros with Doc and Chey, but no one was interested. Chey didn't even come down from her perch. Doc just looked at her. She did a quick rub of her genitals on his fingers, then took hold of a sheet that was looped through the mesh. Well, he decided it was a tug-o-war and pulled back, but Luna left.

We went outside with grapes, corn flakes, and peanuts for forage. I'd read other caregiver notes about how she's been rolling in the grass, wading in the pool, and exploring all over the wooden structures. Well, the grass was wet so forget that. She did go across the structure to gather the goodies, but once again, I couldn't get but a few feet away from her. I'd even strung a couple of ropes, but that was all the better to get to me. We sat on the edge of the pool for awhile, and she dipped her hand in while glued to my lap.

When it was time to go in, the keeper bribed her with yogurt. Both the keeper and I were at the night house door, and Luna was high on the structure. She started whining and reaching towards us with her hand. She'd decided, yogurt or not, she was not going to walk through that wet grass. Of course she had done that earlier to get to me. Anyway, I had to go get her, hoping she'd let me walk her in, but I had to carry her to the night house door. Once there, she entered by herself.

She played alone in A for awhile because Doc and Chey had been shifted to the tunnel and B. There were workers down the aisle, and Kelly and Rudi had gone outside.

I set up the squiggly water toy thing you attach to a hose. I set it by the tunnel. Doc and Chey had a blast. Luna was scared at first, only touching their wet fingers, but she finally got into the fun. Wasn't much touching, just together type play. Then when she wanted to wander down the aisle, I put her back into A I gave Chey a T-shirt because she was trying to stuff a sheet with hay. (She'd rolled it up.) She stuffed the shirt awhile, and then tried it on, in a fashion. Doc came in, bit her, and snatched the shirt. He then put it on over his head and around his chest. Earlier, when he walked by Chey, she'd reached out and slapped him, just for good measure. Maybe he was just retaliating.

Chey and Doc were shifted back to D, E, and F, so I set up ropes in B, the tunnel, and C, with the creep door between the tunnel and C. I put some grapes and corn flakes in assorted containers, and shut her in B.

I was out of sight and out of there as soon as the next caregiver arrived.

July 13, 1999

Back to the zoo today after 19 days of not seeing the gang. I sent each a postcard from the Black Hills 2 weeks ago, but so far they've only received the one I sent to Doc.

Luna didn't rush to give me a hug (guess that would be expecting too much), but when the a.m. caregiver left, she didn't whine or try to cling to her. I gave her a container with some crackers which she took up to her little hammock. When I reached for her, she put on her play face and tried to bite me. Hmmm...... However, the play face was a good sign she was glad to see me.

She's completely off formula now, but she gets 50-75 cc of water in the a.m. and p.m. Not much else has changed in the 19 days.

It was raining when I got to the zoo. Lynn had opened the outside door so Doc, Chey, and Rudi had access to the tunnel, and that's where they were sitting. Kelly was in B, her place for the day and night.

Doc and Rudi were playing, kind of wrestling. First time I'd ever seen Rudi do anything like that. Doc would put his head down and charge into Rudi. At one point he pushed Rudi across the tunnel. Rudi probably let himself be pushed. Anyway, it was neat watching them.

Luna really didn't do anything new and different. She played in A by herself for an hour. Then we went to E and F where the morning caregiver had strung ropes and the canvas hammock. She ate her lunch there. After playing alone for awhile she started whining.

I tried to divert her attention with crackers, but the whining was converting to quiet shrieks. I went into the cage and sat quietly in the corner.

There was no Luna Show due to the weather. I was glad as she's getting hard to handle during the show.

She was back in A from about 2:45 p.m. on, except a brief trip to the aisle to give her the cereal. Chey was in C, Rudi in the tunnel, and Kelly in B. Doc was outside as the rain had stopped. I gave Chey a bite, then Kelly, then Rudi. On round #2 Rudi still had his cereal in his mouth, and I skipped him. On round #3 Rudi totally refused a bite. I guess real men don't eat rice baby cereal.

A funny thing happened earlier. Lynn put a banana in front of the tunnel to entice Rudi to the tunnel. (I think he was in C, but I was down the aisle so not sure.) Anyway, Lynn came back into the night house, and noticed Chey was eating the banana. She'd gone outside, pulled a big weed for a tool, came in, and swiped the banana. Lynn says, "Chey is just evil." However, she says that with lots of love in her voice.

When I left Luna to take a potty break she didn't whine, but when I returned in less than 2 minutes, she had her thumb planted firmly in her mouth. As soon as I sat down she started playing again.

The keeper Kelly doesn't like closed tonight, and every time she had to walk past her cage, she got a mouthful of water spit at her. Sometimes Kelly is just not very nice!

July 15, 1999

I entered the night house at 7:45 a.m. Lynn said Luna was fussing when she unlocked the night house. I gave her the bottle of water, and she took it to her hammock to drink it all. It was really cold water, having been in the fridge all night. I guess it hit the spot on this hot summer day. She's so cute the way she takes things up to the little hammock.

Had great intros with Chey and Doc today; actually more with Chey, as usual. They were going to go outside, so Lynn said to do as much as possible with them before they left. Chey was in B and Doc in C. Chey was tearing a plastic basket apart, and poking bits of it through the intro door. Luna was busy swinging about cage A, but I enticed her to come to me about 8:15, and we went into the aisle by the tunnel. Chey came immediately to the front and gently touched Luna. She then got the blue barrel, pulled it over, and sat on it. Luna was reaching through the mesh tickling Chey's feet. Chey was making the low guttural sounds and kiss squeaks. Doc came into the tunnel, and Luna gave a quick bite on his fingers. I hooked ropes onto B and the tunnel, putting both ends on the same cage. That way Luna stayed close and didn't go back and forth. Chey stayed close because she was trying to figure out how to undo the clamps. She was using her fingers, bamboo, and her mouth.

Luna led me back to A after awhile. I left for a potty break. I gave her a vitamin and told her I'd be right back. Lo and behold, when I came back she was not sucking her thumb, didn't have her bone pillow, and wasn't on hairy mama. We're making progress!

I then set up the squiggly water toy thing so it would spray into B and the tunnel. I also anchored the rolling cart to the tunnel. Then the games began! The three of them went nuts. Doc was literally bouncing off the walls. They were gulping water, splashing water, and all three got plenty wet. Doc and Luna had on their play faces. It was great fun! We had to quit so Lynn could get out to clean the yard. Luna and I went back into A. Lynn gave me three monkey biscuits to feed Chey through the intro door, and told me to encourage Luna to go there. I didn't have to. Luna saw Chey had a mouthful of biscuits, went to the mesh, pulled Chey's head towards her, and tried to steal a biscuit. Chey closed her mouth, of course. Then she actually offered Luna a biscuit with her mouth a couple of times. I couldn't really see, but I think Luna took one and dropped it back into Chey's cage. She did get a piece of the plastic basket that Chey gave her.

After Chey and Doc went out Lynn was hosing A, B, and C. I was holding Luna as she was eating a piece of endive. We were walking about the aisle, chatting with Kelly and Rudi. Luna was munching away, perfectly content to be in my arms, to be held, and loved. I realized I must cherish such moments because it will all end soon. How I will miss the hands on; the hugging, kissing, tickling, teasing. The loving won't end however.

July 20, 1999

What a fun day at the zoo! When I arrived Luna was playing in D, E, and F with no complaint. I thought it might be a rather boring day. WRONG!!

As usual, Luna was fiddling with the locks of the cages she was in, but not whining. I figured I'd reinforce that big girl behavior by letting her out before the whining began. Therefore, 30 minutes after I arrived, I decided to take her back to A. Chey was in B. Well, actually, Doc and Chey had access to B, the tunnel, and C.

Lynn had spread 2 jars of baby food on the threshold and walls of the intro door. Chey and Doc had worked on retrieving it. However, there was plenty left when Luna and I arrived in A, so I sat down with her by the intro door. She immediately started licking it up. Chey came over and tried to touch Luna, after she shoved Doc aside. He was there first. She really didn't try to eat any, just seemed to want to interact with Luna, who was too busy eating. Then Doc put his big old hand on Chey's face, and the wrestling match began. They tussled quietly while Luna kept eating. They got a little noisy once, but Luna did not run, just sat on the outer edge of the door. After she licked up all visible signs of the baby food, I noticed some in the crevice of the threshold. Being a good mama orangutan, I decided to teach her how to use a tool to retrieve it. So I got a ginger twig and demonstrated scooping it out. Then I gave her the end of the stick to lick off. She learned she should lick the stick, and then put the stick back in my hand to scoop more out. Made a "monkey" out of me. I tired of this after 5 or 6 times so I laid the stick down. She picked it up and scooped in the crevices. She was paying attention. I laughed when I told the zookeepers how trainable I was.

There was a large crowd at the Luna Show. Luna was a bit clingy, hanging onto me with one hand as she sat on the jungle gym. I think she was frightened of the speaker that was on a nearby table. Lynn's voice was "booming" out of it, as much as Lynn's quiet spoken voice can boom. I'd taken a ginger stem, a bamboo stem, a rope and paper toweling to keep her amused. She mostly chomped on the ginger stem. Someone asked if she did tricks. Lynn said no, only the ones she wants to do, and they aren't trained to do tricks because they are wild animals. Well, a few moments later Luna started applauding. Then the crowd applauded. She did it again; so did the crowd. This was repeated several times. Guess she's her mother's daughter as Kelly applauds all the time. What a ham! Seems she was doing a good job training humans today. She also stood tall on the top of the jungle gym, and gave her best royal wave to the crowd. Lynn was laughing, I was laughing, and the crowd loved it.

Back in the night house I put her on the ropes and the cart in the aisle between B and C. No intros took place except she had a quick sniff of Doc's fingers. He was in C. Lynn made door #2, between B and the tunnel, a creep door. She told me if Chey and Doc tried to pull it up, tell them, "No, release the door." Then I was supposed to reward them with some dry rice cereal saying, "good girl" or "good boy." Well, they quickly decided pull on the door, get food. So then I just did the "good girl, good boy" and no food. This was the first time the door had been like that, and Doc and Chey just didn't know what to think, except the door should be open or closed, not open just a little bit. Chey laid her head down on the threshold, and peered under the door. Lynn said she probably thought there was some secret thing she was being left out of on the other side of the door. She and Doc also grabbed at each other under the door.

When I fixed Luna's cereal I made extra for Doc, told him to give me something to put it on, and he pushed out a large, 12" by 24" tub lid. So I put his cereal on that. Then I went into A, fed Chey some cereal through the intro door mesh, and handed Luna her little flat dish of cereal. She drank it, spilling some, of course, to be licked up later. Well, Doc saw this action and took his lid to the creep door and started to pass it through, looking for more handouts. I mixed more. He went back to C and gave me his "dish" again.

Luna played alone in A from then on, with frequent trips to the intro door and no complaints when I left.

July 22, 1999

Luna was on the cage front when I entered the night house. She started squeaking when she saw the bottle of water. She took it up to the skylight and guzzled it right down. She definitely likes the cold water. As usual, after she finished, she took the bottle apart. I only saw the rim on the floor. Later in the morning, however, I found the nipple and bottle in her little hammock along with leftover snacks, a cup, a cardboard roll, paper etc.

When I took her into the aisle to weigh her (still 20 lbs.), Chey came immediately to the front of her cage (C), and I put Luna on the mesh for intros. Chey wanted to touch her and did so - gently. She also made the guttural sounds to her, and Luna presented her genitals for Chey to touch.

About 8:15 we headed outside. I took her sweet potato and avocado with us. I climbed to the top of the structure, laid out the buffet, and she ate quickly with one arm around my leg. I was sitting with my knees bent, and after a few minutes, I stretched my legs out. Luna literally picked one of legs up, bent it back the way it was, and wrapped her arm around it again. Can we say clingy? The whole time we were on the structure she had one hand on some part of me, except for a few brief moments when she ventured about four feet away. However she kept checking that I hadn't moved.

I decided to go back inside for a brief intro with Doc and Chey, figuring that was more productive. However, a large bird was in Luna's cage A, and that worried and scared her. Forget the intros – she just wanted that bird out of her cage, and she was not letting go of me while I shooed it away. Fortunately, it was a slightly gimpy bird and shooed quite easily. It gimped down the aisle toward E and F where Kelly was, and that got a rise out of her. Like "oh boy, that's a clever enrichment item." It finally found an escape route to the outside.

We then went back out on the exhibit, she continued to stay close with one hand attached to me. I carried her to the pond, and she splashed while sitting on my lap. When it was time to go in I had to carry her. She did cross the threshold by herself, and was rewarded with yogurt and her vitamin.

At cereal time I fixed three dishes and sat down in front of the tunnel. Doc and Chey came into the tunnel, but Doc took his dish and went back into C. He's always afraid Chey will take his food. Chey stayed put and ate hers while Luna ate. She was hoping I'd share some of Luna's with her, and of course I did After that I put Luna on the mesh for more interaction with her. Lynn had put some bamboo stems in the tunnel for Doc and Chey. Luna pulled on one and Doc grabbed it real quick and hurried into C. Poor guy – he probably figures he can't win with these greedy gut females.

The funniest thing happened. Luna was playing with a sock, putting it on her hand. Then she smeared soaked monkey biscuit on it, so I gave it to Chey. A few minutes later, after she'd sucked the monkey biscuit off, Chey dipped it in her water bowl along with Doc's cereal dish, and proceeded to wash the dish. She scrubbed that dish with the sock for about 5-10 minutes. It was hysterical! Now who taught her to do that? Well, she does see us washing dishes in the sink, and they learn by observation.

The rest of the morning was uneventful. I smeared baby food on the inside of the intro door for them to share. Doc gave up as Chey was front and center. He did stretch an arm towards me so I could dab some on his finger. I let him lick the jar down in F while Chey and Luna pigged out.

When I left Luna was busy playing in A, and the separation was easy.

July 27, 1999

I was an hour late today because I was waiting on a furniture delivery. The morning caregiver was already gone and Lynn was "babysitting." She said Luna pitched an absolute hissy fit this morning when the caregiver left her in A while she set up a playground in D, E, and F. She screamed and screamed. Lynn said she told the caregiver to ignore her; just keep doing what she was doing.

When I arrived Luna was playing quietly in the corner of E; had a wet pillowcase to go in and out of.

The Luna Show went well. She was very active on the jungle gym during the show. I'd taken a rope, bamboo branch, and paper toweling. Lynn gave her a hibiscus blossom as soon as we arrived. She'd never had one, but it must have been delicious. She gobbled it down very quickly. She did a couple rounds of applause for the crowd, and the human primate crowd responded appropriately. They are so trainable! She also stood tall and did her grand, open arm wave to the crowd. Little showoff!

Kelly was inside today. Lynn said when Luna was pitching her fit, Kelly spit a mouthful of water at HER; got the whole right side of her head. Kelly was obviously blaming Lynn for her baby being upset.

Also, when I arrived, Kelly was lying on her back on the blue barrel with a wet gauze stretched across her face. (2 x2 gauze bandages were part of today's enrichment.) She looked so silly. Guess she had a case of the "vapors." I took an extra one she'd stuck in the mesh, dampened it, and gave it to her for a refresher.

At 3 p.m., after the Luna Show, Kelly had been shifted to B, and Luna had access to everywhere else. She was one happy baby playing in all of the cages. The squiggly water toy thing was squirting into the tunnel and B. That way she could play in the water where Kelly could watch her.

Lynn left early as she'd adopted a puppy in her neighborhood that was being neglected, and she wanted to get home to check on him. She left me instructions to set up the cages after Luna went back to A. I got to put in everyone's diet etc. I didn't dump anyone's food in a pile. I hid it in boxes and under things. They need a challenge.

Luna played in the other cages by herself for 2 hours this afternoon. She is getting so independent, just like she should, but it's a reminder that it won't be long until the "hands-on" care is over. How I will miss the hugs!

July 29. 1999

Well today the lunatics were running the asylum! Lynn entered the night house first to give Luna her bottle. She then set up a rope playground between D, the squeeze, E, and F. Chey was in E and F and Doc was in D. They were going out later so Lynn suggested doing what I could to get interaction going. Luna was thrilled with the playground and started playing immediately. When she got close, Chey tried to touch any body part of Luna's that she could. She was making kiss squeaks but Luna didn't care. She was having too much fun on the ropes. Then she got bored and led me back to A. I decided to disconnect some ropes so she would have to relate to the adults. I went back to A to get her, and upon returning to the aisle, I saw Doc had the end of one rope. Well, how did that happen? I thought I was so careful. Doc thought he'd gotten the prize and was having a blast; pulling, twisting, knotting, and wrapping. I attempted to get it back, but one doesn't win a tug-o-war with an orangutan. Just yesterday, Doc broke a rope clamp with his teeth, and Lynn said we should not hook them directly on the mesh because of that. Well, they weren't! He got a loose end. Then Luna rolled all the way back to A, so I locked her in there again. I went back down the aisle and saw Chey had part of another rope in her cage. I tried to get her to go to the other side of her cage for a treat and she did, but kept one hand on the rope. I took Luna back to attempt intros but no luck. Instead, she raced up the mesh, out of reach, and I had to get the rake to get her down. I finally decided to take her outside. She was a bit clingy. She did sit alone on the jungle gym nearby, but watched me closely. At one point she came over, climbed onto my lap, and just cuddled real close for a few minutes. Baby orang just needed to cling to "mom" for a bit. I love these moments. They are few and far between anymore.

I also had a pair of full length emerald green satin opera gloves to give Luna today. I first showed them to both Kelly and Luna, and how to put them on. Kelly was so funny. When she saw I had the gloves, she traded me a clamp she had as fast as she could; she wanted one so bad. I gave one to her and she tried to get it on, but of course her hand was much too big. She gave it back to me. I then gave her a pretty painted tray and she was happy. Luna put her glove on and she looked lovely. It went all the way to her shoulder and was still too long. I put a spinning rope over her wading pool, and she was a sight with her glove, spinning and splashing. Wild crazy baby!

When I left the zoo I felt like I'd been run through a wringer. I was pooped!

August 3, 1999

Chey and Doc were in today so I knew there would be lots of intro attempts and intros. New memos regarding the a.m. caregivers have us still arriving at the same time, but not entering the night house until 8:30 or 8:45. The zoo keeper does the early stuff. So on Thursday I'll be involved with that schedule.

I was also reading today about how the placing of Luna with Chey will be done. It'll be done after Chey has eaten. (She'll probably be in a better mood if not hungry.) Apparently, a creep door will allow Luna access to Chey, and it will be her choice. Caregivers will still be present after the introduction because she will need that extra security of "friends" nearby.

Luna played in the aisle on the cart by the tunnel, and also had lunch there. We shared some peelings with Chey. One green satin glove was still present; one was gone. In reading the Luna notes, it seems Chey took one in the last few days. However, I didn't see it anywhere.

Luna was a bundle of energy during the Luna Show. She had a huge bamboo branch, paper toweling, and a rope. She went from one thing to another. At one point she took off and grabbed Lynn around the legs. I was exhausted by the time we got back to the night house.

She played independently in her cage a lot today, but I also took her into the aisle for intros. Doc was put into B for the night; Chey in C and the tunnel. At one point I hooked the squiggly water toy thing up by the tunnel and B, and a good time was had by all. There were three very wet orangs and one very wet caregiver. Of course Doc and Chey both managed to grab the toy at different times, and it was very difficult to get it away. The cart was full of water too, and Luna did a lot of stomping up and down.

The intros were good even if minimal. Gentle touching by Chey and lots of kiss squeaks. Luna put her hand through the mesh and touched Chey's face too. When she and Doc were interacting, he would put his fingers through the mesh, Luna would try to bite them, he'd jerk them away, and they'd do it all over again. He also had on a big play face. Later Luna and Doc shared pudding I'd spread about the intro door. It was so funny; when Luna saw I had the pudding, she headed straight toward the intro door, knowing that's where the goodies would be.

WELL – Lynn said we had an interesting incident. Rudi and Kelly were out on exhibit. She went up on the roof and tossed in a large red "popsicle" for Rudi, and a smaller one for Kelly. (She'd frozen juice in drink bottles.) Apparently Kelly grabbed both. Then Rudi grabbed Kelly and forced copulation in front of the astonished crowd at the Plexiglas window. After that, he lifted her arms up and nursed her; nursed her dry on one breast and then the other. Lynn said she went into the crowd to try and offer her educational viewpoint for all of this behavior. She said Kelly's nipples were white, all the color literally sucked out of them. Rudi is a nipple man; we all know that. THEN, as if all of that wasn't enough, he pushed her head down for her to perform oral sex on him. She said Kelly was having no part of that. Lynn said when THAT happened, parents were ushering their kids away quickly. Poor Kelly. Lynn told the closing keepers to check her over for any obvious injuries.

I met a man today who helped hand raise Bubba, Luna's daddy, at a zoo in Jackson, Mississippi. Lynn said he remarked that Luna looked like Bubba did as a baby. She said she thinks Luna looks like Kelly. I think she probably looks like many baby orangs her age.

Another funny thing today. Doc was lying down with part of a T-shirt across his shoulders. I told him he needed a whole T-shirt, and gave him one. He put it on correctly and proceeded to walk about. It was too small (I think he probably takes as XXL) so he didn't wear it long, but it was so funny. I laughed and called him Macho Man.

August 5, 1999

Well, fortunately Kelly suffered no lasting physical or mental injuries from her rape, and other sexual humiliation, on Tuesday. Lynn said she was a bit subdued yesterday, and her nipples appeared bruised. This morning she was playful again, prancing around her cage with a blanket on her head, playing ghost.

Rudi refused to go out today, plus he was cantankerous about shifting cages. His stubbornness made for interesting cage arrangements, and there was very little opportunity for Luna to interact with Doc and Chey. For a time Doc was in with Rudi, and they had access to four cages, but Doc was steering clear of Rudi. When Rudi was asked to go out, he displayed loud and long. Was throwing the big green ball and other stuff about in his cage.

As we, the caregivers, don't go into the night house until 9 a.m., there was ample time to read charts after I fixed Luna's food and cut ginger stalks. I read up on Rudi and other adults. Apparently aggressive sexual behavior is not unusual for Mr. Rudi Valentino. I noted he recently raped Chey too. She is a better candidate as she's been known to go for sex with Rudi herself. It just amazes me these orangs have these person like sexual tendencies. None of them are fertile types, except Kelly and Doc. He's still a teen, however, and hasn't yet been given the okay to be a dad. They just like sex. Hmmm……..

Luna was a nut outside. The grass was dry so she rolled and rolled, side over side, not head over heels. Six or seven times she rolled toward the door, but it was awhile before the keepers were ready to have her go in. She did go in all alone when it was time.

It was a rather quiet morning. She played alone in A. Had a great time with water in her wading pool and a black tub.

August 10, 1999

I knew it was Kelly's turn to be inside today, and there would be no introductions. I gave Kelly a handbag left over from a garage sale. I put a couple of crackers in it. As only Kelly can do, she amused herself for a long time with this strange new enrichment article. At one point she walked appropriately with it over her arm. Silly woman!

Someone or ones brought in a bunch of new tubs, storage bins etc. Luna had a deep bin in her cage almost full of water. That was great for splashing. A couple of times she got in the water all the way to her tush. She had access to all the cages except C, where Kelly was, but didn't want to play long anywhere but her own cage. I'd set the other cages up with fun stuff but….. She was more whiny than usual with me. When I transferred her from D, E, and F into B, she got on a rope and I exited quickly. The whine soon turned to shrieks. Well, that behavior doesn't faze this mean mom! I just stood quietly in front of the cage with a small dish of cracker crumbs until she stopped carrying on. Then I gave her the crumbs, and she raced away to gobble them. I also gave her a sheet that Kelly had traded me for some cereal and a pink cord, the kind we tie Luna's hammocks with. She played alone until 4 p.m. Then it was time to put her back into A so Lynn could ready the other cages for the night.

Interesting note – when Luna was shrieking, Kelly did not budge from her spot. No interest in her baby whatsoever. That's really kind of sad.

Someone put a small tire swing in Luna's cage. Just her size. What fun!

Today Luna seemed to want to do a lot of chewing; on the rope knots, a branch in her cage etc. I'm wondering if there are some molars starting to come in.

August 12, 1999

I entered the night house at 8:45 a.m. after preparing Luna's food for the day, and walking over by the clinic to cut some forage greenery. I clipped a couple of hibiscus stems and blossoms on the way back. Figured the p.m. caregiver could use them for the Luna Show.

Doc and Chey were going out. I was to do intros until 9:50 a.m. Doc was in C and Chey was in B. I put a rope on each cage, plus set up the squiggly water toy thing between the tunnel and B. Doc and Chey loved the water. Luna loved trying to pick the locks on their cages. No interaction whatsoever! Luna wanted to go back to A. I let her go for about 10 minutes, and then tried again. By that time Doc was busy masturbating with the plastic glove the keeper gave him, and Chey was playing by the intro door. Therefore, I took Luna back to A, spread a jar of baby sweet potatoes on the intro door, plus sprinkled a few corn flakes about. They shared nicely. When I tried intros again, outside the cage, Chey showed slight interest, even offering Luna a branch, but Luna only wanted to pick locks. Meanwhile, Doc was playing wildly with a couple of plastic tubs. I put Luna back into A.

At 9:50 I asked her if she wanted to go outside, and she led me eagerly down the aisle. We went out through the squeeze today. She was clingy, but did get off of me briefly to sit a few feet away on the structure. When she was attached to me, she not only had one arm about me, she grabbed my hand and wrapped it around her. It seems every time we start to increase, encourage, or insist on her being more independent, she gets whiny and clingy. When it was time to go in, she only went the last couple of feet alone. Had my hand before that.

I tried to get her to play alone in the other cages, but she wouldn't unless I stayed with her. So I swept the cages and she played. She was perfectly happy in her cage alone. And why not? It has every toy known to orangs. I filled the bin with water, hung a rope above it, and that was great fun, dangling her feet in the water and splashing.

(Side note—I read in Kelly's notes that the other day she waded into the moat up to two feet deep to retrieve her "popsicle" that had rolled in.)

Luna is still chewing on hard objects. I do wonder about molars coming in.

Rudi got to stay in today with Kelly. The keeper had filled the blue barrel with water, and when they were shifted, he did his usual display – throwing things etc. He took the barrel and sent a flood of water into the tunnel. Kelly headed for the rafters. After that they both just lazed around.

I heard from another caregiver that October is when Luna will be put in with Chey.

August 17, 1999

Well, Doc and Chey were in today so intros, at least "attempts at" were in order. Luna was happily playing in cage A when I got there. I tried to get them to interact about 1:15 p.m. but no go. I put Luna's lunch and yogurt in the intro door so the three did congregate there, but Luna took off after the yogurt was gone, and her mouth was full of a piece of pear. The next attempt was dry rice cereal thrown so Luna could lick some up from outside of B and the tunnel, while they did likewise from inside. That worked for awhile. No touching except once Doc touched Luna's fingertips, ever so gently. Then Chey was shut in B with her food for the rest of the day. Doc was in C and the tunnel. After Chey ate, she held a sheet up to the intro mesh, peering through it. Luna went over several times, presented her genitals, which Chey kissed through the sheet, and also after pulling the sheet down. I put a swinging rope over the wading pool filled with water that was right in front of the intro door, hoping to keep her there, or at least to entice her every once in awhile. That worked fairly well. When it was cereal time, I spread it all over the intro door mesh and walls so Luna would stay there and lick it up. Didn't take long for all of that to be over and done with.

THEN at 3:45 p.m. I put the squiggly water toy thing in the intro door, jammed it in a crevice, and anchored it with a rope. Chey got busy with a bamboo branch trying to get the toy, Luna became a cling-on so I couldn't exit the cage, and no toy would suffice. I got Lynn to bring an ice pop so she'd let go. That worked, but after the ice pop was gone she managed to get the water toy loose, and took it to the back of her cage to play. I anchored the hose so she couldn't pull anymore into her cage than what was already there. She played and played and got her cage very wet. Chey was busy munching alfalfa and ignored Luna.

At 4:30 the keeper came by to say they were going to start closing. We also mentioned the word bottle. Luna's thumb went into her mouth when she heard that.

When I was getting things out of A that are prohibited at night, Chey grabbed a rope. Well actually I think Luna took it to the intro door and gave it to her. I was busy untying a sheet hammock. I anchored the other end of the rope, and Lynn traded Chey a cracker to release it.

When Luna finished her bottle at 5 p.m. she handed it back through the slot. I rewarded her with a piece of banana. The other notes showed she has done that two or three times lately. Smart little girl.

August 19, 1999

Well, this was one of those "where do I begin" days. I prepared Luna's food, and then walked around the zoo cutting bamboo, ginger, banana leaves, and hibiscus. Went into the night house, where it was 90 degrees, at 8:45. Rudi and Kelly had already gone out, so I needed to figure a way to get the intros going with Doc and Chey. (side note: I always get down really close to Doc and Chey to say good morning. Doc, especially, always comes right to the mesh and stares intently at me. I always wonder what he's thinking. I always hope he thinks. "Oh, this is the fun person who gives me treats. I like her.") Luna had finished her bottle of water and had taken it apart. The bottle was fairly close to the slot where it slides through. I showed her the vitamin, and told her to give me the bottle. She kept reaching for the vitamin, but the request didn't compute. So this "orangutan mom" made a tool with a stalk of ginger, put it in the bottle, and said "give me the bottle." She then took the bottle and put it in the slot. I gave her the vitamin and lots of praise. We then went down the aisle to see the others, but there wasn't much interest. So I sprinkled the corn flakes in the well of the intro door, and she and Chey shared there.

After Doc and Chey were shifted to D, E, and F, I set up ropes and other things so Luna could play there. Chey had an oblong plastic tub, half full of water, and she was playing boat, scooting around F, splashing like crazy. There was brief touching by Chey, and Luna reached through the mesh and grabbed her arm. She also pulled a large stalk of bamboo out of Chey's cage. Chey just watched and didn't try to grab it back. Meanwhile, Doc was quietly going about gathering up all of the monkey biscuits for himself. At one point Chey got the end of a rope. Well, Doc had actually grabbed it, but Chey took it away from him. An avocado slice and corn flakes weren't a good enough trade. The keeper offered a taste of baby food. That did it, but only after Chey tossed a few buckets around in protest. I spread the remaining baby food on the mesh for all three to share.

When it was cereal time, back in A, I spread it on the mesh of the intro door. I also made Doc a separate dish with a large portion, and Chey a dish with a smaller portion. Chey was busy licking the cereal off the mesh so I handed Doc his. Well, Chey saw that, reached over his head, and grabbed it. I had to give him the smaller portion. Poor guy. Later Chey was busy playing with a sheet in the tunnel, and Doc went to the intro door mesh to lick off the last bits of cereal. However, he kept glancing over his shoulder to see if she was coming.

Luna stayed in A the last hour and a half I was there. The keeper had brought in a huge box filled with a bunch of little boxes, and she was in orangutan heaven. Doc and Chey were busy wrestling so it all worked out fine.

Oh!! Today Chey would get herself all wet in the "boat" and then climb up and sit in front of the vent. Good plan for a hot day. How intelligent, these wonderful creatures.

August 24, 1999

I never thought THIS day would come - when I was actually bored at the zoo. When I got there, Doc and Chey were outside. Rudi and Kelly were in, so no intros planned. Luna was in A, playing alone. She had not been out all day. A keeper had entered her cage for five minutes to hang sheets for playing, but Barbara (she does the a.m. shift) said we are trying to get her to be independent like this. She thought I might be able to take her into B later. However, there were huge claps of thunder and rain, so Doc and Chey were brought in at 12:50 p.m. Well, Kelly had parked in C and wouldn't shift, so Chey was put into B, and Doc in D. I couldn't do any intros because Kelly was too close. She also had access to the tunnel. If only Doc had been in C; then maybe I could have tried some intros.

Luna played like crazy all afternoon in A; perfectly happy. She had all kinds of enrichment articles including a huge box full of papers, jugs, boxes etc. At mealtime I put her food either in a box or on a cardboard, and slid it under the door. She took her food to the back of the cage to eat, as if someone else would get it.

Chey was busy aggravating Kelly in the tunnel. She stayed glued to the front of B, passing things out so Kelly would grab them. These two ladies really don't like each other. Anyway, Chey paid little or no attention to the intro door. At one point I got out the bubble soap. Mild interest from the ladies; zero from the guys. Kelly wiped off all the bubbles that hit the mesh with a rag. She also used the rag to wipe her arms if they landed there.

Luna did latch on when I was leaving her cage to get her nighttime banana. So I did get in one hug. October 25 is the projected date for letting her in with Chey.

August 24, 1999

Got to the zoo about 7:40, but didn't enter the night house until 9 a.m. I did go about the zoo and cut a few hibiscus, ginger, and some banana leaves. Then I read some in my primate book. Luna was busy playing in A. The keeper had given her the breakfast items, including an egg (Thursday item). Upon looking into the cage, I saw she'd only eaten half the egg and the avocado. The keeper had also tied a sheet to the cage front, and she had a great time with that; playing hide and seek. Doc and Chey were out when I entered, so I knew there would be no intros.

I'd brought laundry baskets and animal sippers today, one for each. It was fun watching Kelly when she found hers. She tried to turn the basket inside out, and also spit mouthfuls of water into it. Amazing - it wouldn't hold water! Even Rudi, who usually sits in his cage and looks bored, paid some attention to his sipper. He took the lid off and sat with it for a minute. They are animal shaped with a straw end. At one point I even heard Kelly slurping.

I served Luna her cereal and banana by sliding it into the cage. She tossed the banana aside but wolfed down the cereal. At 11:15, after the keeper had cleaned B, we set up an elaborate playground with ropes, sheets, boxes, forage; everything but bells and whistles. I took Luna in, at least getting to give her a quick hug, and she got off my hip immediately to start exploring. It was great fun watching her have fun, being such an orangutan – like sitting on overturned buckets and sliding about the cage, tearing up paper, foraging for cheerios etc. And so independent! As I said to the keeper, "I remember those days, not so long ago, when she screamed when we tried to separate. We thought we might never get to this point." I'm so thrilled she is so independent, and so good at being an orangutan.

August 31, 1999

Well, I was only at the zoo 2 ½ hours today. I traded shifts with Barbara as I had 10 people coming to dinner, and she told me to come in at 10. I took along two huge boxes, pieces of foam, bubble wrap, small boxes, balls, and crisp tissue paper. Luna was playing in A, but as soon as I got there, I took her to F to share cereal with Doc and Chey. I smeared it on the mesh with a toothbrush. Then she made a beeline to C, marched in and proceeded to play there, in the tunnel, and B while the keeper cleaned. When the keeper took her break, I hosed C out and squirted Luna with water. She thought that was great fun. I tried intros later down at F, but she wasn't interested and she marched down to A. There was some minimal interaction at the intro door after Doc and Chey were shifted to B and C. Their forage was placed by the intro door, and I'd put Luna's forage in the intro door.

I gave Luna the crisp tissue paper. She had a blast with it; crunching it, putting it on her head, wrapping it around her, and carrying a piece around like a security blanket. Also, somebody brought Luna a little purple plastic chair and she loves it. Even sat on it properly at one point. She carries it, wears it, and pushes it around.

Doc was so funny. He was at the intro door when Chey was elsewhere. He picked up all the monkey biscuits, one at a time, looking over his shoulder to see if Chey was coming. Then he took them to the water bowl for dunking before eating. Chey was busy with the bubble wrap. Then she settled into foraging through the small boxes into which the keeper had put monkey biscuits, seeds, crackers, etc. When Doc walked by her, she pulled her "loot" towards her. He made a sweeping gesture with that big old hand, scattering a few of her seeds and cracker pieces.

The keeper said last week she gave Doc one of the huge foam pieces I'd brought. She said he was so funny. He first tried to bite it, then tried to tear it, then squeezed it back and forth like an accordion. He finally put it on the floor and started jumping up and down on it. Today he dipped the smaller piece in the water bowl, and let the water drip on his face. Then he tore it up.

The keeper set up a hose to spray into the tunnel. Chey parked there, getting her whole self wet. I had a huge light weight ball that I was playing with on the tunnel mesh. I would bounce it off Luna's head. She had on a huge play face. Then she went back to A.

As I left, Chey and Doc were taking turns using the water spray for genital stimulation. Whatever turns you on, I guess.

September 2, 1999

I arrived at 7:30. We have not officially been given the okay to come in later. Went around the zoo and cut banana leaves, hibiscus, and other edible flowers. Then I went to the educational center to make caregiver note copies. That took awhile. I, and the person working there, had to figure out how to make it copy both sides correctly.

Entered the night house at 9:10. Didn't enter Luna's cage but talked to her, and got her to trade her bottle rim for a peanut. Then later, after getting a bottle from the kitchen as an example, she gave me her empty bottle for her yogurt. I also showed her a nipple, but her nipple was so far back in her cage, I couldn't get her to understand to go get it. Another caregiver brought limes, one for each orang. When Luna got hers, you could almost see the joy on her face as she feasted, sitting on the back bench.

Doc was busy in B playing with some PVC pieces that the caregiver had brought. The keeper said when she entered the night house, he was using it to masturbate. When I arrived he was just busy putting the pieces together. Kelly was in C, Chey in D, and Rudi in E and F. I didn't try any "out of cage" intros in case Luna bolted towards a cage she shouldn't. The keeper let Rudi out first, knowing when he saw hibiscus blossoms waiting for him, he'd go immediately. She then went to let Kelly out, but there was all kinds of "trash'" in the tunnel. Kelly needed to pass it to the keeper. There were many pieces of a plastic laundry basket that she'd torn up the day before, making "tools" to try to reach a mirror that had been propped up in front of the tunnel. That had kept her busy all that afternoon. Anyway, she cleaned the tunnel up. When the keeper opened the door she raced out. However, Rudi decided he wanted to come back in. As the keeper closed the door, he put his big hand through and grabbed it. He planted himself there for about 10-15 minutes, hand gripping the door which was open about six inches, and his face pressed against the opening. The keeper ignored him, left for her break, and he finally got bored and left. I called her, and she came back and closed the door.

I tried intros but Luna wasn't really interested. They shared cereal off the mesh, but Luna was more interested in climbing to the rafters, grabbing things off the shelves etc. At one point she marched down the aisle and caught her image in the mirror propped against the wall. Well, that was interesting; that other little orangutan. She touched it, kissed it, pressed her face against it, and looked behind the mirror for it. At one point, when it did what she was doing, <u>she</u> jumped and grabbed for me.

She was a bit of a whiny butt today. When I left the night house for a potty break, there was a whine, then a minor shriek, and the thumb went into the mouth. When I came back, she refused the banana piece offering, pushed my hand away, and held out for a grape before she took her thumb out. A haggler!

September 5, 1999

WELL – When I bought the first two journaling books, I thought that would be more than enough. But today I began writing in my third, and probably my last. Maybe I write too much. I'm just so afraid I'll forget something. I want to be able to go back and read and remember all of the wonderful days as Luna's caregiver, and observer of the rest of the orang gang. The book store had no more journals like the first two, so I selected one with a cute teddy bear cover. Luna was so attached to her stuffed bear, even <u>after</u> Doc removed the stuffing. This cover will stir fond memories.

Today is a Sunday. I traded my Tuesday afternoons as I'm relieving a friend who works at an adult day care center, and is currently on vacation. I met the Sunday morning caregiver who is also a zoo docent.

Chey and Doc were inside which surprised me. They were in on Thursday, and I thought Kelly would be inside. I was not disappointed for several reasons. First, I knew the Luna Show would not be happening. She is getting so hard to handle during the show. I also knew some intros could take place. And another reason – Chey and Doc are just so much fun to watch.

Luna was playing alone in A when I arrived, and it was an easy caregiver exchange. Doc and Chey had large bubble wrap which is always great fun to pop. The keeper was busy cleaning the cages. When she left for lunch, she set up the hose to spray into C so Doc and Chey could play in the water. Naturally Chey took over the spot and thoroughly soaked herself. She was also sliding across the wet floor. She could have used one of those slip and slides. The spray was significant today; good water pressure. After playing awhile, she just parked for what could be considered feminine hygiene, but in her case she stayed much too long for just cleanliness purposes. After she was "satisfied" and mellowed out (all she needed was a cigarette) she went into B to the intro door. Doc took over the hose, or sex toy as it had become. He also thoroughly enjoyed what that spray could do.

Meanwhile Chey was having great interaction with Luna. Luna reached through and took hold of Chey's arm and fingers. Chey scooted closer to the door and kissed Luna's head. Chey stayed near the intro door for the next ten minutes. Luna went back and forth, but each time she went to the door, Chey touched and kissed her. Maybe the secret to the ultimate intro is Chey being satisfied sexually, and she'll be all calm, cool, and collected.

When Chey returned to play in the water, Doc went to the intro door. Luna grabbed and bit his fingers. He had a big piece of foam. Luna tried to get it, but only managed to get a tiny piece when he wasn't looking. She got a piece of cardboard and placed it against the mesh like he sometimes does.

Meanwhile Chey was back at the hose doing exactly what she did before, but also playing. The hose was spraying to the back of the cage. She'd turn her back, and push along on all fours to the end of the spray, then turn around and let it hit her on top of her head. When the hose was finally turned off she had "bad hair day" plus. Doc was behind her trying to play in the water too, just grateful for whatever he could get..

When the keeper set up their cages, she hid their food in boxes, and also put pieces of fruit in bubble wrap and taped it shut. Well, Doc had trouble finding his. He knew there was more food somewhere, and he looked all over his cage. He checked the shelves, looked in buckets, and peeked into the hammock. He finally found it! He <u>hugged</u> the big wad of bubble wrap, and carried it into the tunnel for his feast. There were papayas in the mix, and he really seemed to enjoy that.

The keeper did training with Chey and Luna, and I'd say they both got an A. Chey was a bit unsure about the brushing the teeth behavior. That's a fairly new one. She doesn't have that many teeth to brush but still……. It was terrific seeing Luna do her stuff. She was especially good at "presenting her arm for a shot." The only thing she hesitated about, for more than a moment, was giving the gold clamp back to the keeper that she was asked to retrieve. After all, it was shiny, pretty, and fun to have.

When it was cereal time, I spread it on the mesh of the intro door so Luna and Chey could share. Really wasn't any touching.

Luna played independently in A the rest of the afternoon. Got a little whiny when I took a potty break. She took part of her jungle gym apart. She is so strong. I fixed it while she had her bottle. Tried to get her to trade her bottle for a treat, but she was too busy trying to take PVC apart again. It's <u>amazing</u> how strong she is. For the first time today she reached for the orangutan on my T-shirt. Seemed quite interested.

September 9, 1999

I went in at 7:30 a.m. as usual, (We're still waiting for the official instruction to go in later.) I went about the zoo to cut hibiscus, banana leaves etc., and went by the flamingo exhibit. They have babies and there are still some eggs too. Saw one little guy about 6 or 7 inches tall. He'd stand and then sit back down. Two slightly bigger ones were swimming. One about three months old was standing in the group. The keeper was there and told me his age. He's all gray, but fuzzy. The little ones are white. Anyway, so much for the flamingos. There's always something interesting at the zoo.

I read the orangutan profiles while I was waiting to go into the night house. Lynn wrote them recently for the SSP. Not too much history about Rudi except he was hand raised. It did mention his sexually aggressive behavior. I also saw a note that he puts his erect penis through the mesh for certain zookeepers. It was kind of strange reading about when he was a youngster.

There was a note that Cheyenne possibly had a miscarriage at one time. Not too much known about her either. Did note she was very depressed when she first arrived at the Houston Zoo.

Kelly was hand raised from about six hours old. Apparently her mother had her between 1 and 2 p.m., laid her on the cement floor, and was totally not involved.

Doc was also hand raised. His mother was dragging him about by his arm when he was two days old.

One thing; notes about Luna will <u>never</u> be considered sketchy.

I went into the night house about 9 a.m. Luna was busy playing, actually sitting in the intro door when I entered. She did come to the cage front to greet me, and resumed playing. At 10 a.m. I entered her cage. I didn't say anything to her; just smeared her cereal on the intro door mesh. She, Doc, and Chey all shared but there was no touching. I was surprised Chey let Doc have any, but I'd spread it all over so he'd have room and a chance to eat too. At one point Luna licked a bit off the end of Chey's finger.

I took her to the outside of B and C to get her to interact with them, but Doc was too busy acting very silly. He had a piece of bubble wrap that he was dipping in water, putting on his head etc. Luna <u>did</u> watch him quite intently. Chey seemed to want to touch her and tried, but Luna kept pulling her hands or toes back. She seems so content in A. I finally gave up and went back in there. I swept while she played. She did manage to pull the jungle gym apart, and break it. That took care of that! Later when I'd left her cage, she traded me two sharp pieces of the PVC for some Rice Krispies.

When Lynn shifted Doc and Chey to D, E, and F, she suggested I hook up some ropes between the cages in the aisle. I did, but Luna wanted to climb higher. At one point, Lynn asked me a question, I turned to answer, and Luna went all the way to the top. Chey went up too. It took 5 to 7 minutes <u>with</u> the rake before I could grab a leg to pull her down. She was determined but I won the battle, if not the whole war. It was about time to leave so I put her into A as it's easier for the caregiver exchange.

On September 12 we are having a caregiver meeting. Time is winding down. Oh how I will miss getting my hugs from this wee soul.

September 12, 1999

Well - I had a birthday yesterday, and Luna will have one <u>next</u> Saturday. She'll be two years old.

We had a caregiver meeting today from 1 p.m. to 4 p.m., so I didn't spend much time in the night house.

This coming week will be the last week of the Luna Shows. On Saturday at 11 a.m. there will be a birthday party for Luna; caregivers and keepers invited. Then at 2 p.m. there will be a media presentation and birthday party. I think we can attend that too. We got so much information today; it's hard to keep it all straight. Thank goodness it will all be written down in great detail.

We are not going to be needed at the zoo until 10:30 a.m., and starting September 20th, we'll leave at 5 p.m., with 15 minutes being knocked off each week. We need to have physical contact only to shift her to other cages, and to touch her at the mesh, giving treats etc. We will completely eliminate the ropes from her multi-enrichment program, except maybe one attached to the cage front for her amusement. The target date to open the creep door giving her access to Chey is October 21. The caregivers will not be present for that as the less people, the better. Barbara, the curator and now also a caregiver, will be there along with Lynn and one other zoo keeper. This way no one caregiver "lucks out" and gets to watch. We will continue coming for at least 30 days to observe and document. As we all know her so well, we'll be able to note any odd behavior. As this is all beginning next week, I can note the procedures in this journal as I go. Because the shifts are being shortened, I'll just come on Thursdays. Another caregiver will take over my Tuesdays.

Today I gave Luna a 5 foot long piece of lavender cello wrap and that amused her 'til time to leave. (I felt sorry for Kelly so I also gave her a red piece instead of saving it for Luna.) Luna wrapped hers around herself, squished it up, put it over her face, put her arm in it, stuck her arm through the mesh, and then took it up to her little hammock where she stretched out and put it over herself. What a great enrichment! A good investment of 99 cents.

We volunteer caregivers are getting together to give Luna a TV/VCR for her birthday, and all of the orangs can watch TV. There is someone checking on the definite okay to do it.

I also asked today if I'll be able to help clean the orang night house, knowing I can't touch Luna etc., when I am just a volunteer keeper in Primates. Lynn said that shouldn't be a problem because Luna wasn't particularly clingy with me. I'll probably volunteer on Friday mornings.

Luna played with the lavender cello wrap non-stop for 35 minutes.

September 16, 1999

When I arrived at 10:30 this morning and entered the night house, Lynn seemed really "down." After a few moments of "hi" and "how are you," I commented to her that she seemed down. She said a siamang died last night. They found her dead this morning. Lynn said she felt terrible, and just wanted to go home. She said the siamang had some illness in the past year, and the last couple of days she had been kind of "off" her usual behavior. I love the way these keepers are so loving toward the animals, so concerned about their welfare, and so upset when there's a problem. They are all special people.

The new rules didn't allow me to have contact with Luna except through the cage front 'til 1 p.m. When I entered she was in the intro door. I told her "hi" and she came toward me, but stopped halfway and resumed her activities. Wild play ensued.

Kelly was in so I knew there would be no intros; just needed to make sure Luna stayed amused. I swept out cage B for Lynn, and when she left to do her time sheets, I cleaned D, E, and F completely. Figured I might as well keep busy. At 1 p.m. I put Luna's lunch in different containers, and put them in B. She'd watched me "load" the containers. I let her out of A and took her immediately to B . She got off of me right away, grabbed the little dish with the yogurt, and headed to the far corner of the cage to eat it. Lynn came in about that time, and I left to go eat my lunch. (Bringing food is a necessity on a 6 ½ to 7 hour day.) When I came back, Lynn was in A and Luna was in B. Lynn had smeared baby food on the intro door mesh, and Luna was very busy licking it off.

Today was the next to the last Luna Show. On Saturday, her birthday, it will be a media presentation. She was well behaved during the show. As we left the building and she was clinging to me, she kept taking my hand and putting it around her. Little sweetie!

When we returned to the night house, I put her in D with access to E and F. Her big stuffed gorilla was in D, and she went right over to it and just hugged it. It's been strapped to the big hammock in her cage for days and it was like "Oh, my friend." She dragged it about, and also rolled on the floor with it. She played well until 4 p.m. when I moved her back to A. Of course she was happy about that. I remember the days when she didn't want to be alone in A, let alone all the other cages. She has really grown up. Her p.m. water was served in a commercial water bottle, and she took it to her little hammock to drink. I left the night house at 5 p.m. with no complaint from Luna. I'd given her an interesting box with her forage in it.

September 18, 1999

Luna's 2nd birthday and what a grand time was had by all!

THE ORANG GANG ET AL - LOVED, HUGGED AND PEED ON

The celebration started at 11 a.m. with all but one of the caregivers, the Primate keepers, and Barbara. We gathered in the administration building conference room for yummies, conversation, videos, and slides. Barbara started the festivities with a tearful thank you to all of us. We all got choked up too. There was fresh fruit, delicious "roll ups" with luncheon meats, and a chocolate cake with two candles. Her official birthday cake was there for our viewing. It was a 3-tiered construction of bananas, then grapes, then more bananas, and topped with a stuffed ape. Two of the caregivers had made a HUGE Happy Birthday poster, and poster board laminated pictorial displays. As we lunched, we watched a video of Luna from the beginning to now. That was great; seeing her as a tiny one. We all shared our worst day as caregivers. I told of my fall off the ladder a few months ago, and the 7 minutes last week when I worked to get her down with a rake. One told about the day Luna got loose and was on the mesh of Kelly's cage while she, the caregiver, was going nuts trying to get her down. As she did this, Kelly was looking at her wondering what on earth she was doing, and paying no attention to the baby. Another shared how, on a hot day last summer, she pulled her T-shirt up to cool off. Luna went up under it and bit her very large breast. The next day she had her annual mammogram, and had a lot of explaining to do. One said her worst day was the day after Luna's dad, Bubba, died. She'd been called and told the night before so she could prepare herself. She said she psyched herself up for the empty cage etc. The next day Kelly had an enrichment item which was black window screen like material, but very flexible. Kelly spent the entire day shrouded in the black mesh in the corner. Doc, who is Bubba's half brother and was his cage mate, spent that day huddled in a corner. She said she "lost it." Lynn spoke of when Luna was tiny, still at the clinic, and they stayed with her 24 hours a day. She was alone with her one night, and had to use the bathroom. She knew she couldn't put her down as Luna was crying. So Luna was up on her shoulder, kind of wrapped around her head as she dashed to the bathroom. She held her with one hand as she managed her business with the other. All went well until she flushed the toilet. It scared Luna and she grabbed Lynn's hair and held on, very tight. Barbara said the absolutely worst day was the day when Luna was 6 weeks old, and they put her back in with Kelly. Kelly tossed her three times, and they heard the thud of Luna's head against the hydraulic door. They got a pickle to entice Kelly away from her. The next caregiver spent the entire shift checking her neuro vital signs.

Barbara gave each of us a very pretty glass vase, letting us choose from a selection of them. She also gave each of us an orang greeting card with a very nice personal thank you. I still can't believe I've been so fortunate to have this incredible experience.

We also looked at slides. We got to see Rudi, as a youngster, and Bubba. We saw when Doc was introduced to Bubba. There were photos, including several of Kelly as a brand new mom with Luna snuggled on her chest. It was all so much fun! We presented the 20" TV/VCR combination for Luna and her friends.

At 2 p.m it was time for Luna's last public appearance. It was held on the outdoor stage. There were banners, little posters, and 8 x 10 photos displayed. When Luna arrived she was a little clingy. She hasn't been outdoors for awhile, plus there were so many people there. Barbara said a few words prior to her arrival, and recognized the caregivers. The regular Saturday afternoon caregiver was with Luna. Another one gave her a big gift wrapped box. It held other wrapped boxes containing a book, peanuts, etc. WELL, the wrapped box scared her, and she started to walk to the exit. "Hey, I'm outta here!" They showed her that beneath that paper was a plain cardboard box filled with lots of interesting stuff. That got her attention! The crowd sang happy birthday to her. I thought that might scare her, but it didn't. She started looking around like, "Oh, yes. That's for me and I deserve it!"

They presented her with a small cake made of cooked rice, and bordered with orange slices. She liked that. Her big official cake was brought to the stage. We thought she'd go for the grapes, but she wanted the stuffed toy. She held it tightly through the rest of the presentation. Barbara took it away from her when we all went over to Primates. She seemed to be rubbing her eyes like she was allergic to it.

In Primates we had pictures taken of all of us together with Luna. She looked around like, "Wow, all of my mommies are here at the same time." I felt so proud, so happy, and so lucky.

Happy, Happy, Birthday, Luna!

September 23, 1999

Arrived at the zoo at 10:30 a.m. Luna was at the front of her cage. I said hi to her but didn't touch her. After I put my belongings down, she left to go play again. I knew there would be no contact with her until 1 p.m. Lynn came in and asked if I'd mind sweeping some empty cages. She was headed to the clinic as they were euthanizing a very old macaque today, one who was probably in her 40s. She'd been at the zoo since 1962.

Kelly was the only orang inside, so four cages plus the tunnel were empty. I was glad to not just sit around twiddling my thumbs. Swept and hosed down B, C, E, F, and the tunnel. Even sprinkled a bit of bleach here and there. At 1:10 p.m. I put Luna's lunch in assorted containers and put them into B. I took her out of A to B. She got down immediately, grabbed a couple of the containers, and headed to the far corner to eat. I then proceeded to clean her cage. What a mess it was. She must have had a party last night which included a "wrapping" with toilet paper. She played in B, the tunnel, and C until about 2:15. Lynn needed to set up cages, and she was going to clean D after she shifted Kelly to C. I left to go eat my lunch and watch the Luna birthday party video on the TV we'd given her for her birthday. I never tire of seeing this baby on video, in pictures, whatever.

When I came back, Rudi, Doc, and Chey were brought in, and Kelly went outside. This is kind of a new routine for all of them; the half day in and half day out business. Lynn said they're all acting a bit strange. She said the first day, last Saturday, she switched them at 3 p.m. Doc came in, clutched his blanket for security, and didn't go after his food right away. Lynn said he must have been afraid he was going to be sedated or something. Chey's diet had been placed by the intro door along with a black tub with beta chips and cheerios for forage. Luna was at the intro door but Chey shared nothing. She even took the tub across the cage, dumped it, and parked there to forage for the cheerios. Lynn said she's worried 'cause Chey just doesn't seem that interested in Luna anymore. I told her Chey did touch Luna's foot and finger when she first came in. I also told her that maybe the new has worn off. Of course she's worrying that this whole intro thing won't work.

Luna continued playing independently the rest of my shift. Chey went to the intro door every now and again, and peeked into A to check on Luna's whereabouts. Luna went to the intro door periodically too. I'd given Chey a magazine to browse through. I also gave one to Luna. She took it up to her little hammock.

Separation was easy. She did suck her thumb as I was putting things together to leave. I'd do a bit, then sit back down like I was staying awhile. I gave her forage items, and her bottle of water after a few minutes. She grabbed the paper sack I'd put soaked monkey biscuits in, and headed up to her hammock. I left the night house at 4:45 p.m. – not a peep.

September 30, 1999

I arrived at the zoo at 10:25 a.m. loaded down with enrichment articles as usual. I entered the night house about 10:35. Luna was at the cage front passing a two foot piece of PVC through to me. I put some corn flakes into a little box for a trade. She took them up to her little hammock for munching.

Kelly was inside. Therefore I knew there would be no intros until Chey and Doc came in midday. However, Lynn said the old system was back in place, and they'd be in at closing. She said Chey hadn't been as attentive lately, plus the switching was upsetting to all of them. She also said Luna had been awful the last couple of days, whining constantly and screaming at intervals. Also very clingy. Upon reading the notes, I noted another caregiver had a terrible time with her two days ago. Apparently Luna was screaming most of the day. Poor little thing. Also poor caregiver. At the end of her notes she wrote, "I hate this day."

Luna played well independently 'til almost 1 p.m. She got antsy about 12:40 pm. I don't know if it was because she saw us setting up C,D, E, and F, and she anticipated going into those cages, or if her internal clock just knows when it's nearly 1 p.m., and the caregiver will unlock the door and move her.

Kelly was put into B after the extra screen was put on the intro door. After Luna was moved, Lynn came in and said Chey was upset outside. It's like she knew Kelly was in B, and she thinks that is her space. Anyway, I put Luna's lunch in different containers, and put them here and there throughout the four cages. Lynn put corn flakes and dried monkey biscuits here and there also. Luna didn't complain at all when I moved her. I also took a couple of bed sheets with us. She's really into sheets lately; playing ghost, snuggling them, wrapping them about her etc. I also put a small stuffed pig in with her; a new arrival in her toy box. She played throughout all the cages. When the maintenance man came to fix a door lock, she retreated to the far back corner of E under the bench. She had a sheet and the stuffed pig with her. She played quietly, coming out once to collect 5 monkey biscuits, but only ate one. One time I gave her some sunflower seeds, tossing them into F. She immediately started sucking her thumb. It's like she knows I often give her a treat before leaving to go to the bathroom or whatever, so it's THUMB TIME. When I gave her dry rice cereal she passed the dish out to me when she was finished. I put some corn flakes and monkey biscuit powder on it. She ate the corn flakes but dumped out the powder. She does know what she likes.

Before transferring her back to A, she thought it was great fun to leap off the hammock in C to a flake of hay on the floor. Did it eight times. Then she'd race up the mesh to the skylight. When I left, I put dry rice cereal and corn flakes in a magazine for her to forage. Lynn and I both left the night house, and she didn't even notice.

October 5, 1999

Entered the night house at 10:45 a.m. Luna barely glanced at me when I spoke to her. She was busy rolling around on the floor with an orangutan colored blanket. I think she thought it was a surrogate. Chey and Doc were inside. Lynn said there had been little to no interaction. Doc and Luna did have a tug-o-war at the intro door with Luna's gray blanket. Doc won. Lynn said Luna whined when she (Lynn) was out of sight. She needed to go outside and Luna complained loudly. I told Lynn maybe the little squirt misses going out. Anyway, Lynn said she smeared a bunch of baby food at the intro door, and sneaked out. Luna <u>did</u> notice, complained a bit, but was then quiet.

When 1 p.m. came Lynn asked me to wait before moving Luna to D, E, and F. She wanted to serve Chey's diet at the intro door, and it hadn't arrived yet. When it did, I put some of Luna's sweet potato and pear, plus two soaked monkey biscuits, in the intro door. Lynn put Chey's diet on her side of the door. Luna immediately swiped a piece of Chey's orange through the mesh, and raced to the corner of the bench to eat it. Well, when Chey came into the cage, she grabbed the sweet potato of Luna's. She then pulled her pile of food <u>away</u> from the intro door and had a feast. Never mind sharing. Luna came back to the door later, and took the rest of her food.

About 1:45 p.m., I moved Luna to F, having Lynn snap a couple of photos on the way. I'm trying to get a good Christmas photo. She got off of me right away because the yogurt was in plain sight. She played in all three cages until 3 p.m. or so. Lynn came in with raisins to train her to go through the hydraulic doors on demand. She was not very cooperative. I went ahead and set up cage A. Lynn said she wanted Luna to move back there early so she could set up the other cages for the night. She needed to finish in order to clean out a corner of the kitchen for the new water fountain. She also had me smear about a cup or so of applesauce all over the sides, floor, and ceiling of the intro door, hoping that would keep Luna there to interact with Chey. Well, Chey parked there for the long haul, but she had no tools to get the applesauce. She was trying very hard with a flimsy piece of cardboard. I got her attention and told her to get the paper towel cardboard I spotted behind her. She <u>did</u> and was much more successful. It became ruined so I got the squeegee, and used it to pull a long skinny cardboard roll from Luna's cage to give her. Lynn had put a bamboo stem in for Chey to use, but she didn't even try it. When she saw I had the long tube, she came for it immediately and had great success. Luna was not really interested in the applesauce; maybe ate ¼ cup, if that. Chey didn't mind. More for her greedy self. She was still parked there when I left at 4:15. I put Luna's banana pieces in a little box, and she grabbed it and took it to the back bench. No complaint when I left.

It was really funny today when I went to move Luna from C back to cage A. I unlocked the door, opened it, and turned so she could get on my back. She kept trying to turn me around so she could hug my chest. I finally did let her grab onto my front, but didn't put my hands on her. She <u>had</u> to cling.

I also took a half gallon rum bottle today for enrichment. All three looked hysterical swigging water from it. Wish I could have gotten a photo.

Speaking of photos – two other caregivers left envelopes for all of us with snapshots of Luna, plus there were two 8 x 10 black and whites. All of us caregivers may need therapy after this is over. How we'll miss her!

October 14, 1999

The schedule this week is 11 a.m. to 4 p.m. so I arrived at 10:45. Had to borrow a wagon to cart all of the boxes I'd brought.

This week we have no contact with Luna other than through the mesh. I'd forgotten that. Last week, when I moved her from C back to A, I should have given her one last hug. Now she's moving from cage to cage through the hydraulic doors.

She was in B and hardly looked up when I entered the night house. Chey and Doc were in, and Lynn had the TV on; had the tape of Kelly's labor and delivery, and early views of Luna in the VCR. Lynn left to work on time sheets. I donned my rubber boots and proceeded to clean E and F. When I finished, I headed to A to clean it. I noticed Chey was glued to the TV. It was close-ups of Kelly and the newborn Luna. Golly, she was a cutie. Of course she still is. Anyway, I stopped working to watch the video with Chey. In the video, Luna whined very loud. Chey immediately looked over to cage B, thinking it was Luna <u>now</u>. One week and the creep door will open. She can actually hold her! Will she even want to? Hmmmm.......

When Lynn shifted Chey and Doc to E and F, I moved the TV down the aisle, and put in a video called Bonkers for Babies, or something like that. It was about zoo babies. Chey and Doc pulled up overturned buckets and watched intently. Lynn said she was glad we bought the TV for the orangs. I was amazed at how they seemed so interested. Wonder what they think as they watch TV.

Luna then had access to C and D, but she would only explore if I had a treat to give her at C or D. She was very happy just playing in B. She was busy building a nest under a bench just like Kelly does. Lynn says she has so many traits that are just like Kelly – unique to Kelly – like applauding. Lynn says she thinks Kelly will be upset when she sees Luna with Chey.

Luna was shifted back to A at 3:30 p.m. Her food is left in her cage in a bag, just like the adults. She's given a whole fruit now. Apparently, she's been given an orange a couple of times, and has not known how to open it, banging it on her cage etc. Another caregiver showed her how to peel it yesterday. Today she had ¼ of a cantaloupe. She was hesitant, but then carried it about her cage while munching on it.

I left the zoo at 4 p.m. I'd kept busy, but Luna was a bit uninteresting today. Never thought <u>that</u> day would come.

Thursday, October 21, 1999

Well, this is THE DAY!! Yesterday I kept thinking about today; the introduction with Chey. Last night at 11p.m. I left messages on both Lynn and Barbara's voice mail to tell them I was thinking about today, and to let them know I just had a feeling it would be all right. We'd worked too hard for it <u>not</u> to be.

All day today I kept looking at the clock, knowing the time of opening the creep door between A and B was getting closer. When I got home from the dentist at 3:30 p.m. there was a message from Barbara to let me know the introduction was going great. (She called all of the caregivers.) Luna was fearful at first, displayed for Chey. Then Chey figured out, if she was soliciting, Luna was afraid, so she just "walked off." Luna then went to her. She proceeded to play wrestle, showed some fear, but Chey was gentle with her, and making all sorts of vocalizations to "this kid" as Barbara put it.

Tonight after arriving home, after dinner and a movie with a friend, there was another message from Barbara at 9:10 p.m. saying the day had gone so well. She said Chey held Luna, there were lots of play faces, wrestling etc. She left at 7 p.m. Said Chey had bedded down on the floor. Luna was a bit confused but returned to A to big hairy mama on her hammock. So far our prayers have been answered. I almost cried when I listened to the message - <u>three</u> times. I'm just so proud of this baby, and also very proud of Cheyenne.

October 22, 1999

Lynn called today to let me know we'll start back next week, observing and documenting. We'll be on duty from 10 a.m. to 6 p.m. We talked about the intro going on. Of course she's also very excited. Said she'd been all over the zoo blabbing to all who would listen. I told her I was telling all I talked to, plus I'd saved the messages so my family members could listen too. I'd also had a friend listen to the first one, and I'd listened over <u>and</u> over.

She elaborated on the bedtime confusion on Thursday night. Apparently, Luna went back and forth no less than six times from B to A to B. Chey was bedded down. Luna got her little soft blanket and laid it by Chey, but no reaction from Chey. She put it on Chey's head; still no reaction. She then went back to her own cage to sleep. Couldn't figure out why her new mama didn't take her to bed.

October 24, 1999

Barbara called today to see if I could work on Tuesday as the regular caregiver can't work that day. Is the Pope Catholic? Of course, I will work! As I bowl on Tuesday mornings, I asked if I could work from 12 to 6 instead of 10 to 6. She said that would be fine.

She said the intro was continuing to be great. At one point Chey was in the hammock in B with Luna on her abdomen. Chey was grooming her. She also said Chey was sitting in a black tub, and Luna kept diving into her lap over and over. Also, this morning when the keeper entered the night house, Chey was resting on a bench in B, like she was still in sleep mode. Luna was standing in the hammock, looking at her like a kid who goes into a parent's room in the morning, wanting the parent to be awake, but not sure if he/she should wake the parent. This is all so neat! How exciting to be a part of it!

Barbara also said Chey had been aggressive toward Doc this weekend when they were together. When back with Luna, however, she tempered it down and was gentle.

I can hardly wait 'til Tuesday.

Tuesday, October 26, 1999

I was so excited all morning; so anxious to get to the zoo. Almost felt like I did before the first day of caring for Luna.

When I arrived Lynn showed me the video of Chey and Luna on the hammock, with Chey grooming her. It was <u>so</u> <u>neat</u>! When I entered the night house, Luna was playing in A and B. Kelly was down in the corner of F, sitting under the bench. She has not seen Chey with Luna yet, but Lynn says she thinks she knows something is going on. When I saw her in the corner, I gave her some bubble wrap, one of her favorite things. She didn't even come to get it. Is this a sad orangutan? Hmmmm….

Doc, Chey, and Rudi were all outside. Shortly after I arrived, Luna stationed in A, Chey was brought into the tunnel, and then let into B. Rudi was brought in first, into the squeeze cage. Of course he came in with his usual flair, pounding on the metal door. After Chey was let into B, Doc was let into C. Rudi was supposed to go back out, but he refused. After Lynn let his 270 pound self sit in the small squeeze cage for awhile, he decided outside was better and left. So did Kelly.

The afternoon was spent observing Luna's wild play in A and B, and the interactions with Chey. Luna frequently whizzed by Chey, grabbing at her, pulling her hair, touching her face, arm, back, whatever. Chey spent a lot of time sitting calmly, thumbing through a magazine. It was rather like a mom in the park watching her kid play; glancing often, occasionally reaching out to touch. Once, as Chey sat high on a prop, Luna was fairly stationary by her. There were play faces on both. Chey did some vocalizing, nibbled on Luna's fingers and toes, and kissed on her. I shed tears while watching. This is just so right that Cheyenne can finally be a mother, and Luna can finally touch an orangutan and have a real mother. As Lynn said, when she called me on Friday, "This is why Kelly didn't nurse this baby." The Kansas City Zoo people told our zoo people that Chey wanted to be a mother; that when a baby orangutan there died, Chey was sad. She had a miscarriage a long time ago, and was then surgically sterilized because she is both Bornean and Sumatran. Maybe I've written that before. Anyway, this was meant to be. That's how we all feel now.

At one point today, Chey lay on her back on the hammock like "Come on, Baby, I'm here." Luna was busy swinging about. Later, Luna was swinging by Chey, using material pieces attached to a fire hose. Chey held the material so she couldn't swing, then lay down on her back again, in a totally submissive position. But again, Luna didn't allow her to hold her. Once today she <u>did</u> get hold of her, sort of held her down, but let Luna go as soon as she squirmed. I think Luna is a little bit afraid of Chey. After all, she's watched her beat Doc up for two years. Chey is so strong, she could keep her held down tightly, but she doesn't. She's gentle with her; that is what is so neat. Luna pulls her hair so hard, but Chey just puts on her play face and reaches out gingerly to touch her. Lynn says she's waiting for the day when Chey carries Luna. She said on Friday it looked like she was going to, but Luna let go, like she didn't know about holding onto fur. After all, she's used to T-shirts.

Lynn gave Chey a little fuzzy soft ball today and she proceeded to scrub everything – the mesh, the props, the walls etc. Kept dipping it in the water bowl. Well, Luna drank the drips of water. However, she'd paid enough attention, and when she got hold of the ball, she scrubbed too. Then later, when Chey pushed it out, Lynn gave it to Doc. He washed the metal wall and hydraulic door in the tunnel.

When they were fed, I gave Luna a whole apple in a paper bag under the mesh of A. Lynn gave Chey her diet (orange quarters, cantaloupe, onion, and sweet potato) in B. Luna took her apple to the bench to eat it. Chey ate her oranges first. Apparently, the other day Luna swiped ½ orange from Chey. The next day, when Luna came to the food pile, Chey covered up her oranges. She did then give her one. Today Luna went back to B with her apple, and dropped a couple of pieces for Chey. Of course she took them. Then Luna cleaned the orange peels, as Chey left some pulp on them. This is food sharing in the orang world. I gave Chey a dish of rice cereal later, and she let Luna take the dish away from her. When I gave them water at closing, Chey picked both bottles up, but let Luna take one from her. This is all so exciting, interesting, and wonderful.

One other note – I asked Lynn if she thought Luna might try to nurse Chey. She said, in the last few days, Chey had actually tried to express milk from her breast. I can't believe this!

One thing I'm wondering about and hoping……….. If Luna is mothered well by this surrogate, maybe when it's time for her to have a baby, she'll get it right. Wouldn't that be great?

October 28, 1999

Arrived at the zoo at 10 a.m. The keeper suggested I go to the viewing area of the exhibit. Pumpkins had been placed there, and Chey, Doc, and Rudi were going to be let out. The whole affair was going to be filmed. Well, Chey and Doc came out. Doc came to the front immediately, and took a bite out of a pumpkin. Mugged for the gathered crowd. Yes, he actually did his smile face. Silly boy. Chey went over to a pumpkin across the yard. However, after closely examining it, she left it to go forage for monkey biscuits. Doc then went to a far pumpkin, and carried it to the back of the exhibit where we couldn't see him. Rudi was still in the night house, having refused to come out. Lynn went inside to try to get him out, and was successful. She said he put on his usual display first, throwing the big green ball, the blue barrel, and everything else in sight. Kelly headed for the rafters, as she usually does when he does that. When he came out, he came to the front of the exhibit, gingerly holding a hardboiled egg in his massive mouth. He proceeded to eat it one tiny bite at a time, ignoring the pumpkin that was intact up on the platform. Doc had come forward, opened his pumpkin at the front, and was munching. Chey had a mouthful of monkey biscuits (not a pretty sight), and wasn't interested in even eating <u>some</u> of the opened pumpkin. We all left, including the cameraman. The action probably started then.

I helped the keeper clean cages. After C was done, Luna shifted there. I'd put in her big stuffed gorilla, and she immediately started wrestling with it. After D was cleaned, she was also allowed access to there. She played back and forth between the two cages until 1:30 p.m. Then she was moved back to A and B in preparation for Chey coming inside. She shifted without problems; got a food reward for doing so.

The interactions were just great today. It's still hard for me to believe I'm a part of this. History in the making, so to speak. Again, Chey seemed to know what to do to get Luna to come to her. On Tuesday I noticed Chey seemed more arboreal than usual. I thought maybe it was wishful thinking, since Luna spends so much time up high. I mentioned it to the keeper, and she said Lynn noticed it too. I guess I'm not crazy. I learned how to use the fancy video camera today (at least I hope I got it right). I got some neat stuff on video. The camera is so fancy – Lynn says it does everything but fix dinner. Anyway, the interactions were frequent. Six or seven times Chey lay on her back, in a totally submissive position, as an invite to Luna. Luna seems a bit hesitant to just go cling to her, even though I envision Chey holding her lovingly. Chey got under a blanket, and Luna would run at it or somersault over to it. Twice she got right under there with her. Chey did get hold of her once. Both were on the floor. Chey wrapped her arms around Luna and proceeded to groom her. There was lots of lip smacking as she had her mouth all over the baby's body. Luna didn't let out a peep. Another time Chey was high on a prop and groomed Luna as she swung by. Later, Luna was hanging by her feet from the skylight, and touched Chey's genitals. Chey had earlier kissed hers. Normal orangutan behavior. By 4:45 p.m. I think Chey was wearing down, but Luna was still quite energized, grabbing at her. Poor Chey – she's finally a mom but she got a two year old. Yikes! Lots of play faces on both.

Chey had a big box today that still had big staples in it. She gave them to me for food, of course.

November 4, 1999

Arrived at the zoo at 10. Kelly was inside, still looking depressed, stretched out at the back of F. After D was cleaned, Lynn put a bunch of enrichment articles in there that I'd brought. When Kelly was shifted she was quite playful. I was glad to see that.

Luna was in C when I arrived. She had all sorts of stuff to play with, including a red silk pillowcase. That was great fun. She came to the mesh to greet me, I gave her little hand a squeeze, and then gave her some soaked monkey biscuits.

When she shifted back to A and B, she took the pillowcase with her. She stuffed bamboo in it. (I noticed in the notes this stuffing activity had gone on with Chey in the last week, and she apparently learned it.) She kept putting the case over her head, getting into it, climbing about with it etc. It was a sight!

This baby has some of Kelly's genes. For example, she applauds just like her, and is arboreal. However, she has learned qualities from her surrogate mom, like stuffing things with stuff.

It was really fun reading the notes from the past week. She was a pest on Monday, following Chey everywhere. I also read when Chey got hold of her and Luna squeaked, she let her go when the caregiver asked her to do so. Also, one day when little pumpkins were given to them, Chey shared hers with Luna. When Luna took hers from A to B, Chey opened it and put half of it down for Luna to pick up.

Today there was minimal actual interaction, but Chey was very playful, even on her own, as Luna played nearby. When she did get hold of her, she was very gentle; grooming her and kissing her fingers and toes. I also read in the notes that one day Luna went up to Chey, wrapped her arm about Chey's arm, and Chey kissed the top of Luna's head.

Again today, Chey stretched out on her back two or three times in a submissive position, but Luna did not go to her. I sat with the video camera ready but they weren't cooperating. Apparently, the film I took last week did turn out okay.

Lynn told me when she let Rudi out after Doc and Chey were brought in, he picked up both ice pops she'd put out on the exhibit; one for him and one for Kelly. She went up on the roof of the night house to check on them after she let Kelly out. She saw Rudi had both ice pops, and Kelly was pounding the ground in frustration. Of course she now knows better than to take one from him, even if it is hers.

There was food sharing late in my shift. Chey let Luna take a piece of her onion that was lying on the floor. (Chey was eating another piece of it.) Then as Chey ate her sweet potato, Luna picked up pieces of it that were on the floor, and also took a bite of the piece that Chey was eating. Then she actually took it away from Chey with no reaction.

November 11, 1999

When I arrived Kelly was inside; the others out as usual. Luna was playing in A and B. I helped Lynn clean cages. Luna started squealing at one point and kept it up for at least ten minutes. Mind you, she continued to play but screeching as she did so. We ignored her, and when she finally quieted, I gave her a treat.

Lynn gave Kelly a coconut which she pounded on the floor to break open. Special treat today. Lynn said the last time she gave Chey one, she pushed it out the drain area in the tunnel for Lynn to open. She did, with a hammer.

Chey and Doc came in about 12:30 p.m. Luna went into B immediately to be with Chey, but there was minimal interaction; a touch here and there. About 1 p.m. some visitors from NASA came by. They stayed by the door to observe Chey and Luna. Lynn had me use yogurt and a metal clamp to get Luna to station in C. That way they could get a better look at her. At one point Chey was sitting in the tunnel near a door. Luna went by her, put her hand on Chey's head, and then kind of sat down on the threshold of the door. Chey put her arm around Luna, and even gave her a little kiss on the cheek. All of this in front of visitors. WOW!

Lynn gave Doc a coconut which he broke open by pounding it on the floor. Before he broke it open, he'd damaged it enough to suck the milk from it. After he'd eaten most of it, he returned to his loud play. He was sitting in one black plastic oblong tub, and wrestling with a second one over his head. He loves this activity. I wish I knew what was going through his mind when he wrestles in the tubs.

When Lynn gave Chey a coconut, she pounded it on the floor but not very hard. Lynn was telling her to do it harder. Then she pounded it on the cage mesh. She pulled off some of the coconut "hairs" like she thought she could peel it. Then she took it into C and pounded there awhile. (Guess she thought the tunnel floor wasn't hard enough.) She picked up a paper towel tube like "Maybe a tool will help." She then put it down on the floor, and pushed it as hard as she could against the bottom of the mesh, using her foot to maybe squish it. Finally, she took it back to the tunnel and shoved it into the drain moat. That way Lynn could open it with a hammer. Well, hey – it worked last time.

Very gentle touching by Chey (not often) when Luna was near her. No lengthy interactions, and none far back in the cage that I could video. A rather uneventful day but fun as always.

November 18, 1999

Both Kelly and Rudi were in D when I arrived. He'd refused to go out this morning. Lynn had moved large, heavy objects out of D in case he decided to display. It's a smaller cage, and we wouldn't want Kelly in the line of fire. However, when he displays and she's nearby, she generally heads for the rafters.

Luna was in C while A and B were being cleaned. As usual, Chey and Doc were outside for their early morning outing. I cleaned E and F while the keeper had her break. Rudi <u>did</u> display right before we were ready to open A and B for Luna. He pounded on the door between C and D, roared, and threw a few things about. Luna grabbed big hairy mama. I told the keeper, if Chey had been nearby, the display might have been enough for Luna to fly into her arms.

I put some food in assorted containers in B for Luna to forage through. Also gave her a crinkly bag to play with. She loved that. Even took a couple of photos.

Rudi refused to go out midday so he was shifted to E and F. Doc had C and D. Poor Kelly had to be outside by herself. But at least she got both ice pops.

Chey and Luna had some good interactions today and I got a couple on video. Chey does seem to grasp her a little tighter than she used to (another caregiver noticed that yesterday), but readily lets her go.

A lady from the city newspaper came today. She and Barbara spent about an hour watching Chey and Luna. They had one really good interaction while she was there, so that was neat for her to see. She'd been there before; knew Rudi well. In fact, she said the last time she was there she'd been in sandals, and he was fascinated by her bare feet or toes. Today she took off her shoe and sock, and shook her foot at him. Well, he was in love immediately; vocalized loudly, and presented his nipple hoping to get it touched. What a guy!

Big day this coming Monday. The plan is to let Chey and Luna go outside before the zoo opens. We've all been invited. I plan to work as a cleanup volunteer that morning. Might as well since I'm driving there to see this next milestone. Hopefully, Luna won't whine because the grass is wet.

Next Thursday is Thanksgiving so I'll not be working that day. Our time is winding down anyway.

November 20, 1999

I saw another caregiver at a hockey game tonight. She said she'd worked as a docent today, assigned to the public area at the orangutan exhibit. She was to answer questions, and keep an eye on people so they wouldn't throw things into the exhibit. Apparently Kelly was throwing bark nuggets at the public. She even managed to get one clear over the moat. She was probably hoping they'd throw her something as a trade.

Monday, November 22, 1999

Another big day for Luna today; her first opportunity to go outside with Chey. I went to the zoo as a volunteer. I wanted to be there for this "debut" and decided I might as well help clean while there. The grass was wet so we all feared Luna wouldn't want to get her feet wet. The keeper put bark chips about on the exhibit, plus pine bedding, to make a path for her.

Four of us "mommies" were there with video cameras ready. There were people from the newspaper; the same lady from last week plus a photographer. Naturally Barbara and

Lynn were there, and assorted zoo people. Chey went right out, sort of waited for Luna, but Luna refused. Meanwhile, a bunch of birds of different varieties were feasting on the cheese, raisins, and monkey biscuits the keeper had placed here and there for Chey and Luna.

After awhile the keeper shut Chey and Luna back in cage B. She and Lynn strung a rope from the tunnel over a free standing cliff on the exhibit, and anchored it on a log. <u>Then</u> Luna climbed the rope to the cliff. She stayed and played there except for a very brief moment when she descended to where Chey was sitting with an ice pop. While on the cliff, Luna ate greens growing there, pulled weeds, and the most fun of all; she discovered loose dirt which she threw on top her head, and then brushed out with her hands. She repeated this process over and over. She was out for about an hour, and we did get some good video. Then they were both sent back inside and we cleaned cages.

I watched the tape before leaving the zoo. It was great.

December 2. 1999

I went to the zoo as a volunteer today and to do a little observing of Chey and Luna. Lynn said Chey actually carried Luna yesterday – on her front. Luna was kind of hanging on her, and Chey pulled her up into position by her rear end. Later she wanted to hold her like that again, and Luna was trying to get away. Chey pursued her and Lynn said they had to distract her with an ice pop..

When I went around greeting everyone this morning, Rudi pressed his nipple to the mesh. First time he's ever flirted with me. Later he spit at me twice. Guess it was a short "affair".

After Lynn opened the door for Chey and Luna to go out, she went up on the roof. I stationed myself in the viewing area across the moat. I had two ice pops and Lynn had me call Chey. She seemed to want to carry Luna. However, it ended up with them walking to the platform, side by side, with Luna holding on to Chey. They had intermittent interactions while out, and Chey was gentle. Some noise scared Luna. She went right to Chey, put her hand on Chey's head, and Chey put her arm around her. Later, a bird frightened Luna and Chey reached out to touch her.

Lynn told me that, a few days ago, Luna was feeding monkey biscuits to the fish in the moat. Apparently she threw one into the moat, or pushed it in when "sweeping" the platform. She was fascinated when she saw the fish go after it. Therefore, she proceeded to push more in to watch the fish.

Today I told some teenage boys, standing by the moat, to applaud, and maybe Luna would do it too. Sure enough, "Monkey see, monkey do."

Doc is kind of in a funk. All this change in routine has upset him. He spent a large part of the morning clutching a big soft blanket. Poor guy. The keeper gave him a peanut butter cup, and he ate it one tiny bite at a time. It's funny to watch him hold something so small in that huge hand, and eat it like that. He's wonderful!

It started raining, so Chey and Luna came into the tunnel. Chey was on her back, and Luna jumped off the threshold and landed on her abdomen. OW! A little gentle wrestling match took place.

I left when Chey went out with Doc and Rudi.

December 9, 1999

Today is Rudi's birthday. He's 22. I wonder if he'll get a little something special.

I arrived at the zoo at 9:20 a.m. Lynn asked me to observe Chey and Luna out on the exhibit, and video tape their interactions. They were out for two hours, 9:30 to 11:30, and then brought inside due to rain. They were so good together – Luna walking along beside Chey, holding on to her, or Chey with her arm around Luna's shoulder. She even carried her briefly. Chey did get sexual with Luna, rubbing her genitals on Luna's. No complaints from Luna, but I did distract Chey later with an ice pop. Luna seemed tired of Chey sitting on her face. A docent and I were there and the zoo had opened. We thought the public would wonder about this activity, so we decided to put a stop to it. However, the behavior is normal. Lynn said Chey is probably ovulating, and she's concerned she might become too aggressive. Apparently, this has been going on for about a week.

Chey groomed Luna quite a lot while they were out. Chey just seems so fulfilled, finally being a mother. It also seems Luna is more and more confident in letting her be a mother to her.

When we went inside Lynn said I could keep all of them entertained for awhile. I gave them all alfalfa; they love that. Also put Rice Krispies in a phone book so Doc could forage. Rudi spit a mouthful of water at me for no good reason. Took some pictures of all of them. I also went around and gave all of them Rice Krispies. Actually, I think I was keeping myself entertained.

December 16, 1999

I went to the zoo strictly as a volunteer today.

First thing this morning they had a drill for a Code 99. I learned this is the type of emergency which brings men with rifles, and the volunteers are safely locked inside the night house. Doc was very interested in the "goings on" and climbed high on the tunnel mesh. He's still somewhat nervous about all of the changes in routines. When he was temporarily shifted into B, he latched onto a small, soft blanket, and kept it with him when shifted back. Poor baby!

Luna and Chey went out about 9:15, strolling side by side with Luna holding onto Chey. The tunnel was left open as it was quite cold. After they foraged for the best treats, they took up residence in the tunnel. We tried to get them back out. The keeper even went up on the roof and tossed ice pops into the exhibit to lure them out. Chey figured that one out. She grabbed an ice pop and raced back inside. Later, when the keepers were in a meeting, another volunteer and I were trying to convince them to go out. He went up on the roof and called them. They went out with Luna riding on Chey's back. Chey continues to be a wonderful mom to the little one; attentive and gentle.

December 23, 1999

Arrived at the zoo a bit late today. Chey was busy washing a little plastic chair that had decals on the seat. Maybe she thought they shouldn't be there. She was using her hand, dipping it in her water bowl. I went to the shelves to find her a "dishcloth" and Rudi spit at me. He was in Cage D. Don't know why he's decided I'm a good target lately – big butt, big target, I guess. Luna had stuffed a little net produce bag with paper toweling. (Remember, Chey taught her the art of stuffing.) Then Chey took it, stuffed it completely, dipped it in the water bowl, and squeezed it out, over and over.

I gave Doc a huge crispy plastic bag (it did have air holes), and he promptly put it on. He walked about, scooted about, and generally had a great time with it.

Chey and Luna went out about 10:15 a.m. Luna didn't want to go; kept pulling Chey to the far corner of the tunnel. I think she thought it was too cold. Chey wanted to go however. She finally picked Luna up and out they went. They were out for about three hours. Another volunteer and I cleaned cages, but Kelly wouldn't shift out of D. Therefore, Lynn suggested I go out and watch Luna and Chey for fun. The docent wasn't there when I first went out. I let the crowd know I could answer questions, and provide them with a bit of education about orangutans. Two or three times Luna took hold of Chey's hair and pulled her towards the night house. Then they'd walk together with Luna holding onto Chey's arm. I couldn't see them when they'd go around the "cliff," but soon they'd come around the other side. I think Luna was cold and wanted to go in. Chey didn't get up on the structure, but sat underneath while Luna was up on top. If Chey started to leave, Luna would go immediately to her.

While we were out, Doc was in B with all sorts of stuff to play with. At one point he had the little plastic chair on his head.

When Lynn let Chey in with Doc for awhile, Luna whined and planted her thumb in her mouth. I gave her a monkey biscuit and played with her a bit. Chey didn't pummel Doc or even get a good wrestling match going. I did notice he's much bigger than she is now. Maybe Chey's thinking twice.

January 1, 2000

I decided to go in and help clean cages today. However, the nighttime arrangements had been such that some creative shifting needed to take place before we could clean. The keeper asked me to go out to watch Chey and Luna on the exhibit until a docent came. I went back for the video camera as it looked like there might be some good stuff to film. Chey and Luna went up to the top of the structure a couple of times. Luna continues to use the hair on Chey's head as a handle to walk along beside her or pull her along. They're getting along so well. I never tire of watching them together. There was food sharing, play wrestling, and snuggling. At one point, Chey carried the heavy baby on her front for a short distance. Then Luna disembarked and grabbed the hair on Chey's head. The docent didn't arrive until about 11 a.m. so I was in hog heaven after the viewing public started coming. I was able to tell all about Luna, Chey, and the others ad nauseum. Meanwhile, the keeper cleaned three cages. However, she said if I hadn't been there, she would have had to do the observation. Chey carried a crossword puzzle book out with her today. After she and Luna were back inside, I cleaned up the mess she'd made with it. The keeper put forage around on the exhibit for Rudi and Doc. We then cleaned two other cages. Kelly was in D and the keeper said she'd clean it later. She was there 'til 6 p.m. so she had plenty of time.

An interesting incident. Chey was in B and Luna was in A. Luna choked on a drink of water. She seemed to aspirate a little and coughed like crazy. Chey was at the intro door in a heartbeat, reaching through for Luna. What a wonderful mommy she is!

When I left the zoo, I spent about 45 minutes watching Rudi and Doc out on exhibit. Doc was trying to get play wrestling going. I hope he doesn't regret that.

January 6, 2000

Arrived at the zoo about 8:30 a.m. with lots of boxes, containers, etc. from Christmas.

There was a volunteer to help with the orangs so the keeper had me go watch Chey and Luna when they went outside. I took the camera and got some good footage, including Chey carrying Luna. Chey is cycling (it's been four weeks since last time) and she spent a lot of time getting sexual with Luna. Luna didn't put up too much of a fuss. However, we did distract Chey a couple of times with ice pops when she held Luna down a bit too long.

They did a lot of food sharing, and of course Luna pulled Chey around by the hair on her head. Also observed a lengthy grooming session.

BIG NEWS! Cage A, the nursery, has been dismantled. The jungle gym is gone. All orangutans can be in all the cages. Also, the creep door is history. Another major milestone in Luna's life. Doc, Rudi, and Kelly are thrilled to get to check A out after two years.

The gang got coconuts today. Chey was having her usual problem of not being able to open hers. I told her to hit it against the floor and demonstrated the action. She did that and I praised her. She also held it over her head and banged it against the cage. She put it in her water bowl. But when I left at noon it still wasn't open. She and Luna were in cages E and F. So there was no way she could roll it out to me, so I could offer an assist with a hammer.

January 13, 2000

Quite an uneventful morning at the zoo. Chey and Luna went out and I helped clean cages. Did touch the little sweetie before she went out. Doc had a plastic glove and of course we know what he was doing with <u>that</u>. Rudi refused to go out. Therefore, when Chey and Luna were back inside, Doc was on exhibit alone.

January 20, 2000

Lynn was back today after being out a week with the flu. She was in orangs and glad to see me. I tidied up the yard and put out forage. Then I observed Chey and Luna out there for 1 ½ hours. I threw ice pops to them right after they went out. When Luna's hands got sticky she rubbed them together. When <u>that</u> didn't get them clean, she wiped them on the top of her head. At least it took care of her bad hair day. No unusual happenings between Chey and Luna. They did have a gentle wrestling session.

When the docent arrived, I went inside and helped clean. Kelly and Doc were being silly, making up games. Rudi was being Rudi, sitting and staring. Had a blanket over him most of the time. He looked lovely in pink. ☺

January 27, 2000

Arrived at the zoo at 7:30 a.m. Went around and cut browse (hibiscus and banana leaves) first. It was very cold and windy so I knew Chey and Luna would be staying in. They were in A and B. Luna put her hands out for a love. Even had a little smile on her face.

Doc was clutching a big pink blanket (his security). I cleaned up the yard and the door track of the tunnel; the one leading to the outside. It was full of "gronk." Fed everyone biscuits and corn flakes while I waited for Lynn. Put some hibiscus just outside of the door hoping Rudi would go out without problems. Meanwhile Chey got a big mouthful of water. Dumb me – I thought she was just thirsty – but VOILA! She plastered me at a distance of about 5 feet.

Rudi and Kelly went out quickly, and I proceeded to scrub cages and the aisle with soap and water. Also had time to sweep Doc's empty cage. I had to leave at 11:30 due to plans in the early afternoon.

February 2, 2000

I took Lynn to lunch today at a restaurant called Mi Luna. Appropriate choice! She said a keeper was resigning if I wanted to apply again. I declined but said if there was ever a part time position, let me know. I also learned her birthday is the same day as Sterling's, my granddaughter.

February 3, 2000

Arrived at the zoo about 8 a.m. Luna was sucking her thumb and didn't greet me like usual. Not too much going on. I helped the keeper clean cages. Rudi refused to go out. Kelly went out early and came in at 10 like a good girl. However, we had to bribe her with a pickle to shift from C to E and F. Chey and Luna went out for awhile. Luna wanted Chey to climb to the top of the structure, and kept pulling on her head until she complied. It's been four weeks since Chey's last cycle, but she showed no signs of it today. Doc went out at 11:45. We did get Rudi to go from A to B, but that's as far as he went. Earlier he actually played a bit with Doc, when Doc initiated a wrestling session.

February 10, 2000

Went to the zoo at 8:30 a.m. Miss Luna greeted me with one hand through the mesh and a little smile on her face. I stroked her cheek and scratched her head.

I cleaned the exhibit and then helped clean all the cages. We finished at 10:30 so I went out to watch Luna and Chey on exhibit. Chey did something strange but funny. One of the vets had been by earlier to check a sore on Doc's tongue. Afterwards, she stopped by the moat to say hi to Chey and Luna. Chey "hid" behind a pillar of the structure. Mind you, her whole body was showing on both sides of the big pole. Since her face wasn't showing, I guess she thought she was not visible. After that, Chey just acted weird, and Luna kept hiding in the wood structure too. Sometimes vets have a strange effect on these orangs.

February 24, 2000

I missed last week as I was in Montana snowmobiling etc. When I arrived, Lynn said to go tell all the orangs "hi" while she fed the babirusa. Said they'd be glad to see me; they'd probably missed me. I thought "Yeah, right!"

Well, Luna came right over to the mesh, put her little hand out, took my hand and just held it for a few moments. Didn't sniff it or anything. She even had a smiley face. And Chey was front and center too. They were in C and D. Doc was in E and F. He came to the mesh, pulled up a bucket, and sat on it while I chatted with him. Kelly and Rudi had shared A and B during the night. (Something new.) They were at the front of their cages too. Maybe they did miss me!

As I walked about, getting things ready to tidy outside, Luna kept coming to the mesh close by. I tickled her feet, scratched her head, scratched her back, stroked her cheek, and poked her Buddha belly. She is such a sweetie!

Rudi didn't spit at me; just made raspberry sounds. That's new from him. At least to me. He and Kelly went out first 'til about 11:30. Then Chey and Luna went out.

Luna is still pulling Chey around by the hair on her head, but Chey is disciplining her when she doesn't like it. Lynn said the first time she pulled Luna's hand away and bit her fingers. Luna put on a play face. The next time she bit harder. Luna whined and looked at her fingers like, "What is that all about?" Today I saw her check her fingers one time when Chey bit her. Poor Chey – her head must be sore.

Also today, Chey traded me a 5 inch long bolt and four assorted size washers for some corn flakes. I looked all over cages C and D for where they'd come from but couldn't locate the place. It was funny 'cause she gave me the biggest washer, then the bolt. When I gave her the corn flakes three more washers were spit out; plink, plink, plink. Sounded like a slot machine pay off.

March 2, 2000

Well, I guess Rudi has decided I'm okay. Today when I entered the night house, he started "purring" and presented his nipple. Then he immediately broke off a two inch piece of hay, stuck it in his nipple, and pressed against the mesh wanting me to pull it out. I told him I wasn't going to play that game. He then presented his other nipple. The keeper was nearby so she touched it, and he was a happy camper.

Doc went outside first. Kelly and Rudi had C, D, and the tunnel while we cleaned A and B. Luna and Chey were in E and F. After Doc came in, and Luna and Chey went out, I noticed Kelly had a bamboo branch about four feet long. She played a bit of tug-o-war with me, and then went into the tunnel and started poking Doc with the stick. He was sitting up high in cage B, but she could reach him.

After we cleaned E and F, we moved Kelly and Rudi there. Kelly picked up one of those microwaveable dishes (enrichment), dipped it in the water bowl in F, carried it very carefully into E, climbed onto the bench, and didn't spill a drop. Dumped it into a hard hat. I don't know how many trips she'd made as I just saw one. However, she eventually filled a big bowl with water (maybe used some from the hard hat), and put her whole face into the bowl. Maybe she was having a hot flash.

Nothing special with Luna and Chey. Luna came to the cage front, but didn't put her arm through today. Chey is still disciplining her by biting her fingers. Now, most of the time, Luna walks along beside Chey with her hand on Chey's shoulder.

March 9, 2000

Really a short entry today as I was only at the zoo 2 ½ hours. Lynn and I cleaned everything between 9 and 10:30 a.m. Doc and Rudi were out when I arrived. Doc will be sedated tomorrow so they can check the sore on his tongue. Poor baby; he's so afraid of needles.

After they came inside, I went to F to say hi to Rudi. He actually came to the cage front to see me.

Of course Luna came to the cage front to greet me when I arrived. Had her smiley face on.

Kelly spit at me through her teeth every time I walked by.

March 10, 2000 1:30 p.m.

I just called the night house to check on Doc. Lynn said he's fine, coming out of the sedation. She said the keeper got him on the first try.

As we spoke, she said Chey had Luna in a tight embrace. They all get so scared when they see a vet. Apparently Chey grabbed Luna, and made her scream she was holding her so tight, but then Luna was falling asleep. (Another way they handle stress.) Wish we could get a picture. Chey tries so hard to be a good mommy.

March 20, 2000

I'll be in South Carolina on Thursday at the IPPL (International Primate Protection League) conference so I worked today, a Monday.

Greeted Luna and got a little touch. Stroked her face a bit. She and Chey went out as soon as I finished cleaning the yard. Chey took a tub into the tunnel, hoping she could sneak it outside. However, the keeper wasn't falling for that trick.

Kelly traded me seven cents for some peas. Later the keeper was talking about how Rudi was becoming playful and decided to test him. She put a brown paper against the mesh and he stuck his tongue through it. Then he'd stick his tongue out and she'd grab it.

I told her another one of the caregivers said he'd recently had a bag on his head. So the keeper gave him a huge plastic trash bag with some air holes torn in it. He put it on immediately. It covered him completely. He continued playing with it for awhile. When he went outside Kelly claimed it for fun and games.

The keeper said Doc had been a bit slow to recover completely from the sedation ten days ago. She said he'd grab the mesh, would miss it, and fall back. She said she left him in the squeeze cage (where they recover from sedation) all night so he wouldn't hurt himself. Then she said she worried because there was a storm that night. She thought he might be afraid being locked in the squeeze. She also said he now weighs 196 pounds. Yikes!

March 22, 2000

I called Lynn to get an address. She said this morning, when she entered the night house, Luna and Chey were asleep in the same black tub. Looked like one orangutan with two heads. Yes! We've been wondering if Luna slept with Chey.

March 29, 2000

Decided to work today, a Wednesday, as I have a meeting tomorrow in the early afternoon. I took Lynn a poster of a baby bonobo (3 poses) that I got at the IPPL conference. It was taken by a wildlife photographer, and I had him autograph it and address it to Lynn. She was thrilled. We discussed the conference. She also showed me the video she will present at the Great Ape Conference in May. It was the training of Kelly during her pregnancy, the sedation so Luna could nurse, the nursing through the mesh, and the aggression toward Luna when a reintroduction was attempted. She is still working on the next video of the introduction process to Chey and the happy ending.

I also learned there was some upset among the keepers because I was there today to help Lynn in orangs. I told Lynn I was willing to work elsewhere as I was a volunteer for all Primates. She feels those of us that parented Luna have priority to work in orangs. Three have said they only want to work in orangs. That is my preference too but...........

Luna came to the cage front today, but would pull her hand back when I tried to grasp it. She did sniff my hand, let me scratch her head, and stroke her face. She had her little close-mouthed smile on. Lynn said she has started playing the tease, keep away game like the other orangs. We're all still proud we made her into one.

I cleaned the yard, then cages. Lynn helped some but she had time sheets to do and she knows I don't mind cleaning alone.

On the way to orangs today I picked five hibiscus blossoms for them. Rudi didn't eat his so we gave it to Doc later. We also gave him a huge box which he thoroughly enjoyed. Lynn let me give Luna and Chey their cheese reward when they stationed in the tunnel. It's nice she let me feed Chey too. I told her if the zoo had a part time keeper job, I'd apply in a heartbeat. She made me feel very good saying she'd <u>hire</u> me in a heartbeat.

April 5, 2000

Arrived at the zoo about 8:45 a.m., and picked five hibiscus on the way to Primates. (There's a bush located just inside the employee entrance.) When I passed them out, Rudi again just set his aside. Doc savored every last bit of his, one tiny bite at a time. He's so funny the way he daintily eats his favorite treats. Holds them gently in those huge hands.

After Rudi and Doc went outside, I gave Rudi's hibiscus to Kelly. She had the remains of a broom skirt in her cage. Lynn said when she got it yesterday, she put it on over her head, peeking out of the waist hole. Then she let it fall down over her. Lynn said she was flapping her arms with the skirt "blowing in the wind." She looked lovely.

I cleaned cages while Lynn did time sheets. She then had a meeting scheduled with Barbara and the keepers. She needed to shift Kelly into E and F from C with cheese as a bribe. Well, Kelly decided to play Lynn like a violin and wouldn't go. Lynn had to go to the meeting, and asked me to let her know if Kelly shifted. <u>Well</u>, no sooner had Lynn locked up and disappeared (Kelly watching her the whole time); she shifted. She's "evil"; that's all there is to it. Interestingly enough, however, she did <u>not</u> come to the cage front to get her cheese reward. She was more interested in foraging for the oatmeal scattered about.

I interrupted Lynn again to unlock C and the tunnel so I could clean. After I finished, I went around to check on "the boys" out on exhibit. Right before I left the night house, Rudi was pounding loudly on the tunnel door wanting to come inside. Consequently, when I went outside, he was not visible, remaining behind the cliff by the door. Doc was holding court at the window watching the children watching him. One had dropped an M and M right by the glass, and he was <u>very</u> interested in that. I talked to a lot of the visitors. I love to tell them about the orangutans. There were some teenage girls there, and Doc happened to be "popping" a zit on his lip as they watched. Typical teenager. Well, as Lynn said, it was better than Doc masturbating as they watched.

Luna let me hold, pat, and rub her little hand today. Scratched her head and all. She made lots of play faces. I watched as she and Chey played together also.

I did all of the cleaning today except for Lynn sweeping A and B. Was at the zoo 'til 2 p.m. I love it there!

April 12, 2000

Well, today the most exciting thing at the zoo was I fell down in the aisle. It was wet and slippery as Lynn and I cleaned. Scraped my left arm. Put ice on it immediately, but then noticed swelling on the back of my left hand. Might have broken a vein.

April 13, 2000

Woke this morning and noticed my hand was <u>very</u> swollen extending down into my fingers. Very discolored too. Went to the doctor and learned I have a tiny "crack" in my wrist. He said it would heal slowly, and prescribed a splint to wear off and on. Thank goodness I didn't need a cast. I think I need to get some new work boots.

April 19, 2000

Well, it's almost Easter. That inspired me to take Easter baskets to my orange buddies. I'd asked permission to bring coconuts and limes for their baskets. I bought five Easter baskets, and tried to personalize them as much as possible. Each orang got a small plastic ball and an animal sipper cup. Gave all but Rudi T-shirts. Put a necktie in Doc and Kelly's as they like to weave things. Put tiny stuffed bunnies in Luna, Chey, and Kelly's, and crinkly bags in Doc and Rudi's. AAA books went into Luna, Chey, and Kelly's. Gave each of the guys a coconut and each girl a lime. I also gave Rudi an orange as his basket looked kind of empty.

Lynn let me put uncooked oatmeal in brightly colored plastic eggs, and I put them out on exhibit. Rudi spotted a bright pink one on the structure immediately. Kelly went for the three near the observation window. She gathered all of them and then noticed Rudi headed toward her. She gave him a look like, "Oh, oh. I have all of these eggs. Will this be cause for a sexual assault?" However, he just gave her a glance, and proceeded to the oatmeal I stashed in the open pipes below the window.

I then started the cleaning inside, slipping again but not falling. Lynn caught me. I'm convinced I need new boots! Lynn agreed wholeheartedly. Therefore, I washed my boots at the end of the day, and gave them to the orangs.

I gave Chey and Luna hand held scrub brushes to keep them busy while I cleaned cages. Chey scrubbed things after she brushed her hair. She scrubbed the mesh, the door track, under the door, the wall, a bucket etc. When she was done she took the brush apart. Luna just played with her brush.

Doc shifted into E and F. I'd put his Easter basket in for him. He sat down by it, and took things out one at a time. Was thrilled with the coconut.

Luna and Chey were shifted to C and D. Luna grabbed her basket and headed to the skylight. They really seemed to enjoy the limes. The sipper cups too. Naturally Luna loved the little stuffed bunny. She used to have so many stuffed toys.

Luna and Chey were moved to D to bring Rudi into C. He displayed like crazy, dumping his basket in the fracas. Then Kelly refused to come in so Rudi was shifted to A and B. He didn't take his coconut with him. When Chey and Luna were allowed back into C, they got it. Well, of course Rudi got Kelly's Easter basket which I'd put into A. He was very happy with the lime. Lynn had transferred his orange over. Chey was thrilled with the coconut, but of course she couldn't open it. She banged it on the floor, using both hands at times, pressed it against her hard head, and even tried to push it out for <u>us</u> to open it. When she'd cracked it enough for some milk to run out, she even tried using a tiny bamboo stem to open it. Luna eventually swooped down and grabbed it, and carried it all over the place. She also had one of my old work boots, and was putting things into it and folding it over. She was being generally silly!

I took a whole roll of film today, and hope some of them turn out. It was a great day and I had so much fun!

April 23, 2000 Easter Sunday

I decided to go help the keeper this morning. (I sometimes skip church on Easter Sunday, giving up my seat for those who only go on Easter and Christmas.) The keeper was glad to see me. Yesterday, two Luna caregivers, now Saturday volunteers, put oodles of eggs and other Easter stuff out on exhibit twice; once for Rudi and Doc and again for Chey and Luna. She said the exhibit looked as bad as Doc's cage usually does in the mornings.

I arrived about 8:30 a.m. Another Luna caregiver was there too. Oh my goodness, what a mess the yard was! I took pictures. We actually salvaged a lot of stuff that wasn't broken; eggs and such. The keeper said yesterday Rudi had been mainly interested in the eggs within easy reach, but Doc went from egg to egg, opening each for forage. At one point Doc was sitting in the drinking pool playing with all of the toys. I hope to see the videos. I asked if we could put eggs out on exhibit again since Kelly and Rudi were going out after Chey and Luna. She said no because Kelly's thing was to break the eggs into little pieces.

With two of us volunteers cleaning, we did a very thorough job in a short period of time, scrubbing the cages and toys with soap. We did take a short break to go watch Mac, the gorilla, go on his Easter egg hunt in his exhibit.

The orangs were given egg shaped jello this morning. In Doc's typical manner, he savored it with little bites. Rudi ate his in one fell swoop. The keeper said Rudi has been "sharing" food with her. He eats half of his apple and offers her the other half. He also gives her his orange peel and bits of his banana peel. What a guy!

This morning the other caregiver gave Kelly a cardboard roll from wrapping paper. She used it as a tool to get hold of the bag of trash from the yard that was in the aisle. We did manage to keep the trash from her, but she mainly wanted the bag. She put it on. Then when she shifted into C with Rudi she took it with her. Rudi refused to go outside when it was time for them to go, so she got both ice pops that were out there.

This morning Luna greeted me with a little smile and presented her head for a scratch.

May 3, 2000

Not too much going on with my buddies today. Chey and Luna went out first. When Chey came back in, I gave her a birthday gift. Her birthday is May 13th. Gave her a mini handheld broom and dustpan. She raced off to the next cage with it. Luna then grabbed it, and had lots of fun with the broom. I also had a little squirt toy another volunteer brought. Doc put on his play face, hid his eyes, and opened his mouth for me to squirt water in.

Rudi refused to go out. He stayed in the tunnel even though the outside door was open. He was sedated the end of last week for his check up. He weighs 293 pounds.

I gave Kelly some cellophane to play with and she enjoyed that, putting it on her head.

Lynn put some biscuits and oats on a petal shaped tray for Doc. He added more biscuits to the tray, and was carrying it around. Looked like a waiter. What a group!

May 9, 2000

Today, since I was in her neighborhood, I stopped by the Easter Sunday keeper's house, to give her photos of Rudi. She loves them! She told me Kelly broke the really nice water bowl in cage B. She'd given her a long willow branch, thinking it was so limp she couldn't do any damage with it. (Kelly was in cages A and B that day.) WELL, she waited 'til the keeper left the night house and threaded or weaved it through the grate covering the drain near the night house door. The grate is about 10 inches wide and three feet long. She pulled the grate into her cage, and used it as a weapon to break the water bowl. The keeper said she and a volunteer were in the kitchen watching the video that Lynn will present at the Great Ape Conference. They heard all kinds of racket in the night house, but figured Kelly was just slamming enrichment articles around. It seems Kelly was slamming enrichment articles; articles of her own choosing. She is so smart, it's scary!

May 11, 2000

I had to wear a Band-Aid to the zoo today. My dog got hold of my finger when I gave her a treat last night. I wondered if Rudi would get all excited as he loves Band-Aids.

When I got there, Chey and Luna were already outside, and the keeper was cleaning A and B. Doc was in C and she said Kelly and Rudi were in D. E and F were open, ready to be cleaned. When I said hi to Rudi he started purring, threw a few things about in a display, and then made the loudest long call I've ever heard. I started cleaning. A few minutes later I looked across the aisle and didn't see Kelly. I went down the aisle to tell the keeper the effect of my Band-Aid on Rudi, and asked where Kelly was. She said she was in with Rudi; maybe just hiding. I went back and noticed at that point she was flat on her back, getting raped by Rudi. She kind of looked over her shoulder at me. Maybe she was thinking, "Thanks a lot. I didn't deserve this." After he was finished, and Doc moved to A and B, the door was opened to C. Rudi took Kelly by the arms, dragged her in there, and then left her alone. She went upwards, but as she was stretched out on her back on the diagonal prop coming from the top, I think she looked a bit like a happy camper.

Later, Rudi refused to go out, sat in the tunnel. He purred when I walked up to him. He then presented his nipple, even putting a tiny piece of straw in it hoping I'd pull it out. I didn't. Kelly came inside briefly and poked him. Hmmmmm..........

I also blew soap bubbles for Doc and Kelly. That was fun.

When Luna and Chey were called in, Luna came into the squeeze cage, but Chey was standing just outside. So Luna took hold of the hair on Chey's head and pulled her in. I'd put a 10 inch plastic ball in the cage for Luna. She rolled around on it, threw it etc. Gave Chey another scrub brush, and she got busy scrubbing this and that. Got a few photos. Also got one of Luna on top of one of the high poles on the exhibit.

May 17, 2000

Nothing special or unusual today. Did a really good cleaning. Lynn is gone; at the Great Ape Conference.

May 24, 2000

Lynn was back today. She said her presentation not only went well, but Birute Galidikas was in the audience. She complimented Lynn and asked for a copy of the video. Lynn said we will all get copies. I watched the video today. It's terrific!!

BIG NEWS! The Species Survival Plan people have given the okay for Kelly and Doc to breed. Lynn said she's not ready, especially for the pre natal training of Kelly, trying to teach her to "get it right" this time. I said at least she knows there are those of us all ready if hand rearing is again necessary. She added that she knows we have an appropriate surrogate too.

Lynn informed Rudi and Kelly they were going outside today. I left the night house to watch the video so Rudi wouldn't have distractions, and he went out like a good boy. Lynn then said, "Ready to go outside, Kelly?" Kelly was right at door #2 (in B, right off the tunnel), but the door wouldn't open. Kelly was not happy! Lynn cleaned cage A real fast and set it up for Kelly. She put in all the enrichment I'd brought, including a ten inch ball, and moved her in there. She played and played. She loved the ball – threw it, kicked it, then bit it. Oops! Flat ball. When Lynn tried to get her to play with the hose and water, Kelly got a mouthful of water and spit it at Lynn. Still mad, I guess. Then Lynn went into B and started checking. It seems the door didn't work because Kelly had picked at a wire and pulled it loose. I wonder how many work orders have been initiated because of Kelly's mischievous behavior. The electricians were still working on it when I left.

Lynn let Doc out with Rudi. I went around to throw them ice pops. Doc took his and went quickly to the drinking pool and sat right in the middle of it. I ran to get my camera, but he was out by the time I got back.

When it was time for Luna and Chey to go out, Luna wouldn't go. She was busy playing on a bench in cage E. Lynn told Chey to go get her baby, and she <u>did</u>. She picked up a squirming, kicking Luna and took her to the door. Luna took a towel with her.

May 29, 2000

Decided to go help the keeper today, Memorial Day holiday. Another Luna caregiver was there too, and we did a very thorough cleaning. Barbara came by; says she's trying to figure a way to create shade on the exhibit.

My neighbor and some of her relatives came by (I'd asked permission for their visit), so I gave them the tour. Rudi, Kelly and Doc were inside. Rudi displayed. As we were watching his action, Doc did a little display. Never saw that before. Maybe he figured it got attention when Rudi did it, so why not. After I showed them the action inside, we went to see Luna and Chey on exhibit. I threw ice pops over to them. Chey pretended not to see hers, hoping I'd toss another one, but I was wise to that. Luna took hers to the area of the structure where she's not too visible. She'd peek out when I'd call her name though.

Barbara is anxious for Kelly and Doc to get together. She says at least she knows there are trained volunteers if needed, and <u>this</u> time she'll get the volunteers involved much sooner. Naturally we hope Kelly gets it right this time.

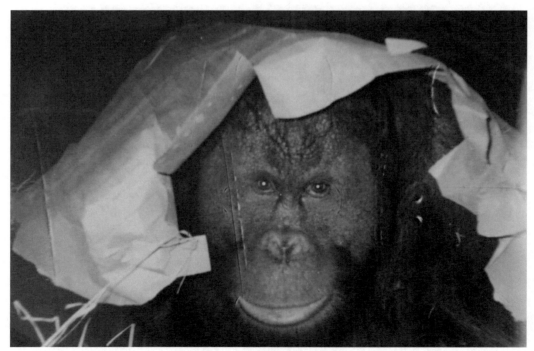

Doc as a teenager

THE ORANG GANG ET AL - LOVED, HUGGED AND PEED ON

Cheyenne enjoying a beverage

Doc likes wearing shredded paper

Elok on his jungle gym

Elok

Doc, all grown up

THE ORANG GANG ET AL - LOVED, HUGGED AND PEED ON

Kelly

Rudi begging from the public

Rudi likes to blow bubbles

Solaris with Daddy Doc

Doc playing with Solaris

June 3, 2000

I decided to go in on a Saturday as the regular volunteers are on vacation. We cleaned like crazy. Had to evict a large frog from the tunnel. (The doors to the outside are being left open at night to make it cooler in the night house.) Also found a large rat in the trap by the supply cart. Had to scrub blood off the floor. Yuck!

Took each orang a new sipper today, all alike. Chey opened hers to drink, but Luna and Doc used the straw.

When a former keeper, who now works in the clinic, came by with a vet tech applicant, Rudi put on a grand display concluding with a nipple presentation (what's new) and Doc displayed too. How impressive! When Rudi displayed Kelly stayed up near the skylight. I don't blame her.

I didn't see it, but the keeper said, when she was letting Luna and Chey out, Chey was being pokey, hanging back in the squeeze. Luna kept reaching for her. She was already on the ground foraging for the rice the keeper had scattered below the door. She finally took Chey's arm and pulled on her like, "Come on." She is so attached to Chey. It's wonderful!

June 7, 2000

First cleaned the yard thoroughly. I had extra time this morning as Lynn had two other areas to go to. Cleaned the inside of the squeeze cage with bleach and it looks <u>much</u> better. Had a lag time when Lynn needed to go catch a monkey who hasn't come inside for five days. I played with Luna and Chey while she was gone. Luna actually put her hands through the mesh, one at a time, and let me hold and stroke them. She also let me scratch her here and there. Put on a few play faces too. I also talked to Chey at length, telling her what a good mommy she is etc. As she pressed her head and shoulder against the mesh, I scratched them a bit.

I cleaned all of the cages today as Lynn was busy. Gave Doc a ball and he bit it open promptly. Gave one to Chey and Luna too. Luna played with it. I gave Chey a scrub brush so she could work.

Right before I left today I noticed Doc chewing on something. When I asked him what he had in his mouth, he showed me he had gum. However, he wouldn't let me have it; just kept chewing. He was stretching it etc. with his tongue. Silly boy - we don't know where he got it. Lynn said maybe he retrieved it from where he'd stuck it some previous time. Hmmmmm.....

A sad note. The baby Titi monkey died. They found him on the ground, hypothermic and dehydrated. They don't know why his mama pulled him off her back. Then the next day, she died. She had hepatitis. So poor Mr. Titi monkey was all by himself today.

June 15, 2000

Two keepers and I were all in orangs so we cleaned very well. I worked hard on the squeeze cage again with bleach. Looks much better!

Nothing of importance or super interesting. Rudi <u>did</u> trade me a wire bucket handle for a little box of corn flakes. He wouldn't give it to the keeper earlier, so I was quite thrilled when he deemed me important enough to make a trade.

June 21, 2000

When I first arrived today Rudi came forward to greet me. There wasn't any "touch my nipple" action. He just sat there. I guess he's decided I'm okay.

Luna and Chey were in C. When it was time for them go out, Luna wouldn't go. Chey was already in the tunnel. Lynn kept saying, "Go outside." Finally Chey went back into C, and started climbing up to retrieve Luna from the prop. She ended up literally herding her into the tunnel.

I had permission to take a pineapple today as a treat for the orangs. They all seemed to enjoy that. Rudi got some as a reward for <u>finally</u> going outside.

My neighbor told me that after her elderly mom and dad visited the orangs, her mom bought both a big and little stuffed orangutan. She named them Chey and Luna.

June 28, 2000

Not too much going on today except the cleaning. Lynn said, when Rudi presented his nipples to her this morning, he actually expressed milk from them. Interesting.

I gave them new sipper cups today. First Rudi took the lid off his and drank some. Then he put his straw in to drink the rest. I forgot to put the fifth one in Doc's cage before it was locked, so I gave the extra one to Luna and Chey. Luna got it so Chey followed her to take it away. Therefore, Luna drank as much as she could hold in her mouth before surrendering it. She looked so funny with her little cheeks and mouth puffed out.

July 6, 2000

It's a Thursday but I was busy yesterday watching Sterling, my granddaughter, so wanted to come help today.

Luna didn't want to go outside. Chey went into the squeeze cage to go, but Luna stayed in E and F. She put on her little obstinate face, and climbed high on a prop.

The keeper kept saying, "Go outside." Chey took action and went into E to retrieve her. Luna then went into F, climbing as high as she could. Chey followed her, trying to grab an arm or leg. Luna went back into E with Chey right behind her. She got hold of Luna's leg, and Luna decided to go out. We praised Chey for being such a good mommy.

My neighbor gave me a bunch of wallpaper sample books. I hope the photos I took of Chey, Luna and Kelly with theirs come out. Luna had hers propped in front of her, couldn't even see her. I called her name and she peeked around the book. We put one each in Doc and Rudi's cages for when they came inside. The keeper said to pick a masculine one for Rudi. I did.

I also brought a plastic bowling set. I put five pins and a ball in for Luna and Chey. Chey picked the ball up, examined it, then looked at the pins which were set up. I'm convinced if I could have shown her what to do she would have done it. However, the pins were in the cage when she came in. Luna had a pin in each hand and was banging them on a bench. I gave the other five pins, a ball, and the plastic holder they were in to Kelly. She examined each item, and then set her brain on DESTROY! She used the holder to bang on the fluorescent light covers, sliding it through the top of the cage above the mesh. She banged it against the cover, moving along to try it in different places. I picked up some baby food fruit and she surrendered it very fast. The keeper thinks she does things like that to get goodies. Wouldn't surprise me.

July 13, 2000

Nothing really noteworthy today. I arrived at the zoo at 8:30 a.m., helped the keeper clean cages and we were done by 11. I really didn't have much interaction with the group. <u>Did</u> give them more wallpaper books.

July 19, 2000

Cindy is being trained in orangs, and we worked together today. She's been working in MYRA, the Monkey Yearlong Retirement Area. One might affectionately refer to it as the Primate nursing home.

Rudi has been in A and B for three days. Won't leave; won't go outside. Today was no different. Maybe when tomorrow's keeper is there. He likes her a lot.

They all had latex gloves when I got there this morning. Doc was doing the usual with his.

One time today I heard Luna screaming bloody murder. Chey had hold of her right foot. Don't know <u>what</u> provoked her. I told her repeatedly to let her go, and she finally did. I praised her and gave her a bite of bagel. Luna favored her foot for quite awhile.

July 26, 2000

Lynn emailed last night that Luna did her first spit yesterday. Apparently she spit at Cindy. Lynn said her form, accuracy, and distance were to be commended.

Nothing but cleaning today. Rudi and Doc went out early. We gave Kelly a straw purse. She loves purses. For fun, Luna was throwing PVC pieces into a tub. Very loud play! Later she was throwing them through the door between C and D. She <u>did</u> let me stroke her little hand for a bit.

Side note: Mac, the gorilla is very ill. Congestive heart failure. He's 47, the only living Eastern lowland gorilla in the United States, and currently the oldest gorilla in captivity. Needless to say, Lynn is quite upset.

August 2, 2000

Going out of town so no zoo. Mac is better at this point.

August 4, 2000

Visited the Ft. Worth Zoo and met their five orangutans.

August 8, 2000

Spent the day yesterday with two other Luna caregivers. They said, earlier this summer, they met Kelly's mother, Maggie, at the Brookfield Zoo in Illinois. I also got my video of Kelly and Luna and Chey and Luna, the one presented at the Great Ape Conference. It's great!

Crisis in the night house yesterday! Lynn emailed me last night. Luna got her arm caught in the mesh of the skylight in cage F. Of course her screaming upset Chey (Also Lynn on the other end of the phone when they called her.) Barbara had to sedate Chey and then Luna. Chey gave her arm for sedation. It seems she realized they needed to help her baby. It was simple to turn Luna's little arm and release her elbow. She's none the worse for wear, but Chey seems a bit down. Lynn says sedations seem to set Chey back psychologically. Barbara came to visit her. She was still mad at Barbara, and tried to pinch her fingers. We just gave her lots of praise for being such a good mommy. Luna sprawled out flat on her back on a pile of hay during the morning, and had a snooze. Guess a little remnant of her sedation.

There was also a power outage at the zoo yesterday. The water in the moat drained down about a foot and a half. It was filling slowly. We only let Rudi out. Lynn said if she let Kelly out she'd wade through the moat and escape.

The best part of the day was giving Doc an orangutan mask I bought at the Ft. Worth Zoo last week. First I held it to my face and looked at him. He reached for it, and when I gave it to him, he put it on. It was upside down but it was so funny. Lynn and I laughed like crazy.

August 16, 2000

Cleaned like a whirlwind today. Lynn had to leave at 10 a.m. to attend a symposium with Barbara. By the time I arrived at 8:45, she'd cleaned the yard, sent Luna and Chey out, and had shifted orangs so three cages were empty and ready to clean. Finished at 10:45. Rudi presented his nipple to me and started purring when I arrived.

I helped another keeper with the mangabeys and left the zoo at noon.

August 21, 2000

Nothing special today – just cleaned.

August 30, 2000

I'm in Kansas City, Missouri. I went to the zoo for a private tour, and then showed the Kelly and Luna and Chey and Luna video to a group of about 15 people; keepers and volunteers. They were very impressed that Chey, a difficult resident when she resided in the Kansas City Zoo, had become such a good mama to Luna. I will have a copy of the video sent to them when I return home. The head orangutan keeper introduced me to their four adults. Their nine month old baby orangutan died in June of a respiratory virus. His mother grieved, of course, but is doing better now.

They told me a great Chey story. Apparently, when the 15 inch square Plexiglas windows were installed in the ape building (windows at all heights so visitors of all sizes could peek at the apes), Chey watched very closely. When the workers left she took the screws out of one and hid them, leaving the window in place. Then, when the keepers went to lunch, she removed the window and crawled out. What a woman!

Another zoo employee told me when Chey arrived at the Kansas City Zoo, she was so scared, and had scraped all of the skin off her fingers clawing at the crate.

September 6, 2000

I returned to our zoo today to help clean. All five orangs are doing great. I gave Kelly an old white purse. (I didn't tell her it was after Labor Day and white is taboo.) Chey had to herd Luna outside this morning. She's getting good at that. Next week, while in Minnesota, I'll visit the Como Park Zoo in St. Paul, and hopefully show the video. Chey once resided at <u>that</u> zoo too. She has certainly gotten around. Hopefully, our zoo will be her last stop. We love her and appreciate her.

September 13, 2000

Today I went to the Como Park Zoo in St. Paul, Minnesota. 14 people watched the video. One keeper shed tears, saying all Chey needed was a baby. (She'd been a difficult resident at that zoo too.) I told her we like to think the reason Kelly didn't raise Luna was so Chey could have a baby; that it was meant to be. After the video the zoo director gave us a personal tour. We met Joy, a hybrid mother, and Willy, her "surprise" offspring. This is Joy's third baby and the first she has raised. Markisa, a young Sumatran female, is in with them so she can learn to be a mom. She will be bred with Jabu, their Sumatran male. They lost two large Bornean males recently. Some evergreen shrubs above the exhibit had been trimmed, and some of the trimmings fell into the exhibit. It was not known they were poisonous to the orangs. They ate them, and died within five hours of each other. So sad!

September 19, 2000

I received some photos of Luna's birthday celebration on Saturday, sent by email from a Luna caregiver. Apparently, there's a piece of her cake waiting for me in the freezer at the zoo.

September 20, 2000

WOW! The piece of cake they left for me was the piece with Luna's photo on the icing. Lynn suggested I slice it off and keep it.

    Friday is Kelly's birthday. She'll be 20. After Lynn removed the orang T-shirt I brought her from Minnesota, I took the gift bag and put gifts in it for Kelly to "open" for her birthday. I gave her a new sipper cup and a sipper bowl. I took a photo, but I'm not sure it'll come out at the angle I had to take it.

    I gave each orang two limes today. They loved them. I also gave them straw hats to play with. At one point Luna put hers on, but of course it was on and off so fast I couldn't get a photo.

I noticed some wheels about two inches in diameter lying about. Apparently, they'd been on a wooden dolly, and Kelly had jumped up and down on it until it was in splinters. They said she had a big play face on while doing it. Later Doc was rolling the wheels back and forth.

When Rudi came in from outside he dragged in a huge bamboo branch about fifteen feet long. Lynn said she'd get it from him later.

September 22, 2000

Tonight Lynn, two other caregivers, and I, met for dinner. It was a neat evening; all of us so crazy about the orangutans, sharing photos and stories. Lynn told us what happened on Wednesday with Rudi and the bamboo branch. She was in the kitchen doing some charting, and heard a very loud noise that sounded like a jack hammer. She stepped into the service court to listen, and it stopped. She went back into the kitchen and heard it again. She went back out and realized it was coming from the orang night house. Oh, oh! She went in. Rudi was standing up, holding the bamboo branch with the end in the fan; the fan hanging on the wall near the cage he was in. Of course the fan was shaking like crazy. As soon as he saw Lynn he knew he'd been busted, and pushed the branch out under the mesh to her.

She also told an interesting story about giving the orangs their juice at closing time. Generally, when the gang sees the keeper with the pitcher of juice, they look for a container in their cages to put up to the mesh so the keeper can pour the juice in it. They usually grab one of the big buckets, not noticing if there are holes in the bottom allowing the juice to run right through. However, one evening she observed Cheyenne picking a bucket up, looking at the bottom, noticing a hole, putting it down, and getting another one <u>without</u> a hole. Yes, they definitely do think.

Now, on the other hand, she also told us that one day Doc grabbed a colander and was hoping to have it filled with juice. Hmmmm....

September 27, 2000

No excitement today; just cleaning. However, Luna did take my hand, and let me rub her little hand. She also wanted me to scratch her head and back. She had on her play face.

October 4, 2000

Another day of cleaning with only a bit of interaction. There was a slight problem when it was time for Luna and Chey to come inside. Chey didn't want to but Luna did. It took three tries, and then only succeeded when they were allowed to go into A and B, not C and D.

October 18, 2000

I missed last week. Luna was glad to see me. She put on her play face and wanted her head scratched. Cindy said Chey and Luna were out the whole day yesterday. Luna wanted to come in, but Chey wouldn't let her and held onto her arm. Needless to say, they stayed in today. Kelly and Rudi went out first. Doc went out at 12:45. Kelly is to be sedated and examined Friday. THEN intros with Doc. Maybe we'll have another baby next fall.

October 31, 2000

It's a Tuesday but I wanted to give the orangs their jack-o-lanterns and goodies. I went in early so I could help with the exhibit. We put a few streamers up, and put hibiscus blossoms in the drinking pool.

Doc and Kelly are a "couple" now. They are happy! Saw him grooming her at one point. Rudi keeps his eye on them. Hey – he's lost his sex partner.

Chey got her coconut open before anyone else. I gave her the one that looked like it would break most easily. Luna was right in her face wanting to share. Luna used hers to bowl; rolled it up a cardboard ramp. She was also playing ball with her limes.

I also gave them plastic Halloween straws, and Kelly used hers as a whistle. Surprised us as much as her.

November 6, 2000

WOW! Today I felt like I was in a porn flick. When Doc and Kelly were let in together, it was sex, sex, sex – all ways, all morning. When she cycles, if she doesn't get pregnant, it won't be for lack of trying. Doc loves having a real girl. Rudi is a bit upset as Kelly has been <u>his</u> sex toy, and now he must share.

I cleaned the exhibit and all the cages as the keeper needed to do other things. Was there 6 hours.

November 15, 2000

The ropes are up! Yes, the ropes we volunteers bought for Luna's third birthday. They are finally up on the exhibit. Cindy said all of the orangs were very curious, and somewhat suspicious, especially about the epoxy on the ends of each. She said they checked out the connections to see if they could unscrew the bolts. She also said Rudi decided to swing on one but stopped abruptly, and sat down sedately, when he saw Barbara watching. Too dignified to have fun after all.

Apparently, Doc and Kelly were "going at it" on exhibit yesterday, and Barbara was videotaping it which upset some visitors. They don't realize this documentation is important in the SSP program. I was telling a former orang keeper (she now works in the clinic) about it when she came by to see Luna on the ropes. She said they should have been there the day Rudi was having sex with a dead bird. <u>No one</u> could explain <u>that</u> one.

Rudi is upset when Doc and Kelly are together. Today when Kelly was whimpering during sex, he spit at Cindy. What a soap opera!

Luna was a busy girl today, playing like crazy and inventing games. She's so cute!

November 22, 2000

Nothing too much going on except the cleaning. Rudi and Kelly went out early – Rudi grabbing the two ice pops as they went out.

A guy is in the process of installing a new water bowl in F. Yesterday Rudi refused to go out, needing to supervise of course. Chey and Luna were worried about it, and raced outside. Later, back inside, they ate their lunch under a bench hiding from him. He was back today. Chey fretted and tried to pull Luna to her. However, Luna was curious, and wanted to watch what he was doing. Chey set up residence in the squeeze cage, and wouldn't let Cindy close it off to clean. Cindy put baby food on the mesh in D for Chey. However, Chey figured <u>that</u> one out really fast, and raced back to block the door if she saw Cindy go near the hydraulics. Of course when Cindy was on a break, Chey licked the food off the mesh knowing she wasn't there to close the door.

Today Luna had a gallon jug of flavored water. Because it was so heavy, she opened it, and turned it over in a tiny black tub to empty some out. Smart little girl!

December 20, 2000

Back at the zoo today after a month. (Vacation in Hawaii) It was great to see the gang. Luna came to the mesh for a back scratch right away.

Couple of good Doc stories to record. A former caregiver, now volunteer, was leading a group of adults around the zoo on "caroling to the animals" day. As they stood at the moat watching, Kelly was on one side of the structure and Doc was on the other. As the carolers sang Silent Night, it so "moved" Doc he went to Kelly, grabbed her arm, pulled her onto the grass, spread her legs and had sex.

Lynn told me that on one of the really cold days last week Doc and Kelly were outside but had access to the tunnel and cage C. She figured it was so cold few people would be at the zoo. She also knew they would probably take things outside. But, since there would be few people, it didn't matter. Well, Kelly came inside and Lynn went to check on Doc. He was sitting in front of the viewing window wearing a sweatshirt, at least partially. He also had a piece of blue material with big daisies on it wrapped around his head like a turban. It had tails and he rather looked like the Syrian leader, Yasser Arafat. What a hoot!

I strung Christmas tinsel in the cages today. They liked that. No other noteworthy news. Oh, I did give Doc and Rudi huge tree disposal bags. Of course Doc eventually got in his. Rudi was outside do don't know what he did.

December 23, 2000

Went to the zoo early and helped the volunteers put Christmas stuff out on the exhibit. Chey and Luna went out. What fun! Hope the video turns out. I'm going tomorrow to help the Sunday keeper.

December 24, 2000

Part of yesterday's fun was putting fruit out for the orangs that is native to Indonesia; durian fruit and rambutan. (Had the latter in Hawaii and it is very good.) Durian has a distinct, not so pleasant, odor. The keeper said when Rudi went out, he collected a few durian, sat on the structure, lined them up, and proceeded to smell each one. A piece stuck to his hand. He rubbed it off, smelled his hand, and kept trying to rub the smell off. This morning they were still lined up. Kelly knew exactly how good the rambutan was. She collected them and ate them. Rudi ate some after her. Guess she was the "tester." We cleaned. No other interesting stuff.

December 29, 2000

Took my stepmother out to see the orangs today. Rudi put on an elegant display. Kelly was noted to be having her period, so Lynn had her pee in a cup. That was impressive.

January 3, 2001

Nothing special today; just cleaned. Workmen were fixing door #9 so Chey worried.

January 9, 2001

Got a great video today of Chey holding a "Will work for food – God Bless!" sign. I'd put honey at the top of the cardboard so she would hold it upright. Now I hope my friends can use their technology to get the still photo off of it. It was hysterical. We watched it over and over.

Rudi refused to go out. Got him out of A, into B, and even into the tunnel. But he kept his hand on the threshold between B and the tunnel, or sat on the threshold so we couldn't close the door. We even put a mango on the bench in C as enticement. When we weren't looking he raced in there, grabbed the mango and ran back. Stinker!

I gave Kelly my worn out carry on bag. She had a great time with that.

When I gave Chey and Luna their mangos, I gave Chey hers first. I then tried to get Luna's to her without Chey noticing. That big old hand grabbed it. Luna whined, pulled Chey's hair, and looked so distressed. Eventually she got it out of Chey's mouth, and Chey didn't put up a fuss.

February 6, 2001

It was good to see the gang again. Luna smiled as she put her little head and body against the mesh so I could scratch her. I gave them all kiwis. Yum! Luna was a bit of a brat; didn't want to go outside. Then when it was time to come in, Chey didn't want to.

Kelly was acting silly. She was playing with a wet T-shirt; slapping it against the floor as she rolled forward and backward. She and Rudi went out; no fuss.

Doc was his same sweet self. The plan is to introduce him to Luna and Chey on the 8th.

February 14, 2001

I decorated the cages with Valentines (construction paper hearts) today. Cindy said Doc ought to give one to Kelly. Apparently she's been refusing to go outside with him. Guess Doc needs some lover lessons.

During the intro last week, Chey and Doc wrestled, slapped, bit etc., and Chey ended up with five wounds. She's now on antibiotics. Then on Saturday, when Luna was trying to groom her poor injured mom, Chey bit her. Now she's also on antibiotics. Yes, it is like a soap opera.

Rudi expressed his feelings towards Cindy yesterday. Gave her the banana from his lunch. That's his favorite thing.

They are all so wonderful.

February 28, 2001

Was great to see the group. Luna did her usual; pressing her back and head against the mesh for me to scratch. Had a little smile on her face.

Kelly went out with Doc. Yea! Then later she went back out with Rudi. We set up all six cages for intros – Doc, Chey, and Luna. Lynn had gotten permission for me to be present. There were no huge fights. Chey was quite leery but calmed down later. Doc got so frustrated he'd just pound on things, but at least he didn't pound on Chey. Luna just played – up high. At one point though, she was having a short game of tug-o-war with Doc. Doc really seemed to want to play, but Chey was an instigator of trouble. I think it'll all work out eventually.

Apparently, during an intro in the last few days, Chey used Luna as a hostage, holding her between herself and Doc. After about 30 minutes, Doc quietly walked around behind Chey and hit her. Intro stopped immediately.

March 21, 2001

It's been three weeks! It was great to see them. Apparently, Kelly was cycling this weekend and went after Doc for sex. They had an hour's worth, in every position possible, in front of the exhibit window. Lynn answered many questions of the interested viewing public. She said at one point Kelly was just lying there eating alfalfa while Doc was "pumping" away. If it took – baby in November.

They tried to do an intro with Luna and Doc by setting up creep doors. Luna was heading through the doors which upset Chey tremendously. She had diarrhea. Doc was displaying like crazy. Intro was stopped.

I gave the orangs kiwis and tangerines today. Doc peeled his kiwi. He always peels his fruit.

I plan to go to the zoo tomorrow too.

March 22, 2001

Just cleaned and played with my buddies. Another great day at the zoo.

March 28, 2001

Took tangerines to the gang again today. Just cleaned, but I played with Kelly for awhile when I was done. Played the poke game with a weed stem she'd brought inside. She put her play face on as I poked her.

April 4, 2001

Well, boo hiss! Kelly had her period so no baby expected yet. Took pineapple to them today. Rudi was so anxious to have some he was waiting at door #1 (in A) to transfer to C to get his pineapple – the dreaded cage where no one wants to go. Meanwhile Chey was in F kiss squeaking. She saw me putting pineapple slices in D for her and Luna. Kelly and Doc got theirs later as they were outside first today. They all loved the pineapple – lots of slurping while they ate it.

April 10, 2001

I took a friend to the zoo early today to meet the gang up close and personal. Rudi put on a display. We applauded so he did an encore. Took them limes as a treat. We played with them for about an hour.

Walked around the zoo to see all the babies. We have two red capped mangabeys, a baby langur, and twin golden lion tamarins. We also saw a three week old baby pigmy hippo on the other side of the zoo. She's so cute!

April 12, 2001

Took the gang their Easter baskets. Gave them each a slinky, a piece of material, a ball, a new Sippy cup, a coconut, grapefruit, lemon, strawberries, and blackberries. Gave Kelly dill pickles, one of her favorite treats. Hope my photos come out. They seemed to enjoy all of it. Chey even got her coconut opened.

I hung purple tinsel around the cages. Did a very thorough cleaning.

Doc will be sedated on the 13th. He has blood in his urine.

April 18, 2001

Cindy and I cleaned it all in under 4 hours today. Didn't stop to play much as we both needed to finish early.

Doc, Chey, and Kelly were a bit uncooperative in the shifting about. They seem to know when we're in a hurry. Chey spent a great deal of time scrubbing with a brush I'd put in <u>her</u> Easter basket.

A visitor came into the night house and Doc put on a display that would make Rudi proud. His physical exam was okay. No kidney problem and the blood in the urine is gone. He weighs 257 pounds.

April 25, 2001

Lynn said two days ago Rudi took the screws out of the white track in door #2, and another volunteer caught him walking proudly about with the track. He saved back a metal washer, and presented it to Lynn yesterday morning. To quote her, "What a weirdo!" Today, as he went outside, he paused at door #2, checking out the workman's job, noting if all the screws were tight. Then later, when he came inside, he was checking door #8 over. Hmmm…..

I gave Luna a night shirt today. Big hit. She got inside it and was rolling around on the floor. Then she put a box and a soccer ball inside it with her. She was having so much fun.

May 2, 2001

Just cleaning today. I played with the hose a bit as they love playing in the water. Luna was her usual silly self.

May 8, 2001

Just cleaning. Took pineapple for them all to enjoy. A real treat and the slurping is so much fun to hear.

May 16, 2001

Lots of cleaning today. Doc had taken shredded paper out on the exhibit, and it was ALL OVER THE PLACE. Guess they had a good time though.

One time today I looked down the aisle to F where Doc was. He was perched on a barrel with a pile of hay on his head. Looked like a wig.

I gave Luna a piece of netting that had been on a cluster of tomatoes. She put it over her head, of course. Kept it on for quite awhile. I took a photo. Had pineapple for them again. Chey did the loudest kiss squeaks <u>ever</u> to beg for more. And again, the slurping was a joy to hear.

May 23, 2001

Just the usual cleaning and playing. The gang shared a honeydew. I took a photo of Luna with a handful of melon pieces.

May 30, 2001

Much cleaning with uncooperative orangs today. Rudi refused to go out. He had hold of Kelly's leg and preferred staying inside and having sex with her. She didn't solicit it, but she didn't object either. So we let Chey and Luna out. Then, when we wanted them to come back in, Chey wouldn't move out of the doorway. So we bribed them back outside with pineapple. Remember, Chey "Will work for food – God Bless!" Doc was reluctant to move into D while Rudi was in C. He clutched his "blanket" which was a piece of pink plastic today. So it was an interesting day but we <u>did</u> finish by 12.

June 16, 2001

Went to the zoo this morning to only visit the group. I just returned from a mission trip. Couldn't wait to see them. I took honeydews and limes. Due to the Houston floods last week, mosquitoes are EVERYWHERE. Rudi has taken to holding a small blanket to cover his face and head to keep them away.

June 20, 2001

My regular day to volunteer. Cindy and I cleaned everything thoroughly as time will be short tomorrow due to a meeting. Rudi still has his blanket to hide from the mosquitoes. Cindy said yesterday, when Luna and Chey were out, she went to check on them. Chey had a banana leaf smashed against her face to keep mosquitoes away.

    Today Chey pressed her back against the mesh for me to scratch her. Later she spit at me. Ingrate!

June 26, 2001

Well, today Cindy and I inadvertently left the padlock, key, and PVC piece, the one that opens the valve to the exhibit drinking pool, outside. Rudi and Kelly were let out. Cindy went to clean the babirusa yard, and I was scrubbing the squeeze cage with bleach. Cindy came in and told me she went to check on Rudi and Kelly, and Rudi held out his hand to show her he had the padlock. We got him inside cage D and Kelly into the tunnel. I asked him for the padlock. He, somewhat reluctantly, gave it to me for a piece of pineapple, which he just let drop to the floor. ???? Cindy and I went outside to look for the key, and the bright orange cord it was on. We found the cord, untied, but no key. The PVC was also there; intact. Cindy said Rudi <u>must</u> have the key. I went inside and asked Rudi if he had the key. He was looking toward cage F; I was in front of cage D. He wouldn't look at me. I kept asking him, and he _finally_ pulled it from his mouth and gave it to me. The stinker! Then he ate the pineapple he'd refused earlier.

Played "poke" with Chey using a rubber hose. She actually put on a play face.

July 4, 2001

My son, Derek, and I went to the zoo this morning. First time he'd met the gang up close and personal. Rudi didn't display – surprise, surprise. Doc did a small one. When I showed Doc I had a kiwi, he cleared a spot and put his hand under the mesh so I could give it to him. Derek was a bit surprised at how smart that move was. Kelly, down the aisle, was applauding for attention. When that didn't work she got under the white barrel, and scooted across the floor to get our attention. Luna played a little tug-o-war with Derek. Chey did her kiss squeaks. It was fun to introduce Derek to these five special friends of mine.

July 5, 2001

Went to help today. Chey used a hose to get the drain cover grate near the night house door into A. She traded it to me for some baby food. When we went outside to put food out for Doc, after Rudi and Kelly came in, we noticed their drinking pool had not filled. (Didn't get the valve closed) Anyway, Rudi had apparently tried to "fix" it by bending the drain cover so half was sticking up in the air. Never a dull moment in the orang group.

July 18, 2001

Took mangos and watermelon to the orangs today. Rudi apparently doesn't like watermelon, but he was happy about the mango. He refused to go outside but moved quickly to C from B. Why? I'd put a mango _and_ "honey water" in C. I took an empty honey bottle today as enrichment. There was enough left to give him the lid with a bit on it, and I added water to the bottle. Gave him a few sips while he was still in B. I then put the bottle in C. He was sitting at the door waiting to shift.

Chey _loved_ the watermelon.

July 24, 2001

Cindy was sick today, Lynn was off, and so another keeper was in orangs. Doc has been sick with diarrhea. However, he put on a beautiful display when Barbara came by.

Rudi raped Kelly when the door was opened. And he ate the watermelon I was trying to give her. Hmmm.... I also had dill pickle slices for Kelly. I did give some to Rudi, Chey, and Luna. Chey spit hers out. Luna ate hers but made a face.

August 2, 2001

Today I took crepe paper streamers, plastic leis, some new sippers, scrub brushes, a hair brush, and a little plastic chair for enrichment.

Rudi refused to go outside, and then refused to even shift into C from B. He refused yesterday too. He loves being in A and B. Took a couple of photos of Luna sitting in the chair backwards. Chey brushed her hair. She looked lovely. She also scrubbed stuff with her scrub brush. Later Cindy was brushing Chey's hair as she pressed against the mesh. She kept turning to get new parts brushed.

August 7, 2001

Primates was short staffed today. I told the supervisor I'd do orangs, and she could just come in and shift them as needed. I like working alone. I have my routine, and I can stop to play with them as I clean. I took Kelly my old purse. Put some dill pickles deep inside it. I also took a pineapple for them to share and a kiwi for each. Actually gave Rudi two.

August 14, 2001

I had peaches and kiwis ready to take to the zoo today and forgot them. Ugh!

Didn't stop to play much as I needed to leave by 12, and wanted to get as much done as I could by then.

Took some beach balls. Rudi ignored his. Doc broke his and then wore it like a hat. Put several out on exhibit for Chey and Luna. Chey ignored them as the ice pop was top priority. Luna carried one high upon the structure, played with it a bit, then broke it. As I left the zoo she was sitting way up on a pole with the flattened ball on her head. Took a photo.

I put Rudi's sunflower seeds in three boxes and a magazine. I noticed he'd piled them all up. He was eating one at a time, only using his mouth to pick them up, splitting them perfectly, and making a separate pile of shells. It always amazes me that these HUGE creatures can be so dainty in their eating habits.

September 5, 2001

Back to the zoo after three weeks. I took kiwis and peaches. I went to each cage, showing each orang the newborn photo of my granddaughter, Breanna. I explained why I hadn't been there due to helping care for her. Then I gave each a kiwi. They each looked intently at the photo, even Rudi. In reality they were probably thinking, "I'd better look at the photo, act interested, and she'll give me the kiwi."

Rudi refused to go out, but he did move from B to C without a problem. I'd shown him, plus gave him, a sip of juice from a new animal sipper cup. Then I put it in C in view.

Won't be back at the zoo for three more weeks as I'm going on an Alaskan cruise.

September 19, 2001

Well, no cruise to Alaska due to the horrendous terrorist attack on the United States September 11th. Such a sad time for our country. It was good to go to the zoo today. We had to get all the cleaning done by 12. Cindy had a meeting so we didn't take too much time to play.

To entice Chey into cage D from E and F, I bribed her with a peanut butter jar. Trouble was I hid it so well, wanting her to get it and not Luna, that she didn't find it, no matter how hard I tried to help her. I pointed and told her where it was. But she spit on me a few times. I finally looked her straight in the eye and apologized profusely. I guess she forgave me as she turned so I could scratch her back. Eventually, after Doc went out, we closed her in C, retrieved the jar, and set it right in the doorway between C and D. That way she could find it easily when we reopened the door between C and D.

I took them pomegranates today and they loved them. Also took pineapple and kiwis.

EXCITING NEWS!!!!!

"Elok"

We are getting a baby orangutan from the Memphis Zoo. He was born November 1, 2000. He has been hand raised since a few hours old because his mother was aggressive. His name is Elok. Yes, we are going to hand raise him until we can introduce him to Chey. Then she will be his surrogate mother. I am so excited!

September 26, 2001

No special stuff today – just cleaned and played. We could not find any evidence of Kelly's period which should be this week. She and Doc had a lot of sex about two weeks ago. We'll keep our fingers crossed. Kelly was being a silly woman today with the steamers of curly ribbon I put in their cages. Also, she and Doc were play wrestling and, at one point, he was grooming her.

September 29, 2001

Today, two of the other Luna caregivers and I decorated the exhibit with loads of crepe paper donated by the Cindus Corporation. Chey was suspicious but Luna had a blast.

October 3, 2001

Today I had on a Band Aid; covering a stitch where I had a biopsy yesterday. (little skin lesion on my outer thigh) Rudi loved it!! I even pulled the Band Aid up so he could look at the stitch. He got so excited he presented his nipple.

Still no evidence of Kelly's period. Hmmm....... Cindy told me that one day she brought Kelly some earrings, and Kelly presented her ears for Cindy to clip them on. Kelly admired herself in the mirror, then took them off and destroyed them.

October 12, 2001

Showed Rudi my "owey" and that it no longer had a stitch etc. He looked very closely. He was good; went right outside. Of course we'd put some pineapple slices out for him.

Today we had a package from Elok that Luna and Chey were to open. Then we were to read them a letter from Elok. The package contained a stuffed animal and a T-shirt from Elok. That way Luna and Chey could "smell" him. They did a good job of sniffing; especially Luna, sniffing the little stuffed elephant. I read the letter, and also showed them photos of Elok. Got it all on video.

October 17, 2001

Today we showed a video of Elok to Chey and Luna. Chey "pulled up a chair" for better viewing. Luna watched a bit and then seemed to pout. She had a pouty face on as she tried to pull Chey away. Chey did go into B from A, but could still see the video through the door between the cages. It seemed Luna stayed closer to Chey the whole time the video was in. Going to have to deal with Luna's jealousy. When Elok whined in the video, Chey paid close attention. They were <u>both</u> quite fascinated watching Elok suck on his bottle. Elok's father gave a small "roar" on the video and <u>that</u> got Rudi's attention. All very fascinating.

On the 21st we'll have a meeting about Elok.

I took beach balls today. Put two in the cargo net on exhibit for Kelly to play with. She did, briefly, and then broke them.

October 24, 2001

Not much going on today. I had to leave almost as soon as I got to the zoo. Two of the skin cancers I had cauterized yesterday started bleeding. Kelly was fascinated when she saw the blood. Anyway, I went to the dermatology clinic across the street, had them re-cauterized, and then went back to the zoo.

Rudi was very cooperative. Moved from B to C; no problem. I wonder if it was because I let him look at all my "oweys."

Luna and Chey moved into D from E and F with no hesitation either. Such cooperation!

October 31, 2001

Decorated the exhibit with orange and black crepe paper and jack-o-lanterns. That was fun! Kelly and Doc went out first. Festooned the cages too. They had a good time. Gave Chey a new scrub brush and a new hair brush. She behaved appropriately; scrubbed the cage, the door, and a jack-o-lantern. Even Rudi seemed to enjoy the decorations.

December 4, 2001

Well back at the zoo after the two and a half week zoo trip to Kenya and Tanzania. It was my shift to care for Elok. He arrived from Memphis on November 6 and was in quarantine for two weeks. He made his first trip to the night house to meet the other orangutans on November 27th. (Notes about that adventure are filed in his scrapbook.)

He is now 13 months old. Today, a primate supervisor worked with me to "show me the ropes" about him. He's a cutie! But he does want to bite. Maybe 'cause I'm new. I just repeated, "No bite" every time. He's much more independent than Luna was; sitting and playing with things alone or climbing on his jungle gym. At this age Luna seemed to want to have at least one hand on us. He's a big kid; over 20 pounds. Doesn't look that big but he's solid. Luna weighed 22 pounds at age 2.

He doesn't cling very well. I was told I need to keep a grip on him or he'll just fall off. When he does grab – it's tight – and I have bruises on my upper arms to prove it.

He and Chey had some good interactions at the tunnel mesh. At one point she had a sheet over her head and made throaty, clucking sounds. He got off his jungle gym and went to her. Did this twice!! Must be a trait that is inborn. Later, Luna took the sheet away, wadded it up, and held onto it. Jealous, jealous. She was a wild child in cages B and C while Chey was in the tunnel interacting with Elok. Doing all sorts of crazy antics to get attention. Once she got way up on the top of the hydraulic door in the tunnel and draped the sheet over herself like, "Look at me, look at me." She tried to poke Elok's head. He bit her fingers. Good for him. He'll hold his own with this big sister. We took him back to the clinic, where he spends the nights, at 3:30 p.m. He has a wonderful setup there; all kinds of toys and ropes to climb. He hadn't taken a nap all afternoon (was fighting sleep), and at 5:30 he fell asleep on my lap while I was sitting in the rocking chair. Luna took a nap on my lap the first day I cared for her too. And here I am again – How Lucky Am I !.

December 7, 2001

It's Friday and my shift with Elok on Fridays is 7 a.m. to 12:30 p.m. (It's 12:30 p.m. to 6 p.m. on Tuesdays.) I only worked 4 hours today, however, as we needed to go to Austin and watch our youngest, Derek, graduate from the University of Texas. Yea!

I went to the clinic to relieve the keeper who spent the night with Elok. I made his formula for the day, weighed him (23 pounds), and took his temperature. At 8 a.m. Lynn came to get us and take us to the night house. I took him outside on the exhibit. He was a bit frightened but did walk in the grass, played a bit in the pool, and even took a drink from it. Cindy "whistled" us into the night house so he can start getting used to that, the hydraulic doors, and all. He was more clingy today; holding on better. He really has a grip, and I've the bruises to prove it.

He and Chey had some good interactions, and he and Luna did too. In fact, Chey was on the floor of the tunnel, and he and Luna were "relating" halfway up the mesh. So Chey got a bucket to sit on to make herself higher. Luna also showed off again to get attention, and sucked her thumb.

I got loves from little Elok today; no biting. I gave him hugs and kisses, through my mask, of course.

December 11, 2001

Well, what happened to the sweet little boy who got hugs and kisses last week? Today he was Mr. Bitey Baby. I needed to keep something handy to shove in his mouth besides part of my body. He was also a sleepy wee boy, but absolutely would not give in and take a nap. Maybe he'll crash early tonight.

There were some good interactions with Chey and Luna. At one point he pulled hard on Luna's lip through the mesh, but she was nice about it.

Today I also experienced Rudi begging with kiss squeaks when I was giving Luna and Elok rice cereal right in front of him. I did share some. I had bright red Christmas socks and Rudi liked looking at those too.

Elok is at the night house all the time now.

December 14, 2001

Not such a bitey baby today, but he did try a few times. I kept a toy in my pocket or nearby as a distraction. He was a bit whiny, but I think it was because he was hungry. It seemed I was giving him something to munch on pretty much all morning. Only a few, very brief interactions with Chey and Luna, but positive ones.

When the keeper opened the door to the yard, he took my hand and wanted to go out. We walked around the yard. At one point he went off on his own, going 8 to 10 feet away from me. Seemed sleepy too, but there was no way he was going to close those eyes.

Kelly had hernia surgery two days ago. She seems a bit sore, but making an okay recovery. Guess the whole thing scared Chey so much, she refused to come back into the night house. When Luna pitched a fit to coax her in, Chey bit her. What a group of ding-a-lings.

December 18, 2001

My afternoon with Elok. As usual, he started off being bitey. That decreased as the afternoon wore on, with just an occasional relapse. He sucked my thumb a few times, was a tired boy, but no nap. He has so much energy - rarely slows down. I took beach balls today and he had fun with those.

When Chey and Luna came in there was bubble wrap in their cage. Luna was stomping up and down on it; sounded like gun fire.

There were some good interactions between Chey and Elok. She kissed his face and licked his ear. She didn't share any food with him, but did drop a piece of pineapple that he was able to grab.

Kelly was in her bed (hay in tub) most of the day. She seems to be sore and not feeling too well from her surgery.

December 19, 2001

I went in to help clean today. Kelly seems to be feeling better. She was more active, and doing nest construction under the bench as she usually does. She did seem to rest with her legs drawn up; probably felt better that way. She was also having some drainage from her wound. She wiped it off with her hands, and then licked them. There's another part of the 3% DNA we don't share with orangutans.

December 21, 2001

Elok was really quite a sweet boy today, minimum wanting to bite, and even cuddly at one point. Gave him big kisses on his fuzzy head. He did pee on me (first time) but hey – he's an animal and doesn't know all the social graces.

Also saw an example of his "smarts" today. I'd put a bunch of red and green crepe paper on his jungle gym. He was sitting at the bottom trying to pull some down. When he couldn't get it loose, he looked to see where it was stuck, then went there to undo it.

Luna was whiny, sucked her thumb, and tried to pull Chey away from Elok. However, when Chey was busy with her nest building in the tunnel, and Luna was in B, Elok went to the mesh of B. Luna came to him and was friendly. Go figure! Guess it has to be her idea to be nice.

Kelly is much better. Yea!

December 24, 2001

Today, when I went to care for Elok, I took the orangs Christmas stockings. In each was a scrub brush, a toothbrush, slices of pineapple, and a couple pieces of grapefruit, except for Elok's. I put rubber squeak toys in Luna's, Elok's and Kelly's. Also put a hairbrush in Chey's and Kelly's. Later I heard Kelly playing with her squeak toy down the aisle. She seems her same fun, playful self now. Of course Chey was very busy brushing herself, and other stuff in her cage.

Elok was a sweet little guy, but a little bitey. I'd take hold of his face and say, "No" harshly, and that helped. He whined when he was hungry. At one point he was on his jungle gym and I was in his cage cleaning up. Rudi, who was outside, pounded on the door. I looked at Elok. He was looking at me and reaching out his hands. He jumped to my chest, and was a clingy baby for a bit. Gave him lots of hugs and kisses. He and Chey had some wonderful interactions. There was kissing of lips plus Chey kissed his hands and arms. He squeaked to her and she made those mama sounds.

December 26, 2001

Just a day of cleaning. I think there was "hit and miss" the past week without the regular keepers, so I tried to clean extra thoroughly.

The orangs were somewhat uncooperative, but eventually they all moved enough so we could get all the cages cleaned.

Yesterday Doc turned 17.

December 28, 2001

Took Elok outside for awhile. We went up to the top of the wooden structure. He also walked on his own back to the night house. I helped the keeper clean some cages with him on my hip. I also took lots of photos today.

There were minimal interactions with Chey and Luna because they went out early. Luna did suck her thumb when Chey greeted Elok in the early a.m.

January 1, 2002

What a great non-paying job this is!! Elok is just a sweetie. Was a little bitey, but mostly just a neat little guy today. He was a hungry boy, and it seemed he was ready to eat <u>before</u> his scheduled "meals" were ready. He opens his mouth so wide for his cereal. Doc was outside this afternoon, but all the others were inside. I made extra cereal and shared it with all of them, even Rudi. There were some really great interactions between Chey and Elok with lots of kissy face. She did the sheet thing. She covered herself, and poked her tongue through the mesh, through the sheet. She also presented her nipple to him. Luna was a bit whiny and sucked her thumb some. She also showed off, doing wild and crazy things. She did interact with Elok, and gave him a cardboard tube.

    I saw Rudi play a bit of peek-a-boo today. Cindy was joking with him about his juice. He kept shoving bottles under the mesh for more. Then she'd poke him with a hose. He took the hose, laid it down behind him, and covered his eyes. Cindy said he must have learned that when he was little.

    Later, I heard Kelly gathering up monkey biscuits and tossing them in a plastic hard hat. She then took it to her water bowl and added some water. After that, she took her soaking biscuits up to her tub of hay and paper (her bed), placed the hat carefully in the tub, and sat there eating her soaked biscuits. It's so much fun watching them.

    At 5:30 p.m. Elok got on his bed of piled up blankets, and waited for his bedtime bottle.

January 4, 2002

Elok seemed a sleepy boy this morning. He came to me right away – no biting – just wanted to snuggle. He grabbed his bottle as soon as it was heated, but didn't finish it. Sat back on his bed for awhile. He had a good interaction with Luna early. She was offering "toys" through the mesh. They touched hands and almost touched lips. Earlier, when Chey was touching him, Luna tried to pull her away. Chey touched him gently during her interactions.

    He wasn't as animated today as he usually is. I really think he just didn't sleep well. I gave him some wide white crepe paper, and he had fun with that. He's clinging well now. It's a lot easier to do "stuff" as I can use both hands.

January 8, 2002

Went to help clean. Took a pineapple for them to share and they loved that! I also took tinsel garlands and icicles to festoon their cages. What fun! Kelly went outside with Rudi on Saturday. First time she's been allowed with a male since her surgery. Guess they were very "busy" all day.

January 9, 2002

Elok day! Kelly got to go out with Doc today. Cindy said when she opened the door, Kelly sort of looked at him and took his hand like, "Come on Boy, I'm yours." Cindy noticed that later, while they were outside, Doc was gently holding Kelly's hand.

Elok was shut in, and playing alone in A when I arrived, so I just left him there. At 2 p.m. (1 ½ hours later) I tried to get him to take his bottle through the mesh, but he was having no part of that. So I went into A, and he drank it all while holding onto me. Chey and Luna went outside, and he went into B to play. Didn't want to be closed in, however. I sat in there with him for awhile. I noticed he has two upper molars that have poked through, one on each side. Lynn let me give him an ice pop, and he was a major sticky baby after that. It was grape with raisins – yummy, yummy. Got whiny before his cereal at 4:15, but was willing to play alone in his cage for a short time afterwards. At 5 p.m. he was on his jungle gym in the aisle, so I decided to scrub his cage. But he was so tired he just sat on the floor under the jungle gym, and watched me. After that, we just sat in the rocker in his "room" for major cuddle time. When the next caregiver came, he was sitting on his bed by the intro door waiting to go night-night. When she came inside, Chey gave him a little kiss on his head at the intro door.

January 11, 2002

Another Elok day! Was a bit cool when we went into the yard this morning, so he was clingy. But he did get off and marched toward the door to go into the night house alone. I went in first, but he whined as he tried to climb over the threshold. I think he could have made it with a little more confidence. I offered a hand to him and he climbed in. We also had him go through a creep door.

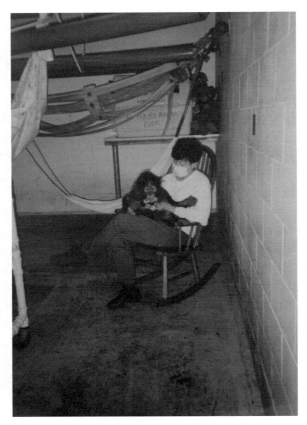

He spent two hours alone in A in the morning, whining at intervals. I tried to give him treats and attention when he did not whine. After his 12 noon cereal mixture, he fell asleep in my arms. I transferred him to a black tub mounted on a barrel in the aisle, after I put a blanket and a surrogate in it. He slept 20 minutes. I then took him back to A, sat with him a few minutes in the rocker, and closed him in again for solitary play.

Luna has a cold. She has been sneezing, coughing, and snorting all day.

January 15, 2002

Cleaning day. I took mangos so they were all very cooperative regarding shifting. Luna, Doc, and Elok all have colds. I noted Elok was clingy and whiny with his caregiver. Poor little tyke.

January 16, 2002

Elok day! Lynn was his caregiver this morning, and she said he was whiny and clingy. His cold is still present, and the antibiotic being given "just in case" has given him diarrhea. He played alone at intervals in A and B, the longest time being 1 ½ hours. Poor little guy; he's having to breathe through his mouth. He has a very snotty nose, but it's not running out like it should.

Chey now has a cold too. Doc is really sick with his. Poor guy.

January 18, 2002

Now Rudi has a cold so only Kelly has been spared.

Elok was a bit clingy, but he <u>did</u> go through the creep door for an orange slice with just my hand extended. He got off his jungle gym in the aisle to walk through the tunnel to the creep door.

I'm going to be gone on vacation for 10 days. I'll miss him.

January 28, 2002

Elok Day! (Did another caregiver's afternoon as a trade from last week.) He wanted to bite me right away. I got him into A, distracted him with red crepe paper, and he played alone in A for 2 hours 20 minutes. Drank his bottle through the mesh; gulped it in about two swallows. Later I put his cereal on dishes and shoved them into him. He ate most of it that way, but I did feed him a few spoons through the mesh. He played alone again 1 ½ hours. From 5 to 5:30 p.m. he was in the aisle on his jungle gym with a brief introduction with Chey at the front of B. She was soliciting for him.

I made him a bed of hay with a surrogate in a tub. Also placed a small blanket pallet beside it. At 5:45 p.m. he was stretched out on the pallet waiting for his bottle. What a cutie!

All the colds are better —everyone is well! Yea!

January 29, 2002

Cindy was sick today so I was the "orang keeper" as Lynn had other things to do. I cleaned the cages, and she came in to shift animals as needed. I took a pineapple for all to share. That's always a big hit. Kelly left her urine in a plastic box on the bench right by her bed. Kept her bed clean. Rudi refused to go out so Kelly and Doc were out for the whole day.

January 30, 2002

Elok afternoon! Was a bitey baby at first. I took him to cages E and F to play while I swept them for Cindy. She was at lunch. The a.m. caregiver said those were the two cages left to clean. B and C had been cleaned, but it was hard to tell as Luna had absolutely destroyed the cages. A regular wild child! Cindy let Doc and Kelly in and Chey and Luna went out about 3 p.m. She decided Luna needed to expend some of that energy outside.

I put Elok into A at 1:20 p.m. and he played alone until 5, except for five minutes when I went in to give him his bottle. I tried giving it to him through the mesh, but he screamed at the first sip. I thought it might be too hot. However, I'd checked it twice before giving it to him. He just needed to be held close while he drank 160 of the 170 cc. Then I put him down and left the cage. No whining. Gave him a soaked monkey biscuit on a lid with a few bites from a spoon. He was a bit whiny at 4:30 when I mixed his cereal. I fed it to him through the mesh, giving a bit extra at the end in his dish under the mesh. He took only one or two bites of that and continued playing, finishing it a short while later.

Earlier today Chey was soliciting to Elok through a damp and torn paper bag. I gave her a bed sheet, and she immediately put it over her head. After a time, Luna grabbed it with a sour puss look on her face. Then I gave Chey a curtain. That wouldn't do so I gave her another sheet. Once again she put it over her head. Later, when Luna tried to get it, Chey tried to grab her through the sheet. Eventually Luna did get it and Chey just stared at her.

When Chey came in for the night, she went to the intro door because Elok was standing there squeaking at her. She kissed him and gave him the lid from her drink bottle. She kept all of her food to herself however.

Cindy scraped her finger. When she came into the night house, she made a big production of getting the first aid kit down, getting a Band Aid, etc. Rudi watched ever so closely. He's so funny.

February 1, 2002

Another Elok day. He has a new feeding schedule. As he only had 125 cc of his 200 cc of formula at 7 a.m., and only ¼ of his cereal mixture at 8:30 a.m., he was one hungry baby at 11:30. He had a mini tantrum and did some minor screaming while I fixed his cereal, which he gobbled. He only gets greens in the mornings, and fruits and veggies after lunch. The only snacking he'd done was some corn flakes as forage. He played on his own quite a bit, but was clingy when I was in a cage with him. Got some good hugs and gave him kisses.

Today Luna had the paper liner from a cereal box on her head and was racing around cage C. It had some air in it and she was pounding on it. At one point she put the blue barrel up on a bench and sat on it. Later she put the barrel on the hammock, was straddling it, and pounding it like a drum. Silly girl.

February 2, 2002

Email from Lynn saying that Elok slept in his bed sheet hammock that is hanging up by the skylight. Progress.

February 5, 2002

Zoo day, but to help clean. I took two mangos for all of them to share plus Cindy had an empty peanut butter jar, (with enough left to matter), so they were all very cooperative shifting about etc.

February 6, 2002

There was drama in the orangutan community today involving Kelly, Doc, and Rudi. Kelly and Rudi were outside together. Kelly was "soliciting" and kept Rudi busy while they were out there. When I got to the zoo they were in the squeeze cage, and Kelly was grooming Rudi. Doc was in E. Chey and Luna were in C and D. Cindy moved them to B as she wanted to move Rudi into D. She asked Kelly if she'd go outside for a minute so she could do that. Kelly backed out into the yard and Rudi went into D. Then she moved Kelly into E, wanting her to cross by Doc into F. However, she didn't, and suddenly she was in E with Doc. Rudi was FURIOUS! He was eating an apple, but kept grabbing mouthfuls of water and spitting at Cindy. He did not want Doc with "his woman." Cindy was _trying_ to get Doc to go into the squeeze, but he's so scared of Rudi and wanted no part of being so close to him. She had the bribes there – banana, a bit of Elok's cereal, but no way. Meanwhile, Rudi kept spitting at Cindy. Doc finally did go into the squeeze when she opened the door to the outside, but he didn't go out. So she quickly shut him in while she moved Kelly into F. She gave Rudi a peace offering – yogurt, pudding, and cheese on a Valentine candy box liner. Doc went back into E. Sometimes it _is_ like a soap opera.

    Chey and Luna were then given access to the yard, but stayed put in the tunnel. I put some pudding on inverted buckets for them to "fish" with bamboo branches. I tried to teach Elok, but he's not yet coordinated enough.

    Chey and Luna then went outside. Elok was in cage A with a bunch of shredded paper, and Cindy festooned B with a roll of brown paper towels, leaving what was left on the roll for him to unroll or whatever. What fun! He played alone for 2 ½ hours except for ten minutes when I took him into the tunnel while they put the intro door mesh back into place. When Chey and Luna were let into B, Chey went to the intro door immediately and checked the nuts and bolts. Elok was squeaking at her at the door, and presenting his back to her. However, after the nut and bolt check, her dinner was her priority.

    Elok essentially played alone the whole 5 ½ hours I was there. He's ready to be adopted.

February 8, 2002

Probably my last "hands on" day with Elok. I had the keeper take our photo.

I took him outside for over an hour. He did some exploring and got down from the structure, via the fire hose three times, and back to me the same way once.

I found myself more willing to tend to him if he started whining today. Guess I was looking for reasons to hold him, knowing it was the last day. I did give him some crepe paper at one point to keep him amused.

Maintenance had to come today to replace some of the bolts in hydraulic door #2. Seems Chey had removed them, and presented them to Cindy yesterday; had them in her mouth.

Kelly was quiet this a.m.. Slept most of the morning. Hmmmm……

February 12, 2002

Tomorrow is the day Elok gets to go in with Chey. Everyone is stressing out. Today we looked at the sheet describing what is to be done and when. It was kind of a dress rehearsal today, shifting animals to particular cages etc. I'm sure it will all work out. We cleaned really well today so tomorrow we can hurry and get it done.

February 13, 2002

I helped clean today so everything could get done by 12 p.m. The intro was scheduled for 1:30, but actually happened at 1:40 p.m.

Apparently Elok only took about 90 seconds to go into B to Chey who was waiting. Lynn said he kind of went limp as she held him, and was biting him all over. Although scary to watch, Chey was gently nibbling on him and he was biting some. She said they had play faces too. At one point Luna balled her fist up and slugged him. Also pulled his hair. She then went about her own business, going wild in the cage; swinging, leaping etc. Lynn said she once noticed Chey "dragging" Elok through the tunnel. She sort of held him upside down and he wasn't clinging. I'm sure it'll all work out. Elok went back into A after 1 ½ - 2 hours.

Lynn also expressed some concern about the caregivers continuing to be there to observe, and Elok not understanding why we couldn't be holding him.

February 14, 2002

I went to the zoo at 2 p.m. to observe, taking another caregiver's place. Apparently, there have been some good, but troublesome, interactions between Luna and Elok, with Luna pummeling him. Some of this was observed later too. Elok went into B and was on some hay. Luna was pulling his hair, yanking him up and putting him down, hay and all. He seemed to go limp. Lynn tried to divert Luna's attention with some juice. That worked, but then Luna, smart little girl that she is, got the idea that doing that to Elok got her juice. So we decided we'd better ignore her. When Lynn told Chey to "get the baby", she did. However, she had him by the arm, spinning and pulling him back and forth. He seemed none the worse for wear afterwards. Finally Luna and Chey shifted to the tunnel, door #2 was closed, Elok recouped on a pile of hay in B, then "stationed" back to A. He ate his banana and had his bottle.

Luna was playing with some beta chips at one point today, throwing them up and over herself. Very funny!

February 15, 2002

When we first entered the night house this morning, I gave Luna juice, Cindy gave Chey juice, and another keeper gave Elok his bottle. Luna and Chey went out early and stayed for two hours. Elok played alone. He whined when he was locked in B, but was a happy camper when back in A. He and Chey interacted at the intro door, and then she managed to pull him into B through the creep door. She carried him haphazardly into the tunnel, and there was good interaction. Later, in C, Luna grabbed him, and yanked him up and down like she did yesterday. He went limp, also like yesterday, but Chey did intervene today. Then Luna dragged him into the tunnel, but he escaped back into A. This will all work out, but it's hard to sit back and watch when we think Elok is going to be hurt.

February 18, 2002 (intro day #6 of Elok to Chey)

Apparently, over the weekend, Elok did not go into B with Chey, except for very brief moments, but there was interaction at the intro door. However, there was one time he was in B, blocked by Luna, and could not go back into A. Chey displaced Luna, allowing him to retreat into A. That was in the early evening yesterday.

As I arrived today, Elok was just going into B. We couldn't tell if Chey pulled him or he went on his own. She carried him upside down into the tunnel. The keeper said she was probably checking to see who had just arrived in the building. She then hauled him back into B, and was holding him at the intro door. Luna was hanging above them, poking at Elok. He was poking at her too, both of his little fists clenched. He went back into A, but then back into B for a short while. Then he stayed in A, playing alone from 12:40 to 2:20 p.m. He got whiny, kept coming to the cage front, and I noticed he'd missed his 12:30 Similac. I called the keeper in the kitchen, and she had me give it to him. He was a hungry boy! We caregivers don't feed him without zoo keeper permission now. At 2:20 p.m. we shut Luna in C and D, and Chey in B, to see if Elok would go into B. Didn't happen. Left the cages closed for 30 minutes. He was content to just play in A. Chey and Luna had part of their diet so they were content to sit and eat. Elok spent a very long time playing in a box.

The keeper showed me video taken yesterday of Luna and Elok wrestling. At one point she picked him up and shoved him in a laundry basket. It was so funny!

Also, this afternoon, Luna looked through the intro door. Elok had a soft baby blanket. He held it as he went toward Luna. Well, needless to say, she grabbed the blanket. Elok went away from the door. Therefore, Luna waved the blanket at him as she reached into A, then she hung it on a rope in A so he could see it. He didn't fall for that trick; went on about his business. She then pulled the blanket back into B. Later I took her photo as she sat high up in C with the blanket, and she shoved it out to me. I gave it back to Elok. She "baited" him later too.

I gave him his bottle at 5:45 p.m., and he was almost asleep on a blanket on a pile of hay when I left at 6.

February 19, 2002

Chey was successful in pulling Elok through the creep door, and carrying him into the tunnel at 7:40 a.m. A great interaction followed! Luna moved into C, and I kept her distracted for 15 minutes. Elok went back into A at 8 a.m. He played independently the rest of the morning. Chey and Luna had access to outside. He even played alone in B awhile without complaint.

I tore up paper for cages today. Gave Doc some to tear up, and he did! He then put it on his head.

We think we saw evidence of Kelly's period today. Darn!

February 26, 2002

Today I cleaned in the a.m., and did the Elok observation in the afternoon. One time this morning Luna had a good grip on Elok in B, while Chey was in cage C. Luna was trying to pull him up onto the bench. That didn't work. (His arm may be longer now, however.) She was also trying to wrestle with him. He still just goes limp, grabs hold of something etc. He needs to bite her, and show her he's able to fight back. Chey didn't intervene until he peeped a bit loudly. She then went into B, and made sure he was away from Luna. After that she sat in the intro door 'til Elok approached it, and she stepped aside to let him through. Later, when he thought about going through the creep door into B, he'd retreat if he saw Luna coming.

About 4:30 p.m. he went through to B and Chey dragged him into C, and they sat together; him in front of her. Then Chey moved into the tunnel, leaving Elok with Luna. Of course Luna grabbed him immediately, and tried to pull him up the cage mesh. She then dragged him into B. Chey followed, but sat about six feet away, nonchalantly "reading" a book. Elok was limp, as usual. Luna yanked on him, and even stood on him, while holding onto a fire hose prop above her. She then put a piece of paper on him, and was hitting him with both palms. <u>Then</u> Chey intervened by walking over there. Luna raced away and Elok went back into A. It's like Chey has decided they need to work out their differences, and she's going to let them have at it, as long as Elok doesn't seem to be getting hurt.

March 1, 2002

According to the caregiver notes of the past couple of days, there have been some lengthy interactions between Chey and Elok. She has groomed him, taken him up onto a bench, and he has followed her up on the props etc.

Today there were just a couple of interactions while I was there, and about the same as I've observed before. Luna got hold of him once, dragged him from D to B, and proceeded to wrestle with him. At one point he grabbed the pole which supports the bench, and she pried his fingers loose so she could continue. Chey intervened and let him go back to Cage A.

March 6, 2002

Interactions of 2 hours and 3 minutes today. There were gentle touches, biting etc. between Chey and Elok. I gave them a bed sheet. Chey covered him with it, then put it over herself so they were both under it, like a tent. After 1 hour and 39 minutes, (we're keeping very accurate records) he went back to A because Luna displayed in C. She had been shut away from them. About 30 minutes later Chey baited him to the creep door with an ice pop, and pulled him into B. She carried him to C and set him down. Luna quickly grabbed him and dragged him back to B. She spent 14 minutes rolling about with him, trying to sling him over her shoulder, putting a sheet over them, putting a broken ball on him and pounding, and also "playing doctor." He lay very still while she inspected his penis. Chey, meanwhile, was sitting nearby on the hammock, "reading" a magazine and observing.

March 8, 2002

Two interactions during the morning; one for 20 minutes and one for 15 minutes. Gentle touching etc. Chey placed Elok on the threshold of the creep door, but he didn't try to get away. He just sat there. Luna was at the front of the cage with her thumb in her mouth for about 5 minutes. She then went over and hung above them. Elok swiped at her and vice versa. Things are improving.

He had a full blown tantrum when Chey and Luna were outside, and he was shut in C and the tunnel. I could not comfort him. Lynn came in and distracted him while I quickly cleaned A and B.

March 13, 2002

In reading the notes of the last few days, it seems there have been some good interactions. However, Elok has also thrown regular tantrums in the mornings when Chey and Luna go outside. He's in cage C, and his caregiver tries to clean A and B, while not paying attention to him. His bad behavior is being reinforced when someone comes in to entertain him while the cleaning is being done.

Lots of interactions were observed today between Chey and Elok and Luna and Elok. Luna continues to pummel him, and he continues to not fight back. She managed to pull him up to the hammock in B twice.

Doc has started asserting himself. Last week Rudi spit at him across the aisle. He thought Doc was going outside with Kelly. Then Rudi refused to go out. Doc did go out with Kelly, but pounded on door #8 as he left. (Rudi was behind that door.) Now it seems every time he goes out, he goes to the door of the cage where Rudi is and gives it a whack.

I'm going to email Lynn about how Elok is playing us like a violin with the daily tantrums.

March 15, 2002

This morning I got some photos of Chey sitting in a tub "reading." I also took some of Chey and Elok in the tub playing "kissy face." It seems Elok is going into B more frequently, even when Luna is already in there. However, he leaves just as frequently when he thinks she's coming after him. He peeks in often or sits just inside the door. He seems to watch her like he's trying to learn to play, wants to play, or something.

Lynn hasn't said anything about my email, but the keeper said she also thinks we are reinforcing Elok's tantrums. So today Elok was in C, and I proceeded to clean A and B, ignoring him. He whined quietly about 15 minutes. He screeched once and I ignored him. Cindy came to the night house door, but tried to stay out of sight. We think he thought he saw someone, started to scream, then maybe thought he didn't see anyone and was quiet. Another time, as he was winding up to scream, I grabbed a handful of birdseed and threw it to him without looking at him. He got quiet. All in all, he did fine and found there was no point in screaming.

Right before I left, Chey was in a black tub in the tunnel browsing through a Martha Stewart magazine. There were some lengths of paper toweling around her. Luna kept pulling at them, making Chey mad as it disturbed her. She kept yanking at it, trying to tear it free, so it wouldn't bother her.

March 20, 2002

In reading the notes of the past few days, it seems Elok's tantrums have subsided as he's not been rewarded for them. He still hasn't gone outside with Chey and Luna. However, Lynn said one day Chey picked him up, and held him by the door like,"Okay, open the door. I'm taking the baby outside."

They had some great interacting early in the morning, but then he played alone about 3 ½ hours. The three of them were shut in cages C and D for an hour. Luna made a couple attempts to pick him up but didn't pursue it. When Luna and Chey went outside at 1 p.m., and he had access to cage A, he didn't go in but stayed and played in B.

Late in the day there was more interacting. He was with them for a total of about 3 ½ hours. Luna did get hold of him, and attempted sex every possible way she could think of.
**Kelly is having her period. Darn!!

March 22, 2002

Neat, neat stuff by 7:30 a.m. today. Elok was in B playing alone. Chey was in the tunnel reading a phone book, and Luna was in C. Then Luna entered B, pried Elok off the bench pole, and pulled him to the hammock. They play wrestled for 14 minutes. When he could have escaped, he didn't. One of them let out a squeal, (I think it was Luna) and Chey came for a look.

Poor Chey, paging through the phone book. Boring! So I gave her a catalog. Much better.

Chey and Luna went out for awhile. Before they left, Chey pulled Elok through the creep door, and carried him upside down into the tunnel, wanting to take him outside. The keeper told her "no" and he retreated back into A.

When they came inside, the keeper tried for 15 or 20 minutes to get Elok into the tunnel. That way we could clean A and B while they all played in C and D. Didn't happen. At one point Chey did manage to get him through the creep door, but left him there on the threshold. He went back into A.

When the keeper took her break, I "hid" from Elok down by the squeeze cage, and tore newspapers for bedding. Chey watched a few minutes and left. Then, when I went to check on Elok, I noticed Chey was tearing paper like I'd been doing. She was putting it into a bucket. She had paper that had already been torn, so I gave her some whole pages to tear. She's so smart!

Rudi has an "owey" on the back of his hand. I noticed the raw area as he sat on the bench. The keeper says he's had it for a couple of weeks, lets others see it, but doesn't let it show when she's around.

Just as I was ready to leave, Lynn enticed Elok into the tunnel. After his bottle, he went through door #4 which was set as a creep door. We watched the three of them interact. He seems to be fighting back, FINALLY, by biting Luna. Some of the interaction was definitely playful, however.

March 27, 2002

From what the keepers have said, the last couple of days have been GREAT, with Luna and Elok interacting more and more. And today they played together a lot! They climbed upon the props, and there was lots of play biting etc. Luna still does some pummeling if he's on the floor, but he seems to fight back by biting her. He didn't race for the safety of cage A every time she headed his direction.

On Friday, March 29, they will go outside together. I'll be there!! In fact, Lynn asked me to bring some of the wide white crepe paper to festoon the structure to keep Luna occupied.

March 29, 2002 - ELOK TO GO OUT WITH CHEY AND LUNA DAY!

Luna was so silly this morning. She kept filling a glass with water from the water bowl, and dumping it on the bench. She would scoot back and forth on her butt, and it made a wonderful squeaking sound. Then she'd stand up, bend over, and scoop the spilled water into her mouth. That bench is somewhat concave and holds water well.

They all were outside together from 8:30 a.m. to 10:15 a.m. Luna went out first. Chey started to go and Elok reached out and followed her. (She'd carried him into the tunnel and had set him down.) Elok played independently for the majority of the time outside. Luna climbed, swung on the ropes, and tried to bait Elok with a ginger branch and some of the wide white crepe paper we'd hung. He and Chey did have some nice interaction, and at one point, all three were huddled together; sort of a group hug.

When it was time to come in, Luna came in first, then Chey – <u>without</u> Elok. He finally straggled in alone, and had a 30 minute nap afterwards.

Today I brought them some large multicolored blocks that snap together; different sizes and shapes. They were a big hit.

March 30, 2002

Today I phoned into the night house to see how things were going. It seems Luna dragged Elok across the grass, and put him into the drinking pool – <u>twice</u>. The second time, however, he had a good hold on her leg and only got his foot wet, as if to say, "If I'm going in, you're going in too."

Luna looks for the number of CPS

March 31, 2002

Apparently, Elok went into cage B and slept in there, but <u>not</u> in Chey's nest. We're still waiting for that.

April 3, 2002

Well, this was the last full day. Elok is doing so well with Chey and Luna. Today he was hardly in cage A at all. He doesn't run from Luna. But one time, when he saw her coming, he did grab the bench pole in C. They had some good play sessions, and he sticks up for himself by biting her etc. When they had their juice this morning, Luna kept taking Elok's chin in her hand, and sucking or licking his face to get his slobbers. She was just a wild child all day long. She zips from cage to cage, making up games to play.

One of her caregivers came by; one who hadn't been here since last summer. Luna squeaked when she saw her, sniffed her fingers, and then put on her smiley face. She remembered her well and that was really neat.

When the evening bananas were given out, Elok ate his in cage B, Cindy giving him bits at a time. Luna pried his mouth open and swiped a couple of bites.

Rudi was cranky today. Who knows why?

April 5, 2005

Today was my last Elok observation day. Its now one big, apparently happy, family. The jungle gym was removed from A, the baby cage, and the creep door eliminated. Chey and Luna loved being able to be in cage A.

When it was time to come inside today, Elok and Chey came in, and Luna stayed behind. Chey had a dilemma; one kid in and one kid out. Luna climbed to the top of a pole near the night house, and was crying. Chey started climbing up after her. Luna started down so Chey went back inside. Then Luna changed her mind and climbed back up the pole. Chey went outside again and sat under the structure. Luna started down so Chey returned to the night house. Luna went back up the pole <u>again</u>. This time Chey walked bipedally to the pole, with a <u>very</u> determined walk, and started up after her. Luna got the hint, came down, and Chey ushered her briefly. Then Luna took hold of Chey's forehead hair, like she used to, and came inside.

Cindy said yesterday Rudi was putting his hand under the cage mesh, and was sort of pointing. She couldn't figure out what he wanted. Finally, he went to the back of his cage, got a water bottle cap and gave it to her. She then realized his water bottle was in the drain, right beside her. He wanted her to fix him a bottle of juice like we do. Earlier I'd asked him for his bottle, he gave it to me, and I fixed him some juice.

April 10, 2002

Well, we have a puny little fellow. Apparently, he was bitten by Chey over the weekend. He was bugging her when she was in her nest, and she punctured his finger. Then Luna got hold of him, and sucked some of the tissue out. Yuck! It's healed, but today he just stayed on the floor. Didn't play and seemed afraid of Luna and Chey.

    Luna tried to get a game going, but he wouldn't play. Chey pretty much ignored him too. The workman came in to fix door #7. Chey grabbed a black tub and climbed upon a bench. She hid behind the tub, probably thinking she might be sedated. The vet had been there earlier, checking Elok out, so she was nervous. Anyway, Elok's appetite was good, he didn't seem feverish, but seems to be catching a cold. We're also wondering if he's a bit constipated. By the time I left, he was holding his left arm up in a weird position—broken?? Maybe just sprained.

April 11, 2002

Email from Lynn. They sedated Elok and checked him over. Nothing broken; just soft tissue injury.

April 15, 2002

Well, the family is getting back to normal after several days of Elok being afraid of Chey and Luna.

April 24, 2002

Went to clean today. Everybody is happy; getting along. I gave Luna my old armadillo slippers. She loved them! Gave Chey two new hair brushes and a scrub brush. Had a purse and shoes for Kelly. She was a wild one today. Gave Rudi a pair of sandals.

May 1, 2002

Nothing too much going on today. I was glad I was there to help as Cindy had a migraine. I was given a tape of Elok, Luna and Chey. I took a lot of the footage. Also got an appreciation for the Elok project signed by Rick Barongi, the zoo director.

Cindy said Elok was sucking Chey's thumb the other day. He wanted to suck mine when I first went into the night house this morning. They are all getting along fine now.

Doc had a coconut today and couldn't open it. I demonstrated how he should pound it on the floor, but he just stared at me. However, when Cindy and I left the night house, we heard him banging it on the floor.

May 8, 2002

Helped clean today. I took an empty peanut butter jar and an empty honey bottle. As there was a bit left in both, I knew they'd like that. I gave Rudi the jar after they all had a bit of peanut butter on their monkey biscuits (open faced sandwiches). I also took a papaya and a pineapple for them to share.

Cindy said another volunteer and two relatives came to visit the orangs. The visitors all had sandals on, plus the volunteer had her toenails painted. Rudi was in "hog heaven" and purred like crazy.

June 5, 2002

Back to the zoo after four weeks. Apparently, Chey was mean to Elok yesterday, but she was fine today. I think, at times, she's just overwhelmed with two kids.

Rudi refused to go out. I wonder if he knew I probably had goodies (I brought mangos today), and he wasn't going out without a treat.

I think Luna was happy to see me. She had a happy face and let me scratch her back.

I really missed them while I was gone.

June 26, 2002

This time back to the zoo after three weeks. Rudi was cranky towards Cindy this morning. He spilled his juice and spit at her. Doc did several displays throughout the morning. He's becoming a manly man!

My neighbor's son and her elderly parents came to visit. Rudi purred for them. Luna showed off, waving her arms in response to me waving my arms, and also copying the "I love you" sign. The parents both use canes, and Chey kind of freaked, thinking for a minute they had something to do with being darted. Poor thing!

Elok is a cute as can be. I think he gets cuter all the time.

July 9, 2002

I took my son, Derek, and his friend (a girl) to the zoo this afternoon for a "visit" with the orangs. All were inside. Kelly spit at Derek. Rudi was "in love" as we all had on sandals, plus the girl and I had painted toes, and she had a toe ring.

July 10, 2002

I worked at the zoo today and took mangos as treats. Plus I had an empty peanut butter jar for Rudi. Talk about Heaven! Elok and Luna are playing well together, but she is still a bit testy with him. He is so cute! Just wish I could hug him again.

July 24, 2002

Lynn was in orangs today. We hustled! Cleaned, without much playing, as she had meetings to attend this afternoon.

Doc has horrendous diarrhea. Don't know if it's stress or if he's caught some sort of bug.

August 21, 2002

Back, after a month. A few days ago, Luna tried to escape while outside. She stacked two computer boxes (enrichment items) together, and wrapped a blanket around her hand to avoid the stickers on the vine she was reaching for. Little stinker. Today she and Chey had metal washers from something, but we couldn't find what they'd taken apart.

August 28, 2002

The zoo has gone private and the new CEO worked with us today, wanting to get to know what goes on in the different areas. I was impressed!

We just cleaned, and I had peaches as a treat for the orangs.

September 4, 2002

Nothing too interesting. Just cleaned cages. We let Doc into A and B when Chey and the kids were outsice. However, he was anxious to get back to C and D to get papaya.

September 11, 2002

Today I spent my birthday doing exactly what I wanted to do – taking care of the orangs. I took a pineapple for them to share; yum, yum. I also took some whistles. Luna figured out how to use them with minimal instruction. Chey tried, and then handed it to me like, "Here, you blow it." Next Wednesday is Luna's 5th birthday.

September 18, 2002

Luna is 5 today! Hard to believe. I had a birthday banner for her, a bowling set, mega blocks, and new slinkys. I took a honeydew melon for them to share. Luna had another plastic whistle, and blew it a lot in front of Lynn. Silly girl!
    Elok put his little feet out for me to play with. Cute the way he does that.
    I gave Chey a new hairbrush.

September 25, 2002

Elok has some bites on his hands and one foot. I guess he caught "mama" in a bad mood. Today Chey was playful; big old smiley face showing the few teeth in her head. Luna was being silly; spinning around on a wet spot on the floor. What a goof!
    I had no special treats for them. And I won't return until November 6. I'm off to the Indian Reservation for a month of mission work.

November 6, 2002

Back with my buddies at the zoo. I think they were all glad to see me. Maybe it was the pomegranates I had with me. Of course Luna wanted her back scratched. And Elok decided he'd like his scratched too. Luna was her usual self; hyper and silly. She was wearing a huge plastic jar on her head a couple of times. Looked like a space alien. One time she was banging on the sides of it while it was <u>on her head</u>. I'm surprised the noise didn't bother her. It bothered me and I was down the hall!

I gave Chey a new scrub brush; always a fun toy. Elok has a cut on his hand. Probably a bite from Chey.

There's a new siamang baby. I saw the video of her (they think it's a girl) when she was 5 days old.

It was great to be back!

November 13, 2002

I'm not sure Chey felt good today. She was back in bed a couple of times; in hay in a tub with a sheet. When I fed Elok his cereal she went into the next cage – wasn't front and center begging. (Of course Luna was.) Maybe Chey didn't get enough sleep or is coming down with a cold. She had a bolt and nut in her mouth when I arrived. We found out later she'd taken it from the hammock in A. Anyway, after I showed each of them I'd brought a honeydew, Chey gave me the bolt, unsolicited. I rewarded her with some oats as the honeydew was for later.

Rudi refused to go out today, but he was very cooperative about shifting cages so we could clean. Luna was her usual wild self and Elok was a sweetie. He's so cute!

November 28, 2002 Thanksgiving

I missed last week – had a cold.

I was greeted with great news today. KELLY IS PREGNANT! At least her external genitalia are that of a pregnant orangutan. She had her last period mid October with no bleeding noted since. She and Doc have been outside together and she's been nicer to him. We figure she's due in late June or July. Who knows? Guess this might explain her sleeping in some mornings.

Another Luna caregiver was also there today and we both cleaned, However, she did most as two of my friends came by to meet the orangs.

November 30, 2002

I went to the zoo to take two other Luna caregivers and Cindy their Christmas gifts. One of the caregivers was having the orangs finger paint. Luna wanted to do it all.

December 4, 2002

Pour little Elok didn't seem to feel good today. He walked like he was achy, and kept lying down on hay. He didn't seem to have a fever or anything, and did drink his formula and eat his cereal.

I gave Chey a whisk broom today, and it kept her busy well over an hour, close to two. She swept the mesh, the door tracks, and the floor. Luna wanted it but Chey wouldn't let her have it. When she started pulling the wire loose that held it together, I traded a slice of pineapple for it. I was afraid she might try to use it to pick the lock later. Cindy said if she got out, she'd probably let Rudi out next so they could have sex.

December 17, 2002

Today was zoo shopping day for members. I bought a finger painting by Luna. Neat!

December 18, 2002

Back to the zoo today after missing last week as I had "stuff" going on. I think Elok was glad to see me this morning. When I entered the night house, he came to the mesh immediately, and put a hand and a foot out for me to love. The press came today to photograph different animals with their Christmas enrichment. I took cherries, grapes, cranberries, and orange slices to decorate the Christmas tree which we put high on the structure. I also put some green and silver tinsel on it. <u>Luna loved it!</u> Elok went up there too, but Chey was "worried" about things today. She stayed below, happy to munch on what fell to the ground.

Chey and Luna were sedated a few days ago; given checkups, vaccinations etc. One of the Luna caregivers, a dentist, cleaned their teeth and removed a broken tooth of Chey's. Chey weighs 170 pounds and Luna weighs 60 pounds.

A ten foot long bamboo pole was put up to use as a curtain rod for a shower curtain to be hung in the aisle between D, E, and F. This is so Doc and Rudi can have a "wall" between them if the spitting begins. Anyway, <u>somehow</u> Kelly managed to use something to get hold of the pole and get it into cage F. Of course she did this while Cindy was at lunch. They are so sneaky.

I finally saw the baby siamang, Raya, in person today. She was hanging on her mom's ankle. For some reason Jambi thinks that is where she should carry her. She's a tiny little thing and so cute.

I received some neat orangutan Christmas gifts; a framed finger painting by Luna, a little statue of two young orangutans, and a gorgeous framed photo of Cheyenne. I was thrilled!

December 26, 2002

I went to help clean today. We sent Rudi (reluctantly) and Kelly out early. Gave them access to the squeeze as it was chilly. Put some sheets and towels in there, and Kelly came in and wrapped up in a towel. Bless her heart. Nothing spectacular going on; just the usual stuff.

December 31, 2002

Two of my friends came to meet the orangs up close and personal. Kelly and Rudi were already outside. Elok threw a tantrum when Cindy wouldn't let him suck her finger. We think he's cutting a molar. He was whiny too.

Chey was sweet as I showed her the picture of herself I'd received. She then looked through the hockey player calendar I gave her. She later showed us how well she spits. Luna was a wild thing, but cute; also spitty.

January 1, 2003

I didn't take a treat today, but I did have a whistle for Luna. Lynn was working in the night house so she got to hear Luna blow it. I gave Chey a hair brush to make herself beautiful. Luna later broke it.

Luna was hyper as usual. I had fun tickling her; her feet and under her arms. She put on her big play face.

Chey was sweet today; no spitting. She and Elok had some good play time. I took some photos of him in a tub. I also tickled him but no play face.

Lynn says Kelly might be a month further along than thought. I gave her a cracker this morning. She immediately gave me two pieces of material, always thinking she has to trade something for a snack.

January 8, 2003

Poor Chey. She has diarrhea and is in the third day of it. She started on Prozac for her apparent PMS a week ago, and they are wondering if that's the cause. (Doc's poop this morning was a bit soft so maybe a "bug" is going around.) Chey had her usual good appetite, but just wasn't herself. She kept making nests and climbing in. Seemed to curl up like maybe her tummy hurt. No kiss squeaks either.

Cheyenne now on medication for PMS

Elok has been routinely pulling the nipples out of bottles or biting the end off. We <u>are</u> introducing a Sippy cup. Cindy says Luna helps retrieve the nipples because Elok won't give them up. Cindy "upped the ante" from juice to raisins yesterday, and Luna held Elok down and pried his mouth open.

Kelly just acts like she doesn't feel well in the mornings. Didn't want her juice this morning, and had a severe case of "bed head." She did go outside with no problem. Rudi went out too. As it was a cold morning, we'd put all sorts of blankets outside. He came back into the squeeze with a soft flannel receiving blanket from outside. He was clutching it the rest of the time I was there. Silly.

Luna gave me a big blanket today. I gave her a raisin. Then Elok was right there, hoping for one. Luna either hit him or pushed him. He ran across the floor whining, went into the corner, and threw a tantrum. A bit later he was still a whiny butt. However, he was hungry. It was rice cereal time.

January 14, 2003

Chey's diarrhea ended a few days ago. No one else got the bug, whatever it was. She was her usual self; playful with Elok, kiss squeaking, begging, giving Kelly the evil eye, and spitting.

Elok was a hungry boy today. He seemed to be eating something all the time. I gave him lots of soaked monkey biscuits. Of course Luna wanted some of those juice soaked biscuits too, so I shared some. Then she started giving me the dried biscuits that were in the cage so I'd soak <u>them</u>. She gave me lots of play faces when I tickled her ears.

I think Kelly might have a little poochy belly. It seems, in looking at her profile, she has her usual tummy, a dent, and then a little pooch. She was slow to rise again today. She refused her juice, licked the baby food off her morning biscuits, and went back to bed. About 10 a.m. she perked up and even went outside for awhile.

January 21, 2003

Well, Kelly must be over her "morning sickness." She was up early this morning, waiting for her juice, which she drank eagerly. She then did her nest building 'til time to go out.

Rudi has horrendous diarrhea. He stayed up on the props, staying off the filthy floor. He does <u>not</u> like to be dirty. I scrubbed everything in his cage <u>twice</u> with bleach and soapy water. I don't know if he caught a "bug" like Chey had, or if John Q. Public threw him something he shouldn't have.

I gave Luna a few of the "thunder sticks" that were given out at the hockey game. She tore two open and put them on like gloves. They were all the way to her shoulders. I also gave her a whistle, but she gave it back. So I showed Chey <u>again</u> how to blow it, and <u>she did it!</u> I also had a scrub brush for her.

Luna with thunder sticks from hockey game

I took mangos as a treat for the group. I put Rudi's and Kelly's outside. Doc got his for moving over to D from F. Chey was mad because I didn't give her one. She spit on me every time I walked by. After we shifted them from A and B I gave her one. I gave it to her in Cage D, and she took it all the way to the tunnel to eat it. Elok followed her there, and she actually shared some bites with him before I gave him one. I also gave them an empty grape jelly jar. There was still some stuck on the inside of the jar, and Luna got out as much as she could. Then Chey took it. We gave her a straw to use as a tool to get it out. I also told her to put some water in it. She finally did get a mouthful of water and spit it into the jar. Made grape juice. They are too smart!

February 4, 2003

Back at the zoo today. Was in Montana last week. This week Elok has diarrhea. Luna had it a few days ago. I took a pineapple for them to share. Rudi refused to go out. Gave Chey some pineapple, before she switched cages, so she wouldn't spit at me. Worked like a charm. Of course we then had to listen to her loud kiss squeaks, begging for more. Kelly seemed to feel a little punky today. She stayed in bed late and refused her juice.

February 11, 2003

Now Doc has diarrhea. Yuck! Poor guy. Chey was playful today, and Lynn came in and played with her a bit. I put the hose where she was able to grab it. Oops! Had to give her a Valentine cookie (with permission) to get it back. And <u>then</u> she had to think about it. Kelly was perky today. There are pictures everywhere of mama orangutans with their babies. Generally they are placed in front of whatever cage Kelly is in. I gave Luna a pair of socks, and she did put one on for a bit.

February 18, 2003

Cindy was sick today so I functioned as the orang keeper, only needing Lynn to shift animals. I never mind as she, as supervisor, has things to do. She did help sweep a cage. I had strawberries so I was liked a <u>lot</u> today.

When I hosed the tunnel, Luna had a great time playing in the water. Kelly was a sleepy head this morning. Doc is over his diarrhea. <u>Not one had it today!</u> Yea!

When Chey, Elok, and Luna got access to cage E, Chey climbed up intentionally to look at the pictures of the orangutan moms and babies hanging in front of the cage. I wonder if she's thinking, "Hmmm, must be I'm going to get another baby."

February 25, 2003

It was really cold today. We knew there would be some creative shifting, as all would probably refuse to go out. However, Doc did go out, but came back into the squeeze a couple of times.

We had Kelly watch the orang video, Just Hanging On. We showed it to her several times. The orangutan in Perth, Australia, gives birth to her 11th baby in the video. Kelly did watch it intently and so did Chey. There was also a lot of footage about Camp Wanariset in Borneo. I wonder, when Chey saw all those baby orangutans being rehabilitated, if she thought, "Oh no, I am getting more babies."

Rudi still has a raw spot on his wrist. He let Lynn put ointment on it last week. Doc has a split lip, like it's chapped.

Elok whined for his cereal this morning. He also whined because he wanted to hold the strawberry I was holding for him. I knew Chey or Luna would take it from him, so I was just trying to give him bites. He did take the berry and sure enough, it was taken from him.

March 4, 2003

Gave Rudi some Band-Aids today. He managed to have one stuck on his hand when he went outside. I gave Chey a new hair brush. She made herself beautiful, as usual. I mainly just cleaned, and played with the gang as I did the cleaning.

A new male babirusa arrived in Primates from quarantine. His name is Basil. He's ugly, but I'm sure Delilah will think he's quite handsome.

March 8, 2003

I, and some friends of mine, visited the orangutans this morning. Luna gave me her tooth. (She's losing her baby teeth.) I guess when she saw I had grapes she decided to make a trade. I gave Chey a new hair brush. That's always fun to do when there are visitors. She always brushes her hair for them. I also gave her a few Band Aids, and she stuck them on her brush handle. I put a Band Aid on the mesh of Rudi's cage, and he put his wrist with the sore against the mesh. He knows that a Band Aid goes on a sore.

I'll be gone for a few weeks. I'll miss the gang.

April 15, 2003

It was great to be back with the orangs. I think they were happy to see me, or maybe it was the mangos I had with me. Seriously, before they knew I had treats, Luna put her ear next to the mesh for tickles and wanted her back scratched—our links. She also put on a happy face. Elok put his little hand out under the mesh for holding, patting, and loving. He got upset when Luna put her fingers through the mesh to get attention while I was stroking his hand. Of course Chey gave me long, very serious looks, deep into my soul. I showed Rudi I had a few "oweys" on my leg (shaving knicks), and he had a long look. Then a few minutes later, when I went back to his cage, he had his wrist "owey" front and center for me to look at.

Kelly's pregnancy was certainly more evident than six weeks ago—my last zoo day. And the most exciting thing of all was seeing the baby moving while she was sitting there. There was that rolling movement across her abdomen. Brought back memories of my own pregnancies. I said to Cindy, "I wonder what Kelly thinks when the baby moves." She said she probably thinks she should have danced all night.

April 29, 2003

Back to the zoo after two weeks. I took mangos again—yum, yum. Elok wanted to be in charge of his, but I held it for him to take bites, knowing Chey or Luna would steal it. I did finally give it to him, and Chey quickly took it. He got most of it though, slurping loudly.

Rudi still has an "owey" on his wrist. He let me put a Band-Aid on it. Silly boy. I think Rudi and I can be considered buddies.

Elok has learned to drink from a straw. He's also starting to put things into boxes. He's growing up. He still has two bottles a day, but the amount of formula is decreased.

May 6, 2003

Another fun day at the zoo. Kelly is HUGE! Looks so uncomfortable. Her labia are swollen and drooping, and she can't sit flat anymore. Has to lean on one hip. Cindy says she has been intently watching the videos of mama orangutans nursing their babies, and is responding by presenting her nipple on command.

I showed Rudi my "oweys." He was fascinated.

Elok threw a tantrum today when Chey wouldn't give him something he wanted. He screamed and threw himself on the floor.

Luna gave me lots of play faces when I tickled her ears.

Once today Chey used a big juice bottle to tinkle. No spillage! She doesn't like to just go on the cage bottom; too tidy for that. Her birthday is next week. I told her I'd bring her a new hair brush.

May 13, 2003

Today was Chey's 31st birthday so I went to see her. I made her a little "cake" of sliced carrots glued together with peanut butter. Added a few raisins too. I gave her a hair brush as promised. She is so playful anymore. Her Prozac dosage was increased and maybe PMS is history.

May 14, 2003

Another fun morning at the zoo. Rudi let me put Band-Aids on his "owey." Gave Chey another hair brush. She brushed her head, her arm, her leg, and even Elok. I gave Luna another whistle. After she broke it, Chey tried to put it back together – and succeeded. We noticed Elok is learning to soak his biscuits. Also today, Rudi was trying to unscrew a loose screw on the hydraulic door in cage F, the door maintenance worked on yesterday. He was working on it, trying not to be noticed.

Kelly went outside first, but was still near the door when Doc was let out. She scurried off, moving very rapidly for a nearly full term pregnancy. Wasn't going to let _that_ guy near her any time soon!

May 20, 2003

I gave Chey a little sponge off a dish scrubber today, and she washed a glass in her dishpan (the water bowl), and scrubbed the cage mesh.

Cindy said Elok threw a tantrum this morning when his 75 cc of formula was gone from his bottle. He wanted more! She opened the creep door and told Chey to deal with him. Cindy said Chey looked at her like, "You want _me_ to take care of him?"

We kept Kelly inside as she was acting rather strange, unusual posturing and all. We wondered if she was in labor. She sat in front of the AC vent for awhile with a wet rag on her head. Later I took her picture stretched out on a bench with a cloth over her head. She is huge, labia huge and dripping, (yuck) and seems generally uncomfortable.

May 26, 2003

A call from Cindy making sure I'd be at the zoo tomorrow. It appears Kelly is dilating and "acting strange."

Email from Lynn to everyone later saying Kelly appears to be in labor, and keep toes and fingers crossed. She's actually due May 27th.

May 27, 2003

Well, no baby during the night, but Kelly looked awful this morning. Major bed head etc. She didn't rearrange anything in her cage after it was set up yesterday. Ate her carrot and orange, but noticed she left her celery and onion. She did some strange posturing, and we think her water might have broken as there was a sudden gush of clear fluid. She had noticeable "gushy," but small, leakage twice more. Couldn't really tell if there were contractions. She looked like she felt awful too.

All of the others were doing fine. Luna acting goofy as usual. Chey was playful.

It was a free day at the zoo yesterday, so the orangs were thrown stuff by the idiot public.

In the "baby pool" I guessed the baby would be born May 28 at 10 a.m., weigh 3.8 pounds, and be a girl.

June 3, 2003

Still no baby!! Kelly continues acting like she doesn't feel too well – off her food and beverages. Didn't want her Metamucil. She perked up when it was time to go outside, and moved quickly to the door. Lynn had a meeting at 11 a.m. so we really hustled with our cleaning. (Cindy was off.) Gave Elok his 50cc of formula. One gulp; GONE. One little screech and he pulled the nipple off. But no full blown tantrum.

As I was changing into my shoes outside the night house, prior to leaving at 11, I heard Luna blowing the whistle I gave her. Peeked in and saw Chey was scrubbing the cage with the sponge I gave her.

June 10, 2003

STILL waiting for a baby. Kelly was "draggy" this morning, but perked up a bit when time to go outside. Cindy throws her ice pops every couple of hours, while she's out, to keep her well hydrated. We're worried there might be something wrong, concerned about the baby, Kelly's health etc.

Took some photos of Rudi and Chey, and one of Kelly outside. Elok and Luna were their usual busy, silly selves. I took kiwis as treats; always a favorite.

Today I watched little Raya, the 8 month old siamang, as she played in the exhibit. She is so cute and busy,busy.

June 17, 2003

Well, Kelly must have gotten pregnant when no one was watching. We don't know when she's going to have this baby.

THE ORANG GANG ET AL - LOVED, HUGGED AND PEED ON

Just cleaned today; didn't play much.

June 22, 2003

It's a boy! Born at 3:27 p.m. today, shortly after Kelly came in from outside. Mom and baby are doing fine, and we're waiting to see if he nurses.

June 25, 2003

Kelly is nursing her baby. Got it on video this morning. Thank God. He is so cute, of course. Has big hands and feet like Doc. Kelly seems very content; tired but content.

I noticed Chey trying to pick Elok up today. Hmm…. She and the kids haven't really seen Kelly's baby. Luna was goofy today, and making noise with props and enrichment to get attention.

July 1, 2003

Was nice to see cute little Solaris this morning. He's a sweetie with an unusual name. Lynn has been sending regular email updates so I knew he'd been named on June 27th. Kelly has not eaten for 2 or 3 days, and has not pooped since delivery. Lynn is giving her all kinds of delectable fruits, and trying to get her to take pericolace.

Elok has diarrhea again; horrible, sticky, hard to clean up, diarrhea. However, we were finished by noon with the cleaning.

Chey, Luna, and Elok are all very interested in Kelly and Solaris.

I saw Kelly patting Solaris on his wee head and back. That was <u>so sweet!</u> She is being a very good mom.

July 15, 2003

Back to the zoo and armed with a pineapple. I took lots of photos of Kelly and "Sam" today. Cindy says everyone is calling the baby Sam, but she's sure Lynn won't approve an official name change. Many of us were hoping he'd be named Sam Houston. He's a big baby and nursing a lot. Kelly is becoming more confident, and moving about without holding his arm or leg in her mouth. He's clinging really well. She continues to pat his little back.

Elok has diarrhea <u>again!</u> It was better for awhile. He threw a few screaming fits today. Lynn says maybe his tummy hurts. Cindy said one day Chey had some of his diarrhea on her, and was quite upset. She washed her hands to get it off.

Luna was acting like a goof all day, trying to get attention.

July 22, 2003

Well, little Solaris is one month old today. He is so cute, and alert. At one point today he was searching for a nipple. He was going all over Kelly's front with his mouth wide open. He finally caught his thumb and sucked on it. He also hit himself in the head when his arms were flailing about. Too cute! Lynn said Kelly got some of his feces on her last week, and was trying very hard to wash it off in the drinking pool. When that didn't work she went to the moat. Lynn said she gave Solaris a bath too, washing his stinky butt. She was holding him out and spitting on him. He was screaming like crazy.

And another tale of poop. Cindy said Elok pooped on Chey's head. She put her head into the water bowl to clean off. He threw a tantrum today, screeching because I forgot to give him his straw after his juice. Little brat. He has the tantrums down to a fine science.

I'll be gone for the next four weeks. I know Solaris will change a lot.

August 19, 2003

Well, the baby has grown and is awake for longer periods. He is so cute. They put the photo I took of Kelly and him into Plexiglas to be used as his "birth announcement" on the exhibit.

Kelly and Solaris July 22, 2003

What an honor! Today, after they came in from outside, Kelly and Solaris were sitting on the floor at the front of cage C. Kelly offered Solaris' hand to us. She's done it to others, but it was a first for Cindy and me. He also has two little teeth starting to show.

The others are also great. Elok had no tantrums today. Luna was her same silly, busy self. I took a pineapple for them and they loved that, of course.

September 2, 2003

Zoo day today and I went with a pineapple. Solaris is cuter than ever. And so alert. He stayed awake all morning, and seems very curious about things around him. Kelly is presenting his arm for an "injection" on command. That way they can give his immunizations when they're due.

Cindy said yesterday Chey waded out into the moat to get some bits of orange that were there for the turtles.

I gave Doc a clear plastic angel food cake container. He loved it! He put a little water in it so he could scrape out all the crumbs that were stuck to the side. Smart.

September 9, 2003

No big events today. Elok started whining about 7:30 a.m. before the night house was opened. The "volume" steadily increased until Cindy opened the door. No one was hurting him. He's just a whiny brat sometimes. Shortly after going in, however, we saw Luna toss the big white barrel, and it nearly hit him. Hmm…was she throwing it at him?

We disinfected the pool today. Cindy oiled the padlock to get it opened. She thought it was totally locked when we went inside. However, when Kelly and Solaris came in, Kelly had the padlock! Traded it for some baby food. Cindy said she'd opened the drain hatch but that was all.

When Solaris started to pee today, Kelly held him out away from her. Didn't want to get herself dirty. This mom thing only goes so far!

September 10, 2003

Today Derek and I went to visit and play with the orangutans for awhile. He wanted to meet the baby. We stayed about an hour. Luna played tug-o-war with Derek. I took grape tomatoes. Lynn said she didn't think they'd had them before. They loved them. Also took some raisins, a popular treat. Both of us had sandals on. Rudi liked that, especially my feet with the painted toes.

Solaris pooped and Kelly wiped his butt with a paper towel. Too cute.

Derek thought Elok was really a cute little fellow. Well, he is!

September 16, 2003

When I first arrived today I asked Rudi if he'd like a drink. I had some Gatorade powder. I told him to give me a bottle, and he pushed an empty water bottle out to me. So smart!

I gave Luna a little lime juice bottle; globe shaped bottom with a long neck. Well, we saw her using it as a sex object. Oh yes! Then she was trying to sit on it for further pleasure. I told her she needed lubricant. Just being an inquisitive, "Ooh, this feels good" little girl.

There are new hammocks in B and D. Luna has decided its lots of fun to twist them. She got the one in D jammed. When Kelly got back in that cage she worked with it 'til it was fixed. Solaris was holding on for dear life while she pushed and shoved with arms and feet. He is so cute; so bright eyed etc.

September 23, 2003

I worked with another zookeeper today. She and Cindy are going to alternate. Rudi purred like crazy when he saw her. He's in love!

Solaris is the cutest thing in the world. He's trying to grab things, but is totally klutzy. Not sure his grab is intentional. He just looks at us like he's trying to figure the world out. It's hard to believe he's 3 months old already.

September 30, 2003

Had the usual fun day today. I took a pineapple and some plums for them. Real treats! They couldn't go outside as the moat is being worked on. I made a new "will work for food" sign and took photos of Chey. I hope some turn out. I'll try again next week.

Kelly kept applauding, wanting more pineapple. She was passing bits of cardboard out to have me put some on it, or to trade. I told her she'd have to wait 'til she moved back to the other cage. She then tried to trade Solaris for some pineapple. At first I thought she was offering his little hand for me to touch. Then she shoved his whole arm through the mesh. That's all that would fit! I don't think Kelly has the complete mother thing down yet.

Elok had a tantrum because Luna got something from the forage that he wanted. Too funny!

October 7, 2003

Nothing particularly special about today. Just cleaned. I took a pineapple again, but at least Kelly didn't try to trade Solaris for some.

Doc refused to go out. Don't know what <u>that</u> was all about.

I took the 20 plus jack-o-lanterns I'd stored in my garage since last October to the zoo. The orangs hadn't ruined them so figured we might as well keep them. I brought home a bunch of the small plastic items to keep 'til after Halloween. Of course Luna tried to hoard all of the 8 jack-o-lanterns I put in their cage. She thinks when there are multiples of anything, they belong to her.

October 8, 2003

I had permission to take a good friend to visit the orangs today. She was so excited to see the baby, and also meet Elok for the first time. She loved it all. I took some grape tomatoes for them. Kelly applauded between each one, wanting another, and Chey did the loudest kiss squeaks I <u>ever</u> heard. Elok would take his tomato and run. Doc wasn't sure about the tomatoes as he's not had them before. I think he was outside the day Derek and I were there, and I gave them some. However, he did eat his when we weren't looking. I also gave each of them a kiwi.

I gave Chey a new hairbrush so she made herself beautiful. I also gave one to Kelly, but she thought she should trade me one plastic bristle at a time as barter. Silly woman.

I gave Luna some Velcro rollers. She loved them and took them into a corner to play. Eventually Elok got hold of them, and wow, he thought he had the prize. He was cute when he first started playing with them 'cause they would stick to his hair. I have several more packages for other days. The dollar stores are great!

Little Solaris was cute as could be, wide eyed and curious about everything. At one point he was grasping the mesh, and I thought he was going to climb right up it.

When we left the night house, we went around to the exhibit to say "hi" to Rudi. He was perched up high on the edge of the structure, "supervising" the workers that were doing whatever they were doing at the edge of the moat. Well, I called his name and he did a sideways glance. We were the only two there so I said, "Rudi, look. I wore sandals today." And I took my shoe off and waved my foot. Anyway, he climbed down and headed over to the window. We walked around there, and he was as close to the window as he could get. We took our shoes off, waved our painted toes at him, and he just stared and stared. He also looked us right in the eyes when we got down close. I took a photo of him looking at my friend's foot. It was so cool! We got so tickled at him. We were also glad we were the only two standing there.

October 14, 2003

Not too much new at the zoo. Mac, the 50 year old gorilla, is quite ill. He's more or less being considered a hospice patient. Apparently a grief counselor met with the staff to help them prepare for his death.

Solaris is adorable, of course. Cindy gave him a few drops of juice, and he thought it was quite wonderful.

Doc is still refusing to go out most days. Today I put peanut butter and honey on top of a pumpkin, stuck a few whole pecans on top, and made a big production of placing it outside. Well, he went right out. However, another volunteer said she went out to see him, and he was mad. I stopped to check on him when I left. He was sitting by the window and, when he saw me, he gave me a pointed glare. If looks could kill, I'd be dead.

October 29, 2003

Today Derek and I went to the zoo. (He had an interview) When we went to orangs, the volunteer said Chey had two screws and wouldn't give them up. Well, I walked into the night house in my regular clothes, carrying my Wal-Mart bag. Even though Chey didn't know what treats I had in the bag, (cherry tomatoes and honey nut & oats cheerios) she offered me the screws. I hadn't said a word to her, but she knew I had some sort of treat when she saw I had the bag. Amazing!

I showed Rudi my bare foot with painted toes. He purred and presented his nipple with a piece of straw in it.

Lynn said Luna put a sweatshirt on yesterday. Got it on totally right and it came down to her ankles. On the front it said "Class of 2006."

She also said Kelly gave Solaris some solid food. She mashed up a monkey biscuit in her mouth, pushed it to the edge of her lips, and he sucked a bit off. Solaris didn't seem too impressed.

I think Doc and I are friends again.

November 4, 2003

I love this job – best non-paying job in the world.

Solaris is so cute! First thing this morning he was bright-eyed, busy, and looking all around. He and Kelly were in D. When I walked to the other side of the cage, he bent his head over backwards to see where I went. Several times today Kelly put his hands and feet on the mesh, sort of showing him how to hang on. She usually kept a hand on his ankle. When she got her juice this morning, he was pursing his little lips like he wanted some too. They are "introducing" Doc to Kelly and Solaris using an intro door. However, there's an added screen so Doc's big fingers can't get through. Lynn says it's going really well, and she hopes they can let them be together soon.

Well, the National Zoo in Washington, D.C. wants Luna. Lynn said she wanted to tell me in person, thinking how upsetting it would be. Another volunteer had already told me, however. Lynn says the answer is "no" for at least a year. Luna needs to keep observing Kelly and Solaris, Elok needs her, and she's too attached to Chey to go. I think the National Zoo would be great because Luna is so smart, and would be an ideal candidate for the think tank there. However, in a year they may not want her, and she'll go elsewhere. Luna is a potential breeding female so she's not ours to keep. I think I'd feel worse if Rudi was snatched away.

And speaking of Rudi, when I arrived this morning and went to greet him, he immediately looked at my feet to see if my toes were visible. Silly man.

Elok threw a tantrum when I gave Chey and Kelly a piece of pomegranate and didn't give him one. Never mind that he had some of his own earlier.

After I finished cleaning today, I wish I could have just stayed to watch Kelly and Solaris. He is so adorable. Kelly did present his hand for me to touch.

November 11, 2003

Nothing special today. The intros of Doc and Kelly are non-interesting. Lynn just hopes they can soon be in together.

Daiquiri came to see the group up close and personal. Rudi enjoyed a peek at her bare feet with painted toes.

Elok whined a few times, Luna was hyper as usual, and Solaris remains adorable.

November 25, 2003

Just a a regular day. Solaris is climbing onto the mesh at times, totally separate from Kelly. Quite an independent little guy. And so bright eyed.

Solaris

December 16, 2003

Back to the zoo after being away three weeks. Solaris "explores," climbing onto the mesh, sometimes a whole cage width away from Kelly. He has four teeth; two above and two below. This morning he got hold of one of Kelly's pudding softened monkey biscuits. It was so cute watching him eat it. Hard to believe he'll be six months old next week.

I took paper shell pecans today. Poor Chey –she gave the first one back to me. She thought she couldn't crack it with her teeth, even though Elok and Luna were crunching theirs. I did crack it for her. She wanted to give the second one back to me too, but I told her to bite it, demonstrating how. She sucked on it for awhile and then did crack it. I gave her lots of praise. The third one she not only cracked, but also got the nut out <u>whole</u>. She showed it to me. More praise, of course.

I gave Rudi some Legos today. We did see him pick one up. However, because he was caught showing interest, he pushed it out to us. He's so silly.

December 23, 2003

Today I took the orangs their Christmas stockings. In each one I put a mango, a kiwi, 2 almonds, and 2 English walnuts. I gave Elok and Luna Velcro rollers, Cheyenne a new hair brush, Kelly a dill pickle, Rudi a coffee bag, and Doc a necktie. We gave Elok his by himself so Luna wouldn't steal his stuff. He was trying to bite through the bottom of his stocking while holding the open end closed. I finally convinced him to turn it over. After Luna got hers, she arranged both her and Elok's rollers on a bench and played with them. At one point she turned a somersault over them, and they stuck to her back. Then she was looking around for them. She finally noticed one stuck to her shoulder, and realized where they were. Silly girl. Chey brushed her hair <u>before</u> eating her goodies.

They have been letting Doc go outside with Kelly and Solaris. Kelly has been apprehensive and staying up high on the structure. Today we just did the intro door, and they did spend lots of time staring at each other.

I wore Christmas socks today, and Rudi gave my feet a very good onceover.

January 13, 2004

Back to the zoo after three weeks. It was so great to see everyone. I took mangos and grapes.

Solaris is steadier as he climbs about; not so jerky. I gave Kelly a piece of foil wrapping paper which she loved. Even played with Solaris with it. And he grabbed it and was playful too. Even put on a little play face. So cute! He stuck his arm through the mesh, reaching for me. He grabbed my finger. Kelly wasn't too sure about that, pulled his arm back in, and sniffed his hand. He was also very interested in what Kelly was eating; putting his mouth on her mouth trying to grab something. He did get a small piece of kale, but it fell out of his mouth.

Elok threw a tantrum this morning. Luna had stolen the macaroon cookie that he gets to curb his diarrhea. He screamed and threw things, not patient about having to wait for another.

Doc refused to go out for the 5th day in a row. It might have been my fault as I'd put a mango and grapes in a box, and put it in cage D for Rudi when <u>he</u> shifted. I didn't think Doc noticed. The keeper fixed Doc a peanut butter sandwich and showed it to him. She also showed him a mango and grapes that she was going to put outside. But he wouldn't go. So she let him into cage D, and he went immediately to the box with the treats. On the other hand, Rudi <u>raced</u> outside to get Doc's treats.

Chey was very playful today too, being silly. And when the keeper and I were paying too much attention to Kelly and Solaris, Luna went wild in cage A trying to get attention.

Elok was playing with a plastic tube about 10 inches long and 1 ½ inches wide. I noticed liquid coming out of it. <u>Well,</u> he had it over his penis and was peeing through it.

Never a dull moment!

January 20, 2004

I took a pineapple today. They were very cooperative. We spent a lot of time deciding how they could shift because someone was going to work on a hydraulic door. Then the workmen decided to wait 'til tomorrow. Life would be so much easier if all the orangs just got along.

I tried to get Kelly to pose with a begging sign, but she tipped it sideways. Got some cute photos of baby boy. He's a busy one and trying to eat different things. Was cute with a bit of kale.

Elok was whiny when I arrived, but he quieted when he got his coconut macaroon. Poor little fellow – he's always hungry.

Just a fun morning hanging out with them and cleaning.

January 27, 2004

Today I took a coconut and two grapefruit for them to share. Lots of kiss squeaks.

It was cold today so nobody went out while I was there. Had to figure how to shift everyone. The big guys were cooperative, but Kelly didn't shift back to D from C for a very long time, even with good bribes. We did get Chey and the kids into B from A, but Chey lashed out at Elok. We heard him screaming and her vocalizing. Made a creep door out of door #1 so he could get away from her. He had a bleeding wound on his foot. He came forward for us, and later for Lynn, and put his foot against the mesh to show us. Poor little guy. The reason for this? Chey didn't want the door shut.

Luna

Elok has a baby sister in Memphis. They pulled her and are hand raising her. Wonder if we'll get her next year.

February 3, 2004

Elok's foot has healed – no problem. However, today he had explosive diarrhea. Bless his heart. He was a bit whiny and once he just screamed. No one was bothering him, but it might have been right before the diarrhea, and his tummy hurt.

I had some Velcro rollers, and Luna turned around so I could stick them to her back.

The keeper tried to put some ointment on Doc's split lip. It isn't an open wound, but we thought ointment might help. However, he was having no part of treatment.

Solaris has 6 teeth now; 4 on the bottom and 2 on top. He reaches out through the mesh a lot, wanting us to take his hand. He is just so cute.

February 24, 2004

Good to see my buddies again after three weeks. Got a great photo of Chey today "reading" a magazine. I also gave her a couple of sponges and she cleaned. Stuck a few Velcro rollers on Luna. Always fun. She and Chey also blew the whistles I gave them. Rudi flirted with me, purring and presenting his nipple for touching. Then he stuck a piece of straw in it, wanting me to pull it out. However, I don't do that. Elok was a sweet little boy. Sometimes I'm not sure his elevator goes all the way to the penthouse, but he can be so sweet. Solaris is a hungry boy; always trying to get some of Kelly's snacks. I gave him a cheerio and later a bite of pineapple. Lynn saw him eating a roach. There's another part of the 3% of the DNA we <u>don't</u> share.

    I won't be back again for another few weeks. I will really miss them.

Solaris learns to climb

March 23, 2004

Well, it's been a month since I was at the zoo. Took a large pineapple for them to share. Put my boots on by Rudi's cage, taking off my socks so he could peer at my painted toes for a few minutes. He was happy.

I took quite a few photos today, including begging signs. Elok threw a fit when he didn't get some of the honey we were putting on the signs. I also took one of Kelly and Solaris. Hard to believe he's 9 months old.

I gave Luna some alphabet blocks. She and Chey enjoyed those. Also gave Chey a couple of sponges. We saw Elok washing the cage with them. Maybe he's smarter than I thought.

I visited Mac, the gorilla, today. He's very thin; only about 260 lbs. He's blind but was feeling his way around the cages. He seemed to know a "stranger" was visiting.

March 30, 2004

Another fun day at the zoo. I took a photo of Elok holding a sign that said, "I want a baby sister." Maybe we should send it to Memphis and try to get Indah, his baby sister. I also got a photo of Kelly holding a sleeping Solaris. So sweet.

I gave Luna Velcro rollers which she promptly stuck on top of her head. Gave Chey a hair brush. Also gave them a package of clothes pins with which they had fun. At one point Elok was trying to put one on his penis. Ouch!

I understand they are doing introductions of Rudi to Chey and the kids, and it's going well. Another volunteer said Chey was just stretched out on her back like, "Here I am, Big Boy."

Little Solaris has his own cup now. He got Elok's cup and Elok got Doc's old cup. Doc has a new one the size of Rudi's.

April 6, 2004

Well, today I took some blank canvas to have Chey paint a picture. She did. Then, like an idiot, I left the brush in her hand while I went to get another canvas, totally forgetting she could move the brush down to the floor, and pull it into her cage. She would not give it back. She tried to poke Kelly and Solaris with it. They were in the tunnel and she was in B. She tried to poke the keeper with it when she bribed her with maple syrup. We also offered her cantaloupe, mango, and baby food. She refused it all, and also decided to spit huge mouthfuls of water at us, soaking us. Luna thought about taking it from her, as she knew it would get her a reward, but she also knows her "mom." Besides, mom was having her period today. Meanwhile, Elok was screaming and throwing tantrums because we weren't giving him any goodies. We moved Kelly into C to get her away from Chey. Doc was in D. Rudi was outside and it had started to rain. He was pounding on door #7 because he wanted in. That made Doc do a huge display. WHAT A ZOO! We even offered Chey a bite of cake. (I'd made a bunny cake for the keepers.) Nothing worked. We got Lynn. She brought in some cheese and Chey gave the paint brush up immediately.

Always an interesting day at the zoo.

Wednesday, April 14, 2004

Decided to work on a Wednesday. I wanted to see Rudi with Chey and the kids when the intro door is put on. Elok was cute as he grabbed a huge wad of hay, holding it in front of him as he walked toward the intro door. He's routinely used hay as a "buffer" if he's anxious. Chey refused to shift to C. She grabbed the peanut butter bribe and ran back to B, so the intro was short. Rudi went back to E and F.

Nothing too special today except Elok tried to put a T-shirt on, but Luna took it and did get it on correctly. It <u>was</u> on backwards, but her arms were in the arm holes, and her head through the neck hole.

April 27, 2004

Back to the zoo. I took mangos for each plus a coconut for them to share. Lots of begging kiss squeaks from Chey. Doc, Kelly, and Solaris were outside together. That seems to be going very well. Kelly isn't "worrying" like she did at first. Cindy says Solaris likes to play in the moat water, but Kelly always hangs on to his arm or leg. I gave him his juice this morning. He's doing quite well drinking from a cup.

There was an intro through the intro door of Rudi to Chey and the kids. That went well too. At first Elok marched to the door with a huge wad of hay in front of him, but later he was there to interact without any buffer. Cindy says this coming Friday they plan to open the door, and let them in together. Chey should have a fun day, finally being with her boyfriend after nearly five years.

Luna put a T-shirt on correctly again. I hope the photos turn out. I also gave her blocks. She stacked them, knocked them over, and stacked them again. At one point she was holding the stack steady with her chin. She is so smart!

May 4, 2004

It was an interesting day at the zoo. Between 8 and 9 a.m. we all, staff and volunteers, were invited to the Children's Zoo to have breakfast, and have a ride on the new carousel. Fun! Then we all walked over to see the cute baby prairie dogs.

Back in orangs, in the midst of cleaning, we heard that Mac, the gorilla, cratered; stumbling, falling, and hitting his face on the floor. The volunteer there came back to orangs in tears. All the zookeepers went over there. Barbara, the retired curator, came in from home, as did two zookeepers who were on vacation. He was given valium, and when I left, he was asleep. Lynn was on jury duty so she wasn't there today.

Orangs were fun, as usual. I showed Rudi my arm where I had a bad abrasion. He then pulled back the hair on his wrist, where he had a sore last year, and showed me his scar. Amazing; the memory. I gave him a Band Aid. He's still not in with Chey and the kids. They are waiting 'til one of the main keepers returns from vacation.

Elok was a bit whiny early in the morning. He knows when he whines and screams we all look, thinking he's being beaten up by Luna.

Solaris continues to get cuter every day.

Apparently a keeper from the Memphis Zoo was here last week. Said the keepers wouldn't mind sending Elok's sister to us, but management wants to keep her. She took a copy of the photo of Elok holding his sign, "I want a baby sister" back to Memphis.

May 11, 2004

Always interesting things happening in the orang night house. Lynn was in orangs today. She gave juice to Kelly, and I gave Solaris his juice. He didn't finish it so I offered it to him later. Of course Kelly came to try to get it, Solaris riding on her left side. I told her, "No, it's the baby's juice." She then pulled him off her, and placed him on the mesh to have his juice. He had some. I gave the rest to Kelly as a reward for being so good. Then they went outside with Doc. The three of them together continues to go well.

We cleaned the middle cages. Rudi was moved to D to interact with Chey and the kids through the intro door between C and D. Elok went right to the door, but Chey was determined to have a sexual encounter so moved into his space. She provided a bit of oral sex, then turned over and backed right up to the mesh for Rudi's convenience. She also touched his nipple and they did a "kissy" face. When Elok tried to horn in to interact with Rudi, Chey did something to him that made him scream. No wounds noted. Things calmed down after awhile, and Elok did some interacting with Rudi. Luna even went over there once.

Chey's 32nd birthday is in two days, so I brought her a "cake" of oatmeal, carrots, and raisins. I had permission to put one chocolate covered cherry on top. However, Luna grabbed it. Might have known.

Rudi again showed me his "owey" when I showed him the sore on my arm.

It started pouring rain and Lynn brought Doc, Kelly, and Solaris in. She creeped door #4. Luna and Elok could go into C and interact with Kelly, in D, through the intro door between C and D. They did go over there. Of course Chey was not happy that her kids were near Kelly, and she parked at door #4. Could not entice her away with a lime (I'd brought some for treats) or baby food. However, when Luna and Elok saw I was smearing baby food on the tunnel mesh, they left the intro door and came back through the creep door.

Luna had a sweatshirt and put it on correctly. Also gave her some Velcro rollers. She plays so cute with them. After she'd stuck them on herself a few times, she took them apart. She placed Velcro over her eyes, then her mouth. She is so silly.

However, the silliest thing today was Elok poking a hole in a lime and putting his penis in the hole. It was hysterical. When the lime fell off and Chey grabbed it, <u>he went after it,</u> so he could continue his fun.

June 8, 2004

Back to the zoo today. Yesterday, while Kelly, Solaris, and Doc were out on exhibit, Kelly was foraging with her back to Solaris. He went over to Doc. He reached for a biscuit and touched Doc's hand. Then Kelly noticed, flew over there, and Solaris clung to Doc's arm. She pulled him away. Apparently Doc didn't even move; probably afraid Kelly would cream him.

Rudi was uncooperative today. He didn't want to come inside. He ended up staying out in the rain. By the time we did creative shifting to get all the cages cleaned, he'd been out in the rain a good long while. When Cindy opened the hydraulic door he almost fell in because he was so pressed against the door.

I took a pineapple today and a coconut. Little Solaris <u>really</u> liked the pineapple.

Lynn got an email today. We may get Elok's little sister by January. Oh, how I hope that happens.

June 15, 2004

Worked with a different keeper today. Rudi refused to go out. Probably because he really likes her. She said SSP told Memphis they need to send Indah (Elok's baby sister) to us. Period! Not much else going on. We just cleaned. Solaris will be one year old next Tuesday, the 22nd.

June 22, 2004

Today Solaris is one year old. We made a banner. We also made little cakes from monkey biscuits, fruit, and carrots for the exhibit.

Chey and Rudi were uncooperative. She wouldn't shift. He wouldn't come in from outside. Sometimes they are <u>very</u> temperamental.

We are not getting the baby from Memphis after all. Darn!

July 13, 2004

I'm tired from having just returned home two days ago from a mission trip, but I didn't want to wait another week to see my orange buddies. I missed them! The Indian couple that helped us during the mission trip was fascinated that I volunteered at a zoo. She, age 39, has never been to a zoo. That's hard to imagine.

Solaris is so cute and such a busy boy. He's all over the place and is really quite speedy. He's still sticking his arm through the mesh, all the way to his armpit, to reach us. Cindy told me a neat thing that happened; Kelly "leaving him with a babysitter" so to speak. Kelly and Solaris were in the squeeze cage, and one of the volunteers was interacting with Solaris. After awhile Kelly went back outside. She sat there looking toward the squeeze with a thoughtful look on her face. She then disappeared for about 30 seconds. She came back with a banana leaf and some biscuits, and climbed back into the squeeze. It was like she realized she could leave him safely with the volunteer while she "went for provisions."

The introductions between Rudi and Chey and the kids have been going well. Rudi is patient, letting Elok fall into his face, and pull hair from his hands with his teeth. He has not lashed out at him. However, Luna tried to interfere once when Rudi was having sex with Chey. He was being a little rough, and she wasn't sure what he was doing to her mom. He lunged at Luna. Lynn says Luna has been throwing things and spitting at him. A creep door is being maintained so the kids have an escape route. Today was the first day the four of them were to go outside together. That didn't happen. No bribe of any sort was going to get Rudi out the door. Chey kept making "goo goo" eyes at him, wanting him to go but no. Eventually she and the kids went out. After they came in, they were put in the other end of the building. Doc, Kelly, and Solaris will be in A, B, and C later.

I gave Luna a red T-shirt that she still had on when I left about 20 minutes later. She also put on the denim hat I gave her.

July 20, 2004

Cindy was sick today so Lynn did orangs. We finished by 11 a.m. Since the orang keeper doesn't do the babirusas anymore, and because we can now put some of the orangs together, we can clean three cages at once. Makes a huge difference.

Rudi has an "owey" on his right wrist. He showed it to me as soon as I got there. Later he let Lynn put medicine on it.

Luna has a sore foot, but no one knows what happened to her. Today I gave her a couple of rubber duckies. Fun, fun. I also had some little rubber animals that could be filled with water. I squirted water at Chey, the kids, and Rudi. Chey and Luna thought it was lots of fun, but Elok and Rudi were not impressed. Must be a guy thing.

July 27, 2004

I worked with another keeper today, and we finished at 11 a.m. Rudi is <u>not</u> in with Chey and the kids at present. Apparently last Tuesday he forcibly copulated with Elok, and traumatized the poor little guy. Elok had done something to make him mad.

Now it's back to the drawing board for the intros. Lynn emailed me that she wished she could explain to Chey and Rudi the reason she had to separate the two of them.

Today we just cleaned with nothing too exciting happening. Elok threw a screaming fit this morning because he thought he should get his juice before Rudi. Then he threw another one when his juice was gone. He screamed and threw himself on to the floor. I told him he was not going to be rewarded for that behavior, and gave him water in his cup with a straw when he quit screaming.

Rudi showed us his "owey" and it is healing nicely.

I took limes and they all seemed to like those.

August 3, 2004

Not too much going on today. I worked with Cindy and I always enjoy that. Rudi has not been cooperating about coming in from outside, so today he stayed in. Kelly, Doc, and Solaris went out early, and the others went out midday. Solaris is <u>such</u> a busy boy. I took mangos and they <u>all</u> loved those.

August 10, 2004

I had a Band Aid on today so Rudi gave it a long look, purred, and presented his nipple. Silly guy. Kelly, Doc, and baby went out early. Then Rudi refused to go out.

Chey and the kids were in E and F and door #8 wouldn't open. We couldn't let them out. Kept telling Chey to push on it, but she didn't figure it out.

Earlier today I caught Chey trying to take a screw out of the hydraulic door with her fingernail. I asked her what she was doing, and she looked at her hand like she wasn't doing anything, just admiring her manicure.

August 17, 2004

Well, today was the last day at the zoo for awhile as I'm going to MT next week, and staying four weeks.

After we let Doc, Kelly, and Solaris out, we went around to see what they were doing. We watched as Solaris walked about 15 feet away from Kelly. She retrieved him. Then, when she had her back turned, he <u>bolted</u>, heading straight for Daddy Doc who was sitting about 25 or 30 feet away. He was about 5 feet from Doc when Kelly noticed. I've never seen her move so fast. She grabbed him, but then sat there awhile just watching Doc. She then took Solaris back to the structure, and climbed up high.

I saw Elok "having sex" with Chey today. She was on her tummy, and he was behind her "going at it" as best he could. I told him little boys who are old enough to have sex are much too old to have temper tantrums.

September 28, 2004

It was great to see the orangs again. And they were glad to see me too, or was it the pineapple I had with me?

Solaris is running all over the place; so cute. Elok is still having tantrums. We <u>really</u> need to get those stopped. And Luna is the same silly girl. She was playing with a burlap bag, walking around with it covering her completely at one point. She also wore a purple T-shirt for about 30 minutes.

I thumbed through a National Geographic magazine in front of their cage, showing Chey the pictures, while I was waiting on the keeper. Elok wanted the magazine, and spit at me to express his displeasure at my not giving it to him. He's just learning to spit, and his aim is not too good yet. I then gave Chey the magazine, and she spent about an hour looking through it.

Doc refused to go out today. Don't know what that was all about.

October 5, 2004

Nothing special today. I took prickly pears, which they'd never had, and they loved them. Elok only had one brief tantrum, for no apparent reason, but only one.

October 12, 2004

I worked with Cindy today. I took some socks and Luna put a pair on correctly. Elok put one on his arm. They also stuffed one or two with hay. And when we cleaned cage A, we noticed Luna even stuffed one with poop.

I took all of the plastic Jack-O-Lanterns, that I stored from last year, to the zoo. Solaris was playing with them, racing around, and kept putting one on his head. Looked so cute. I tried to get a photo, but he took it off too soon.

October 19, 2004

Doc refused to go out today. Who knows why? The keeper and I finished cleaning in orangs by 10:15 a.m. They sedated Joey Mandrill, so we went to help clean the mandrill cages while he was at the clinic. Then I helped clean the patas cages. Left the zoo at noon.

October 26, 2004

Today I took asparagus as a treat for the orangs. Well, Chey thought it was quite good, Kelly ate a few of the tender tops, and Elok tasted it (he's always munching on something). The big guys weren't so sure, although I think Rudi ate one or two of the stalks, and maybe Doc ate one. Luna did exactly as I thought she would; used the asparagus spear as a sex toy. She was also trying to put it into her juice straw.
    Elok threw a tantrum when Luna wouldn't give him her straw while she was drinking her juice. He had a straw in his juice, but that didn't seem to matter. He threw himself on the floor, grabbed the sides of his head, and screamed bloody murder.
    Everyone was cooperative about shifting and that helped.
    I went to see the three week old giraffe. She's really tiny and so cute. I also saw Bella, the two month old elephant. She seems thin. I hope she's doing okay.

November 9. 2004

Well, Doc refused to go out. We moved him into cage D with nothing to play with. He seemed to not care that he was being punished.
    Kelly refused to come inside when it was time. Guess she thought it was too pretty a day to come in early. So we had to move Doc back to F which had been fixed up for Kelly, and he got good stuff anyway.
    I took mandarin oranges and graham crackers as treats. They loved it, even baby boy. He is so cute and playful. And it's fun to watch Kelly play with him.
    We gave a tye dye T-shirt to Luna early. She played with it; put it on etc. Then all three played with bits of it when it was torn apart. Chey used her piece to scrub the door, the mesh, and a little bucket, using the filthy water in her water bowl as a dishpan. Yuck!
    I went to see the baby giraffe again. She is so teeny, but strong.

November 16, 2004

Another keeper said Doc has continued to refuse going outside for her and Cindy. Well, today I showed him the top of the pineapple I brought, and told him I was putting it outside for him. Of course Kelly saw and heard this conversation, packed up her baby, and headed for the door. Anyway, Doc went right out. I went out and saw him sitting way across the exhibit. I told him to go get his pineapple, and pointed to where it was. By the time I walked back, he was over there getting his treat.

Luna "performed" with her whistle. Chey brushed her hair thoroughly. The keeper had never seen that.

When Kelly and Solaris came in, Solaris was walking in ahead of his mom. Then he stopped, waited for her, and climbed on as she walked by. She never slowed down so he had to catch a "moving vehicle."

Kelly made a big deal out of giving us a cardboard "plate." We couldn't figure out what she was doing, and then remembered Cindy sometimes gives her rice flakes when she comes inside.

I gave Chey an empty raisin bag. Well, there were a few left in it. When she'd eaten them all, we noticed her stretched out on her back with the bag torn open and laid across her face. Just tripping out on the raisin scent, I guess.

November 23, 2004

Today I just worked about 3 hours because my husband, stepmom, and granddaughter, Sterling, came to the zoo to see the orangs up close and personal. Sterling is _finally_ old enough to go inside the night house. Luna was in a spitting mood. Doc and Rudi put on big displays. As it was raining, Kelly and Solaris had access to the tunnel. (Doc had refused to go out this morning.) Kelly was very playful with a large plastic tablecloth. At one point she was stomping in the tunnel moat with her left foot; stomping, stomping, stomping. I thought she was playing in the water. <u>Then</u> she handed me a large mashed cockroach. I gave her some pineapple.

I had a hairbrush for Chey so she could show my guests how she brushes her hair. Also gave her a sponge so she could wash things. I gave Luna a T-shirt, but spitting at the guests was a priority.

November 30, 2004

There were two keepers in orangs today, so I helped another keeper clean the howler monkey and lemur cages.

December 7, 2004

I worked with Cindy today. Nice to have her back. Actually she was here, but in another section, last week.

I made a "cake" for Rudi's birthday which is December 9th. Made it with two slices of bread put together with canned pumpkin, and garnished with carrots, raisins, and cranberries. He was a happy camper.

When Luna came to get her juice today, she had two large Legos to spit it in to save it. One had a few holes in it. It was neat watching her check it out, and then use the other one. However, it <u>also</u> had a couple of holes, but she scrutinized it closely to see if it could be used without leaking.

Doc refused to go out so he got no treats, including any of the pineapple I brought.

December 14, 2004

It was cold today so Rudi went out first. However, we gave him access to the tunnel. So he went out, got his pineapple, and came right back in. No exciting happenings; just routine cleaning. Doc <u>did</u> go out with Kelly and Solaris when it was time.

January 4, 2005

Great to be back at the zoo! I'm sure the orangs have a sense of missing people when they don't see them for awhile. Of course Chey stared intently into my eyes like she always does. I showed Rudi my painted toenails and my "owey." (A cat scratched my arm.)

Doc zipped outside with Kelly and Solaris. Chey and Rudi were given access to cages C, D, E, and F. The kids were in A an B. Rudi put on a big display when the doors opened, and scared the bejeebers out of Chey, sending her to the rafters. There was essentially no interaction between them, but she did come within 6 feet of him at one point. The keeper said the last time they were together they had a "heck of a time." Lots of X rated stuff. I guess today no one was in the mood.

Luna had lots of fun in a burlap bag, pulling it down over herself, then laying it out, folding it very neatly, and playing with it that way. She's learning to pee in a cup. As she's rewarded for this behavior, she now pees in different receptacles and brings them to us, showing us what a smart girl she is. At least the cage is staying cleaner at times.

January 18, 2005

Luna continues to pee in bottles and is very proud. Trouble is, today she thought it would be fun to spit the contents of the bottle at us. There's that 3% DNA thing again; the part we don't share.

Everyone was cooperative today. I was popular, of course, as I had a pineapple.

January 25, 2005

Not too much going on. I took mandarin oranges and club crackers for treats. They liked that.

Chey grabbed a huge bamboo branch we had in the aisle, and pulled it into cage A. She wanted to use it to grab a moat grate, poke at the lights etc.; <u>not to eat.</u> She wasn't about to give it back. Even the mandarin oranges weren't a good enough bribe. Cindy got some applesauce to see if <u>that</u> would work. Luna knew what we wanted, and tried to get it away from Chey to trade. <u>No way!</u> Rudi spit at Cindy. Why? Mad because we were hassling Chey, mad because treats weren't coming his way; who knows? She finally gave it up.

Also, little Elok sort of made a trade today. Guess he's learning – <u>finally.</u>

February 1, 2005

Two keepers in orangs today. It was pouring rain, so we had to move them from cage to cage to clean. Chey was not cooperative and later Rudi wasn't. I made some enrichment packages from butcher paper, a time consuming job. However, as there were two keepers and only two brooms, it was good to have an extra person to do the enrichment project.

Luna has a cold, and actually blows her nose using a paper towel or whatever other paper is around. She is so smart!

February 22, 2005

A friend of mine came to meet my orange buddies today. Luna showed off by correctly putting on a pair of slipper socks I'd given her.

Elok had a classic tantrum today. It was really funny. He wanted a little box Luna had. When she wouldn't give it up he screamed, threw himself into the corner on a bench, and was hugging himself. Looked like he was in "time out." Then he turned, screamed, and hugged himself again. After that, he proceeded to follow Luna around the cage whining and screaming. Lastly, he went to Chey, who was inside a barrel in the next cage. She didn't care either.

March 22, 2005

Back to the zoo after a month. I took a pineapple so I was popular. Doc refused to go out, however, so he got none. Poor guy; he was kiss squeaking but to no avail.

Luna's transport crate has arrived. It has been put into cage A so she can get used to it. Chey goes to a cage (D or E) with Rudi. Then the kids are left behind to give Luna a chance to explore her crate, eat snacks placed inside etc. Elok is also enjoying it. We were thinking maybe we should just sneak him off to Luna's next zoo too. Actually, he might enjoy a field trip, just going along for the ride. The plan is for Luna, and her selected mate, to arrive at the zoo at the same time. We've heard he's really smart, like Luna, but rather reserved and shy. Poor guy. She'll probably beat him up.

Today I went over to see Bella, the 7 month old elephant. The other mom elephant, Me-Thai, has sort of adopted her. Her own mom doesn't mind. Bella still has keepers watching her all the time. Today when the keeper walked to the other side of the exhibit, she walked along with him. When he went to an area that kind of jutted out, Bella couldn't figure out how to go 10 feet to the left, through the gate, and get close to him. She started bellowing like crazy. Me-Thai seemed to be trying to comfort her. That didn't work. The keeper had to walk back around the fence so she could figure out how to get through the gate.

Also, before I left, I went to see what Kelly and Solaris were doing out on the exhibit. Solaris was right in the corner by the viewing window with leaves, a cloth, and twigs making a nest. So cute! Kelly was "interacting" with the public, probably thinking, "Isn't my little boy so cute? I'm so proud."

March 29, 2005

Great day today. Elok had no tantrums. Doc cooperated and went outside when he was supposed to go. Everyone shifted as directed. Solaris drank from a straw. Such a big boy and so very cute.

Delilah, the babirusa, died Saturday. She's been ill the past couple of weeks, but I'm not sure what the cause of death was. She was a very neat and sweet animal.

I gave Luna a pair of men's slippers today. She gave them back. Therefore, I put them in with Rudi and Chey. Noticed Chey was using one to scrub the cage mesh, using her water bowl as a scrub basin.

April 5, 2005

Nothing much going on today. Doc went outside like a good boy. Elok had a tantrum, but he was in Luna's transport cage so we only heard it; didn't see it. Solaris is doing well drinking from a straw.

April 19, 2005

When I put forage in the yard this morning I saw a grackle pick up a piece of cracker about an inch square, and take it to the moat to dunk it. I didn't realize they were so smart.

Baby elephant, Bella, was euthanized last week. She'd broken her leg in a fall and the surgery was not a success. Her leg did not heal. Bless her heart. It's so sad. I'm glad I got some good photos of her a few weeks ago.

Today when I "played" with Chey, she put on her sweet smiley face. She's wonderful!

April 26, 2005

Nothing special today. Just cleaned cages. Everyone was cooperative. I took empty frosting containers, and Elok grabbed one and climbed up high so no one would take it. He's learning.

May 13, 2005

Today is Chey's 33rd birthday. I made her a "cake" which was a dish of oatmeal with raisins, 4 strawberries, and a carrot on top. She even shared some with Elok. I took some honey grahams for him and Rudi, just in case.

Luna has left our zoo and we all hope she does well in her new home; Tampa Bay, Florida.

July 5, 2005

Home from Montana and back to the zoo. Yea! In three days I'm leaving again for a two week mission trip, but I really needed my orang fix.

Rudi came down from a high prop when he saw I was putting my boots on. He wanted a glimpse of bare feet and painted toenails.

Elok was sucking on Chey's finger this morning as she sat in B with her left hand through the creep door to him in A. He needs to suck on his own finger.

Solaris is getting bigger and bigger. So cute.

It was hot but good to be back to see my buddies.

August 23, 2005

It was so good to return to the zoo. I attended a PHP (Pongos Helping Pongos) event this past weekend and purchased a wonderful framed photo of Chey that a primate volunteer's husband took. Today, that volunteer gave me another one of his framed photos of

Chey. She said he wanted me to have it as I'd spent so much on the other one. I almost cried I was so touched. They know how much Chey means to me.

I think the whole gang was happy to see me. Or maybe they just think "Sherry and pineapple" sort of like ham and eggs.

Rudi had a close up look at my bare feet as I changed into boots. I gave him and Doc empty peanut butter jars; always a special treat. I also had an empty frosting container for Chey. She fairly ran into the next cage to get it.

Elok had a screaming fit when I gave Chey a package of instant oatmeal, and she wouldn't share. I gave him some when he quit screaming.

We are getting Indah, Elok's little sister, in October. We will hand raise her before letting Chey "adopt" her. Lynn actually told me this at the end of July. I am so excited to have the opportunity to raise another one. We received one of Indah's little blankets from the Memphis Zoo. They gave it to Chey today so she could sniff it.

August 30, 2005

An uneventful morning at the zoo. I took mangos and a cantaloupe for them to share. They loved that. Lots of kiss squeaks.

August 31, 2005

Cheyenne was featured on the David Letterman Show tonight on the Ape or Artist segment. There was a painting she'd done, and David was to guess ape or artist. He said artist. They then showed the wonderful photo that the volunteer's husband took; the one of her reaching out. They also gave a short biography of her. She's famous!

September 6, 2005

I didn't take any treats today, but did have an empty honey bottle. Elok grabbed it as soon as they shifted cages, but of course Chey took it away. He was <u>not</u> a happy camper, and pitched a screaming fit when she wouldn't share. He'd better get a grip when his "mom" has another one to care for along with him. Little bratty boy.

September 13, 2005

Today we saw part of a video of Indah from about a month old to a year old. What a cutie! She's all wrinkly and hairy like Elok was. She also seems cross-eyed. Hmmm.......

September 20, 2005

Kelly's birthday is September 22nd, so today I took a "cake" for her. Made a dish of maple brown sugar oatmeal with raisins in it, and put blueberries on top as well as three macadamia nuts. She was very happy and even shared it with Solaris. She'll be 25.

I also took some pistachios. They <u>loved</u> those. Probably hadn't had them before.

One of the props was broken in cage D. It was holding one end of the hammock up. A piece had broken off and was dangling on the end of the chain. Anyway, when Chey and Elok went through D, Chey stopped and gave it a thorough once over. She studied it closely and looked worried about it. Meanwhile Elok had raced into E and grabbed the empty frosting container I'd placed there, licking the tiny bit of leftover frosting off his fingers as he dug it out. Then he got the nearly empty honey bottle. Chey was still in D looking at the prop. She finally went into E, but stopped and inspected door #8 thoroughly. It had been fixed and now goes up all the way. Cindy asked her, "Are you the building inspector?" She was so funny. When she went into E, Elok took the frosting container up onto the bench behind a "wall" of buckets to hide from her. Later Chey "fixed' the prop by twisting it around the one still attached so it wouldn't dangle.

Cindy said on the weekend the keeper put Elok's dinner on top of a pile of hay, instead of where it was usually placed, and he couldn't find it. He looked around bewildered, then went into Cage B and conned Chey out of her orange. After that he went back to A and saw his dinner on the hay. Duh......not too bright sometimes.

September 27, 2005

Rudi came from cage F into E today to hunker down and watch me put my boots on. He just had to peek at my bare feet and painted toes.

I took graham crackers for treats. Chey was a bit suspicious at first. I also had an empty frosting container. Elok got it as Chey was more interested in the glass of Gatorade I'd made. He climbed high as he could to enjoy it before she noticed him and maybe take it away.

I found a dead baby bunny in the exhibit. I wonder if Chey perhaps loved it to death. This summer she caught one and took it into the night house to make a trade, placing it in the tunnel moat to hand to the keeper. And she'd also put one in a drain outside and it drowned. I think she was probably just looking for a place to save it for trading, but chose badly.

October 4, 2005

Chey and Elok were sedated yesterday for their checkups. They did fine and all is well.

Kelly wouldn't drink her juice this morning, so I put it into a bottle and shoved it into her cage. Then Chey wouldn't drink <u>her</u> juice through her straw. As it has Prozac in it to ease her

PMS, she has to take it. It was orange juice. Yesterday she had some sort of little thing removed from inside her mouth. Therefore, we wondered if it was tender and the juice stung. So I also put hers in a bottle and she drank it all, a bit at a time. Who knows? It might have been that she saw Kelly with hers in a bottle, and she wanted it that way too.

I took plastic Jack-O-Lanterns today. They always seem to like those.

October 11, 2005

Nothing to journal today. We just cleaned and didn't have much time to play. There was a meeting at noon about Indah coming. I'll start caring for her October 24th.

October 24, 2005

This afternoon from 12 p.m. to 5 p.m. was my first session with Indah. She's really cute. Weighs 22 lbs., is quite hairy, like Elok was, and wrinkly. She's a bit cross-eyed, but that doesn't seem to slow her down. Her main caregiver from Memphis has been here with her for the transition, but left today. She was quite tearful a couple of times before leaving to catch her plane. I felt really sorry for her, but she said she knew we were all very caring caregivers.

Indah grazed on sweet potato, mango, kiwi, and a jar of baby food peas to take her medicine. (She takes thyroid.) At one point I thought she was going to take a nap. She got in her tub of hay, and I gave her a stuffed animal and a blanket. She sat very quietly for 30 minutes but no nap. She explored all over the quarantine room, getting into all sorts of mischief, but I was able to distract her. She'd stretch her hand out to me when she wanted me to go with her somewhere. We aren't wearing masks (yea) and that made it much nicer to love on her.

October 25, 2005

Someone made a huge paper mache baseball to commemorate the Houston Astros being in the World Series. We filled it with goodies for Rudi to do a photo op for TV. He complied nicely, tearing it open and being photogenic. Earlier I'd put some cling on Halloween decorations on the metal hydraulic door in his cage. He amused himself by rearranging them, taking them off the door, and then putting some back on the door.

Elok had a great time swinging, using a stretchy surgical stocking I brought.

Doc went outside early and it was quite cool. He took a large piece of butterfly print material with him. He wore it while outside, and was still wearing it when he came in.

I found a water bottle (some kind of plastic sipper with a lid) in the moat. I thought I'd wash it out, but it had poop in it. One of these characters put his/her poop in it and neatly screwed the lid back on. I suspect Rudi. Handling poop; another example of the 3% DNA.

October 31, 2005

Indah afternoon! I took her outside three times today. Wrestled some in the grass with her. She did somersaults too. We were out about 10 minutes the first time. The second was a 30 minute stay. I let her climb on a tree. A man who takes a lot of zoo photos came by and took a lot of her. She also played a game where she would stand up and fall backward over and over. The time changed two days ago. At 4 p.m. her little body thought it was 5 p.m., and she got whiny, wanting her bottle. Therefore, I took her outside again for distraction. She just sat on my lap, wanting to be cuddled. We heard some thunder and she hugged me tight.

Earlier in the day a keeper brought in three huge bamboo branches, and she really liked that. She played and played and munched away.

When she gets hungry, she takes my hand and leads me to the fridge. And when I asked her if she wanted to go outside, she led me to the door.

November 14, 2005

Another Indah afternoon! We're wearing masks now because she had a bit of a nasal discharge 10 days ago.

She played independently a lot today. She had huge Legos to play with, and she seemed to like those. I also gave her crepe paper and a plastic sheet. That was something new and different. She seemed to enjoy the crinkly paper, and playing ghost with the plastic sheet. She did try to lead me, or get me to chase her, through the squeeze cage which is a tight space. I went once! I left her alone two or three times to check on the laundry I was doing, and she did fine.

We went outside for about 30 minutes. She wouldn't climb on the tree, so I sat under it, and she sat on my lap. She needed cuddling. I attempted to make the guttural sounds Cheyenne makes when she solicits for the babies.

She drank most of her formula from a Sippy cup today. As the afternoon wore on and she became sleepier, the poor little girl's eyes became more crossed.

November 15, 2005

I spent the morning with Indah relieving a caregiver who is out of town. She seemed quite subdued this morning. She spent a lot of time on my lap, including 45 minutes under the tree outside, but did not sleep. When she was cuddly, I attempted the guttural Cheyenne sounds again. She was a bit more active when we went inside. After her 11 a.m., bottle she was even more active. I did some rough play wrestling with her. Might as well prepare her for Elok.

November 21, 2005

Indah has moved into the night house. Chey and Elok are both very interested. They met her five days ago for the first time, but it seems Elok is not too happy. Shades of Luna when he arrived on her scene. There was interaction. He grabbed Indah when he could, and pulled her hair. I think he even managed to pull some out, because later he put a strand of hair back through door #1, the intro door. He managed to get hold of her stuffed gorilla, and pulled it into his cage. Indah wanted it back and they had a brief tug-o-war. Later, Cindy retrieved it when she shut Elok out of the cage.

They shared some food; meaning I fed all three from one source. One time it appeared Elok gave Indah a kale stem. Chey offered her a small stick. Indah is a bit jumpy when Chey tries to touch her. I think that's because when Elok touches her, he grabs or pulls her hair. But Indah did solicit attention from Chey a few times, and Chey gave her kisses. One time Chey stopped interacting with Indah, and just played with Elok for about 15 minutes. Poor little fellow; he's a mite jealous. Late this afternoon Chey was mom multitasking. She was kissing Indah through the mesh while letting Elok suck on her finger. Too funny!

Elok also deliberately peed on Indah today. Little stinker!

November 22, 2005

I took care of Indah from 7 a.m. to 12 p.m. today, exchanging shifts with another caregiver. She was awake when I went into the night house. She sat quietly for awhile, and then "peeped" for her bottle which she inhaled.

She was a bit subdued for the first two hours, but had some good interactions with Chey and Elok at the intro door. Chey presented her nipple, gave Indah kisses, and vocalized. Indah showed more initiative in the interactions. When Elok tried to grab her, she bit at him. Connected one time and he gave his wrist a once over. Later he offered her a bit of kale, mouth to mouth.

Chey and Elok were given access to outdoors. Elok wanted to go, but Chey wanted to interact with Indah. Elok pitched a screaming fit, tried to pull Chey, but she didn't budge. So he went just outside the door, grabbed the browse that had been placed there, and brought it inside.

Indah took a 45 minute nap on a big quilt in a tub.

November 28, 2005

Indah afternoon. She seemed subdued when I first arrived, but wasn't particularly clingy. She played independently in A part of the time between 12 and 2 with no whining. Chey was very interested in an enrichment bag that had clips on it, and she didn't really interact with Indah during that time. She did give Indah kisses through the mesh. Elok was at the intro door frequently. He had a scarf that he placed between him and the mesh. He would push his tongue out through it, and Indah would try to grab it. He pulled her hair once, but he wasn't as grabby as he was before. She didn't seem to jump as much either.

I took her outside for the 15 minute "Indah Show." When we headed inside, I set her on the threshold, and I went in. She took my hand, but walked through the tunnel herself. She also took her medicine, fruit, and cereal through the mesh, and then played alone for a long time. (Chey and Elok had gone outside.) She's really good and so cuddly.

November 29, 2005

Regular volunteer morning, helping with cleaning. Nothing special except Solaris was whining, almost like Elok. Oh, no!

December 5, 2005

Indah is more independent as each day goes by. Left her alone a lot more today and she amused herself. She interacted at intervals at the intro door. Elok is grabby with her, but she holds her own in the grab contest.

We are encouraging her to familiarize with the other cages, and to practice going through the doors etc. She played about 10 minutes in B and climbed up on the props. Later she played in C with me there. She would play alone, then jump on my lap and snuggle for a bit.

Once today, when she was swinging on the ropes in the aisle, I started playing with Elok's outstretched hand a few feet away. She "flew" over there and tried to bite him. She did the same later when they were all interacting at the tunnel. If I reached for Elok or Chey, she'd grab hold of me and try to bite them. The little green-eyed monster has appeared.

December 6, 2005

My regular volunteer day. Rudi's birthday is the 9th, so I took him a "cake" of canned pumpkin with some extra spices, raisins, and graham crackers. Also took one mango, just for him. Had a pineapple for everyone to share. However, Doc refused to go outside so he didn't get any. He kissed squeaked all morning.

I took some cute photos of Kelly and Solaris in their black tub. I hope they turn out.

December 19, 2005

An Indah afternoon. She played independently in A a lot today. She also spent 40 minutes in F, but I sat in the corner. I tried to exit into the aisle but she got whiny. She did go through door #9, ten or eleven times, by herself.

We had a brief Indah Show outside. And late in my shift she was quite clingy, but I think she was just getting sleepy.

December 26, 2005

On January 4th Indah will be introduced to her family in the cage. For now, we are continuing to encourage solo play. She played alone in A from 2 to 2:30. She was whiny a couple of times, but after being offered fruit, forage, or formula, she resumed play. Did the Indah Show at 2:30. She was somewhat clingy, wanting to take my hand every now and again.

She also played alone in B and C, using doors #2 and #4 as creep doors, and going through them four times. She played mostly in C. Took her medicine and bottle through the mesh. She had no nap today, and at 4:30 she was so whiny, I put her back into A.

December 27, 2005

I did a shift for another caregiver today. Miss Whiny Butt, AKA "Please Just Love On Me," wanted at least one appendage on me. I was only able to peel her off completely when she was in cage A, but she did her share of whining there too. However, she was quiet during a tour that came through the building. Starting January 4th, Chey can give this baby all the cuddles she needs. She's spoiled but cute. What else can we say?

January 2, 2006

An Indah afternoon. She'll be put in with Chey and Elok on the 4th if all goes as planned. She played independently in A. Seemed hungrier today according to the a.m. caregiver. She was eager to snack on the afternoon produce when offered. There was some intermittent play with Elok at the intro door. I attempted to have her interact with Chey when I had her in the aisle, but she was more interested in just playing in the aisle, so I returned her to A.

For the Indah Show, she came out of A on her own. I picked her up and swung her onto my back. She didn't hold on and slid, then fell, to the floor. She screamed as if furious, not hurt. I took her hand, hoisted her up again, and she hung on as we went to the outdoor structure. She was more independent in her play during the show today. She came over two or three times to grip my legs, but didn't fuss when I put her back on the structure.

Late in the day she was clingier. I tried to get her to play in C, and just sit with her, but she wanted to sit on my lap. So I returned her to A. As it was my last day of "hands on" with Indah, I gave her a hug, told her we loved her, and kissed her forehead. Couldn't resist.

Chey kept very busy this afternoon looking at Christmas cards. Another volunteer brought in her discarded cards. Chey got a stack, sat in a black tub, and spent lots of time looking at each card. She had sparkly gold residue on her thumb from one that she especially liked. Elok was whiny as could be, wanting to suck on her finger. At one point Chey seemed tired, wanting to take a rest. So she lay down on her side with her arm up, finger pointing, and Elok sucked on it. What a mom!

January 16, 2006

First time at the zoo in two weeks. The intros have been going on since the 4th. Today Chey and Indah were together 2 ½ hours. Lots of gentle nibbling of faces, fingers, and toes. Indah went on her own into B several times, and Chey didn't follow except a couple of times. She seems to know to give her space. Elok is being separated during the intros. That way he doesn't bully Indah like he did the first day. We are keeping him entertained so he doesn't have a meltdown. I think they put all three together tomorrow.

January 17, 2006

At the zoo to clean today, but I observed Chey and Indah together for a short while. Elok was separated, but the plan was to let him join them early this afternoon.

Today we festooned the cages with the white waxy streamer paper that my neighbor gives me for enrichment. The streamers are rolled up when we get them so they are somewhat "curly." Rudi was busy pulling them down and rolling them up. Then he stretched them out and rolled them up again. He's so funny! At least he was being enriched.

Doc decided to go out with Kelly and Solaris after much thinking about it. I watched them for awhile after I left the night house. Solaris was running around with a black cloth, playing ghost.

January 23, 2006

Well, the intros have continued with Elok being very rough with Indah; dragging her about, trying to have sex with her etc. She whines, but Chey seems to stay out of it 'til the whine becomes a certain screech. Then she heads over to break it up and Elok backs off. Lynn said Indah did strike back a couple of times a few days ago. She bares her teeth at him, but that only puts him off for a few seconds. She needs to bite him; HARD. After she is separated from Chey and Elok she recovers quickly, and plays quietly in her cage.

This afternoon, when they were together, Indah stopped whining for quite awhile during the time Elok was being sexual with her. Before I left they were both up on the props. She was whining, but this is the first time they've seen her climbing with Elok.

January 24, 2006

I was at the zoo to help clean, but of course I was also able to watch the intros of Indah to her new family. Elok was determined to have sex with her, and interestingly enough, she quieted down, not seeming to mind. This is how they learn. She was on her tummy, being quiet, and he was touching her here and there with his erect penis. She even closed her eyes and almost fell asleep. Hmmm...... Then, as another caregiver described it, he decided on "kinky" sex. He tore a piece of material about 6 inches by 15 inches from a sheet, laid it across her bottom, and was touching it with his penis.

Tomorrow they plan to let all three of them outside together.

January 30, 2006

When I arrived, Indah was whining, as was Elok. They were both in B. Their whines turned into screams as I was giving Indah a bottle, and Cindy was giving Elok juice. They continued with screaming fits at intervals between sips. They finally quieted and played a bit on the ropes. Mama Chey was in the tunnel busy "fishing" for honey on a tub set in front of it. Then the keepers moved Chey and Elok to C and D, leaving Indah quietly playing alone in B.

At 3 p.m., I managed to lure Indah into the tunnel with honey on my finger; yum, yum. However, when the three were put <u>together</u> in the tunnel, Chey and Elok went outside but Indah stayed in. So they came back inside. The keeper went up on the roof and tossed raisins into the exhibit to coax all three out, but that didn't work. Well at least Indah went into the tunnel on her own. That's progress. She and Elok played in the tunnel, but she sought comfort and/or protection from Chey a couple of times.

Between 4:30 and 5:30 p.m. she generally whined loudly or screamed a lot. Bad behavior, I do believe. She was up in her hammock to go to sleep at 6:05 p.m.

This was my last day for awhile.

March 27, 2006

Back to the zoo today to help clean cages, and it was great. I'm doing Mondays now so I can work with Cindy. Indah has settled in well with Chey and Elok. She and Elok were playing together, and it was sweet to watch.

April 10, 2006

Kelly was lazy today, staying in her tub bed 'til quite late. Solaris stayed in there with her quite awhile too.

There was a photo shoot today, with emphasis on recycling. Waste Management provided a big box filled with shredded paper. We fixed up phone books with peanut butter, and put them on the structure along with the box. Great photo op! Well, Doc came out of the night house like "gangbusters," immediately grabbed the box, and threw it into the moat. That was that!

Indah was a bit bratty, not wanting to shift from A into C and D with Chey and Elok. We had to move them back to get Rudi inside. Later we had to bribe her to move. She's catching on to being an orangutan, and learning how to barter.

I'll be gone again for a few weeks. I will miss them as always.

May 29, 2006

At the zoo on Memorial Day – a free day at the zoo. Derek and his girlfriend, Amanda, came by to visit the orangs. They, the orangs, behaved; no spitting. Elok has had diarrhea for a few days; poor little guy. Derek saw Indah miss the rope she was grabbing for and hit the floor, head first. She got up and rubbed her head. She then went through door #1 into B, sat down, and put both hands on her head. Major owey!
   Rudi was happy to see my freshly painted toenails.
   Solaris is adorable. Out on exhibit he reached his hand out like he was begging for food. We don't need another one that does that, namely Rudi.
   We now have a year old babirusa named Remley. She is adorable.

June 5, 2006

Not too much happening today. Poor little Elok still has diarrhea. Cage B was an unbelievable mess! When it was time for the "trio" to come back in, Indah took her own sweet time. Cindy says she does this a lot, and Chey doesn't go back to get her. Third child; what can you say?
   Solaris is so cute and such a busy little guy.

July 10, 2006

I was happy to see my orange buddies today. Showed Rudi my pretty painted toenails. Also had an empty peanut butter jar and coffee bags for him.
   Indah was pokey about going out, so Chey <u>marched</u> (literally) through cage E into F, and dragged her by the arm into the squeeze. Chey wanted that piece of cheese that was waiting when she stationed. Indah took her own sweet time coming in too.
   Elok had several tantrums early in the day. He was all by himself, and we saw no apparent reason. I guess he just felt like a tantrum.
   Kelly applauded several times, wanting treats. Solaris is now three years old and very cute.

July 17, 2006

There were two keepers in orangs today, so I cleaned two cages while they put some new fire hose on the exhibit. Then I went to help another keeper, and cleaned the guenon night house.
   It was so hot at the zoo today, and I was drenched when I left.

July 24, 2006

Elok has a cute new trick. When they are given juice, Elok wants his cup placed on the floor in front of the cage. He then moves it along toward the next cage, and goes there to drink his juice alone. Silly little guy.

Indah refused to go out. Chey finally pulled her out of the tunnel. Then it started raining, so we had to give them access to the squeeze.

August 14, 2006

This morning the yard was full of banana tree stalks, butcher paper, and hay that Indah dragged out. It looked like there'd been a party.

When it was time for Chey and the kids to go out, Indah was hanging back in cage A. Chey went in, took her by the hand, and dragged her into the tunnel. When the door opened Indah tried to climb onto Chey's back, but Chey sort of "encouraged" her to go out with her, not on her. Maybe she thinks Indah is too heavy. She is more of a regular; not a slim.

Chey had a zipper pull this morning that she gave to me. Who knows where she got that? I gave Rudi a cardboard tube from a roll of tablecloth plastic. He tried to poke me with it. Of course when I grabbed the end to poke him back, he pulled it away.

The Malaysian turtle took a monkey biscuit from my hand.

August 21, 2006

Well, today it took Indah just over an hour to come back into the building. Earlier, when it was time to go out, Chey went into A, grabbed her, and pulled her into tunnel. However, Chey does not retrieve her from the yard. Third child; who cares? We don't know what Indah's deal is; why she won't come in like she should. Sometimes we think she just may be a little "slow."

The Malaysian turtle took a monkey biscuit from my hand again. Later I saw it out of the moat, under the structure, scarfing down biscuits. A slider was also there eating them.

September 18, 2006

Nothing special in orangs today. My fingernails were painted so I gave Rudi and Chey close up views.

The zoo is getting a baby siamang gibbon from the zoo in Albuquerque. She is three weeks old. I will be one of the volunteer caregivers to help hand raise her until we can put her in with the siamang family; Boomer, Jambi, and their daughter, Raya. Before being okayed to be one of the caregivers, I had to pass the "Susie test." Susie is a 34 year old wild born agile gibbon, and she has issues with certain people. We will be spending lots of time in the central night house where she is housed with the siamangs.

Therefore, I had to go into the central night house with the keeper to see if Susie exhibited signs of distress or stress. She didn't.

September 25, 2006

Rudi, Doc, and Solaris all have diarrhea. Today they got their medicine mixed in Gatorade powder. Doc was a bit suspicious but he did eat it for me.

Rudi was tearing up a magazine and began shoving pages out under the mesh. So I encouraged him to give it all to me as his cage was the next to be cleaned. He complied and kept shoving trash out. He had a very close look at my painted fingernails like he did last week.

September 26, 2006

Today was my first shift with Sungai, the baby siamang. She's in quarantine at the clinic so we're caring for her there. She's so tiny, so cute, and so sweet. Lynn trained me; that was nice. She took one bottle of 25 cc. We let her suck on a baby's pacifier as she's teething. It was almost as big as her face. I'm going back tomorrow for three hours. I bought her a stuffed gorilla and a black rug as she seems to gravitate towards black.

September 27, 2006

Sungai is way too cute. It seems strange to care for such a tiny primate, especially after little chubby girl, Indah. After her bottle I took her outside for awhile. After going back inside, she fell asleep on her new gorilla with a pacifier in her mouth. I need to ask Lynn if this is going to be a problem. I wonder if they fall asleep on mom while nursing, keeping the nipple in their mouths. Probably do. Later she had 15cc of formula when she woke and was sucking hard on her pacifier. Then she fell asleep again, sucking on the "binky" until it fell out. A keeper brought a sheet from the other siamangs with their smells on it so I put that around her.

October 4, 2006

I took care of Sungai from 12 to 6 today. We went outside for awhile. She grabbed at leaves, but she's still very uncoordinated. She weighed 950 grams today. She took two bottles of formula, 35 cc each, and burped with gusto. She also took two lengthy naps. She found her thumb to suck on two or three times; also sucked on her pacifier. I offered her a cold teething ring from the fridge late in the day. Her eyes opened so wide at the coolness of it, and she then gnawed on it. I think the texture also intrigued her. She's such a lovely little thing.

October 11, 2006

Sungai had her shots today and she felt a bit warm. She slept a lot. The duck pond is being redone, and the water fowl are being housed temporarily by the clinic. While we were outside, one of the swans was "talking" to us. Sungai was quite fascinated. She tries to grab enrichment articles, but her little hands are so tiny. So cute.

October 12, 2006

Another Sungai day. She seemed to want to cuddle on my chest so I put on the black fuzzy vest. I guess she needed the body warmth that a stuffed surrogate doesn't have. She is so bright-eyed and really looks at people.

October 17, 2006

Sungai was active on her surrogate for the first 1 ½ hours today and then fell asleep. When she woke I took her outside for about 45 minutes. We sat on a piece of plastic sheeting, and she played on her surrogate. Every time anyone drove by she'd turn to look. She's very active and alert now. She pulls up on things and has developed excellent grip in her fists. She also wanted to gnaw on everything today.

October 18, 2006

No changes. Sungai continues to get stronger and stronger. Also has a cute little personality. She took two good naps this afternoon. And she listens intently to the siamang sounds on a tape recorder.

October 24, 2006

A stronger baby this week. Pulled herself up on a branch outside; did chin ups and knee bends. She visits her future family every afternoon and that's going well. They all seem quite interested in her. She does like to be held and climbs or moves toward caregivers. Also wants to chew on everything. And her coordination is steadily improving.

October 26, 2006

Did the morning shift with Sungai today. I fixed her a large play area on a quilt on the floor. I blew soap bubbles for her and she seemed quite interested. She took a three hour nap this morning, and I was glad I had some reading material. We went outside but only for a few minutes. The mosquitoes were ferocious. It rained a lot earlier this morning.

October 30, 2006

Back in orangs today to help clean. Nothing special going on. Chey refused to come inside but the kids came right in. She was bribed without success, but when Elok started crying, she finally relented.

October 31, 2006

Spent the afternoon with Sungai. I made a play area on the floor again with different enrichment items. She stayed very busy crawling all over the area and grabbing things. Took a good nap after a short visit with her new family.

November 2, 2006

Sungai moved to WWP (Wortham World of Primates) yesterday. It was chilly this morning, but we spent the first hour and a half outside. I was wearing a sweater and had her snuggled in a blanket. When we went inside we sat quietly for awhile, and then I fixed her a play area in her black tub. Her new family spent a lot of time looking at her. I took her inside empty cages and she touched things, but she kept one hand firmly attached to me. She conked out for about an hour. Then she needed cuddle time on my chest right before my shift ended.

November 6, 2006

Cleaned in orangs today. Kelly played and played with Solaris. She's such a good mother. Chey and the kids went outside like troopers and came in like they should too. Chey was a bit hesitant to leave the tunnel and go into cage B, but when she saw I had pomegranates, she hurried in.

November 7, 2006

Sungai is still way too cute. We are working on getting her to cling, cling, cling. She held on tight to my T-shirt today as I moved about, leaned over, and even when I got on my hands and knees. She's been started on rice cereal and loves it.

November 9, 2006

Sungai was great today about clinging onto my T-shirt. Her formula has been increased to 45 cc since she doesn't hesitate when she gets a bottle. Jambi seemed very interested in her, reaching through the mesh three times.

December 5, 2006

Back with Miss Sungai today after being out of town for awhile. When I took her from the morning caregiver, she sort of reared back and gave me a long look like, "Where have you been?" She napped on my chest for an hour and was awake the rest of the shift. I worked with her in the cages, but she kept one hand tight on my shirt when I tried to get her on props.

December 6, 2006

Got Baby Girl to take a few sips from her bottle through the mesh today. She did cry when I plunked her on the rack and ran to the aisle in front of the cage to offer the bottle through the mesh. After she had a few sips, I retrieved her and gave her the rest through a small mesh door attached to the cage. I did get her to have three of her four extremities <u>not</u> attached to me several times. I took some Christmas wrap and ribbons for her to play with, and she really seemed to like those.

December 11, 2006

In orangs to clean and nothing really noteworthy. It was raining so we just shifted them back and forth to clean.

December 12 and 13, 2006

Two fun afternoons with Sungai. She has discovered how wonderful her thumb is, and <u>that</u> "pacifier" travels with her. She's a little chow hound and is eating bread, potato, zucchini, cucumber etc. I gave her a Granny Smith apple and she had a great time with that. She even managed to get a few bites. It kept her amused while she was sitting alone in the tub. December 20th is the date she's to be introduced to her new family.

December 19, 2006

Well, tomorrow is the day we'll let the trio meet Sungai up close and personal. She was much more independent today as she climbed on the ropes outside. She would keep one hand on me at intervals. This afternoon we sort of had a "dress rehearsal" for tomorrow. I sat with her on the hay in the tunnel, and the keeper brought zucchini and cherry tomatoes to the mesh. Sungai went for them so I left and closed the door. She was quite happy for about 5 minutes. We hope we can do the same tomorrow. I'm excited I get to be the one with her when the big event happens.

December 20, 2006

The morning caregiver kept Sungai awake all morning so she would hopefully fall asleep for the introduction. I took her into the night house at 12:20 p.m. and got her situated in the hay in the tunnel. I'd decorated the tunnel with red and green tissue paper and wide crepe paper. She played actively; was really hyper. About 1:10 p.m. she fell asleep on the hay and I left. I stayed in the primate kitchen with all of the keepers except those who were in the central night house to observe and film. Between the time I left her and 2:45, the trio sort of took turns being with her, but no one picked her up except Jambi at the beginning. Video showed Sungai reaching to Jambi after the brief time she'd held her. Then Sungai cried and cried but wasn't picked up. Those of us sitting in the kitchen listened to her cries, and it was heart breaking. Then Raya and Jambi sort of had a tug-o-war with her. Sungai then "passed out" (fell asleep) in the tunnel. The trio moved, and Sungai was placed in the center cage with the others having access at 3 p.m.
    Later...........
    They had to pull Sungai as Jambi and Raya showed aggression towards her. So she's not going to be adopted by the family, as hoped, and we're back to square one.

December 24, 2006

I took care of Sungai this morning. She's clingier, but no physical injuries. I did get her to completely separate from me to play twice; once for 5 minutes and once for 8 minutes. She's still eating very well. It's not decided what we'll be doing with her to help her learn to be a siamang.

December 25, 2006

I volunteered this morning to help Cindy clean. She was only scheduled to work until 11. (The zoo closes on Christmas now.) We actually finished by 10 as all cages were easy to clean. Kelly's was the dirtiest, as usual. Everyone shifted when we needed to shift them, and it all went very smoothly.

December 26, 2006

I took care of Sungai today from 9:30 to 3. She is still clingy, generally wanting at least one hand on the caregiver. We stayed inside due to cold weather.

December 27, 2006

Today Sungai was much better. We were outside for 2 hours and she was clingy. However, when we went inside, I put a quilt on the floor under a "gym" of sorts. I hung things on ropes; Christmas socks, Legos, etc., and she played and played. I also gave her a red apple; a big hit. This little girl loves red things. When she did fall asleep, she did so independently on her surrogate. Got some cute photos of her today.

December 29, 2006

I took care of Sungai from 6 a.m. to 12 p.m. today. Yesterday I bought assorted plastic toys at the dollar store. Today I hung them on her ropes in the night house, in the kennel, and on the ropes outside. She was much more independent. She napped for about 45 minutes when I first arrived, but was awake the rest of the morning. I took her to the top of the ladder on the exhibit, and she took hold of the mesh with all four of her extremities for about a micro second.

January 1, 2007

I went to help Cindy clean today. I was popular as I had a lot of enrichment items plus three tangerines and a pineapple. I had Chey do a painting for the church auction.

January 2 and January 3, 2007

I took care of Sungai on my two usual afternoons. She's still a bit clingy at intervals, but on 1/3 she was less so, and she didn't suck her thumb quite so much. On 1/2, when we were outside, she wanted to keep one hand on me, but on 1/3 she played independently. At times, she would touch me or sit on my leg while playing with her toys and ropes. She was very active. She's being introduced to Susie, the agile gibbon, and that's going well. Susie grooms her through the mesh and Sungai isn't frightened. It was decided to do the intro to Susie as the intro to the siamangs didn't go well. They want her to again be comfortable with black hairy gibbons.

Her appetite is excellent, and she chows down on whatever comes her way.

January 9, 2007

Sungai was much more independent today, with touching or taking hold of me only at intervals. At the end of the afternoon she sat on my lap, but would then take hold of the ropes above and swing.

January 10, 2007

Today Sungai continued to climb and play independently, only coming to me for a cuddle every now and again. A wire mesh dog crate arrived today for her to become accustomed to, and I "decorated" it. She was quite interested. I took snow peas and a kiwi for her. She was iffy about the kiwi, but loved the peas.

January 16, 2007

Sungai climbed on her ropes and played with hanging enrichment items like crazy today. She took one 30 minute power nap. She ate ½ pomegranate and seemed to love it. (It is red, after all.) I also gave her cheerios.

January 17, 2007

Sungai was again very active and playful. I got to observe a Susie intro. There was lots of touching. Sungai didn't seem afraid, but playful. I gave her extra cuddles today. She could be gone before I return in several weeks. I also gave her an apple and she ate 1/3 of it. Little piggy.

February 25, 2007

Sungai was transferred to the San Francisco Zoo on February 13th. So far the reports are positive. I helped in the central night house and in the lemur building today. It was a Sunday, not my usual day, and another volunteer planned to be in orangs. Not a problem. I don't mind helping elsewhere.

March 7, 2007

Today was Doc's sedation. I helped another keeper in tamarins until 10 a.m. when he was sedated and taken to the clinic. Then I helped the orang keeper clean the building as quickly as possible before they brought him back. The squeeze cage was filled with hay and blankets for him. The vet stayed with him, after giving him his "wake up" shot, until he sat up. I got to pat his back while he was asleep. That was neat. They'd also combed his hair while he was sedated, and he looked so handsome. He weighs 272.8 lbs. which is 8 lbs. less than at the last check up.

Before leaving, I gave Rudi a good long look at my pretty toenails when I put my shoes on. That always pleases him.

Chey spent most of the morning hiding behind something; her typical reaction when vets are around.

March 14, 2007

I helped Cindy clean today. The cages were quite clean considering how messy they usually are. Chey gave me the blankets from her cage at my request. So smart! I gave her an animal cracker as a reward. Kelly spit on me several times. I think her problem might have been the baggie with raisins and animal crackers was where she could see it, and I had not offered her any.

Chey refused to come in after their time outside. Both kids came into the tunnel, but she planted herself on the door threshold. She was still sitting there when I left.

March 20, 2007

Today I took strawberries for good bribes. The keeper that closed last night forgot to give Kelly a black tub to make her nest. Therefore, she had to make a nest on the floor, and she looked like she'd had a bad night.

Solaris is so cute. He's busy as can be and very mischievous. He even puts on little displays. He's something else!

When Chey, Elok, and Indah went outside, I took ice pops to throw to them. Chey was out of sight. Elok grabbed the first two I threw and ran. Indah whined. I threw the third one to her as she was low on the structure. Elok was up high with his "loot." Well, Indah wasn't fast enough, and he raced down and grabbed the third one too. She pitched a fit; loud

enough that Chey came to check things out. Indah only had the ice pop container. Elok had climbed even higher with his treats.
   Side note............
Rudi was sedated recently for his check up. Lynn told me that Chey worried so much that day. Of course she worries when a vet is even nearby, and hides behind tubs and barrels. Apparently, when Rudi returned to the night house, and was recovering in the squeeze cage, Chey wanted to check on him. She put a bucket on her head, and got as close to the squeeze as she could. She thought no one could see her.

April 3, 2007

They were doubled up in orangs today. I helped another keeper clean up the babirusa pen and the patas night house. Also helped with the cages over in MYRA.

April 20, 2007

I helped in orangs and it was great to be back. It had been a month. Chey spent the night outside as she refused to come in yesterday. The kids came in, however. Kelly and Solaris were sedated for their checkups, and Chey apparently fretted and fretted. She wouldn't come in this morning either. Elok went out but Indah refused to go. In fact, she fell asleep in the squeeze cage. She also has diarrhea so who knows what's going on with her. I checked her forehead but she didn't feel feverish. She was cute sleeping in the squeeze and completely covered with a blanket. After Elok came in we let Rudi out with Chey.
   Yesterday the keeper gave Rudi paints and a brush to distract him from picking at his "owey," and being upset about the sedation activity in the night house. She said he amused himself for 3 to 4 hours painting things in his cage. So today we gave him paints again. He painted his cage and his water bowl. Too funny.

May 2, 2007

Today everyone had to stay inside because of work being done on the exhibit. They were all good about shifting so we could clean. Chey and the kids went into the tunnel for ice pops, thinking they were going outside. So we did sort of trick them, but Cindy opened the door to C so they had access while we cleaned A and B. She also gave them gum as a treat. Elok grabbed Indah's right out of her mouth, and proudly showed me he had a big wad of gum. Chey chewed hers with her mouth open, and pulled it every now and again.

May 6, 2007

Lynn emailed me and said a keeper found a toy tractor that someone set out for the trash. She gave it to Elok. He got into the driver's seat and took hold of the steering wheel. She said he looked like a farmer; just needed a hat. Later, while sitting in the driver's seat, he was pulling himself along by the ropes overhead. The keeper took photos.

May 8, 2007

Lynn was in orangs today. She had things to do so I told her I'd do the cleaning, and I did do most of it. I took mangos for treats and bribes. Everyone was cooperative. Rudi got hold of Elok's tractor as Lynn forgot to take it from a cage he had access to. He was quite fascinated and inspected it closely.
    Chey's birthday is the 13th. Plan to make a big deal of it.

May 13, 2007

Chey's 35th birthday! Lynn knew I planned to have a big celebration so she contacted the PR department of the zoo. The media was there. I made and hung a big banner which read, "Happy Birthday Cheyenne!" I also had a shiny happy birthday banner, shiny swirly things, and pastel plastic streamers to festoon the exhibit.

I wrapped her gifts in front of her so she'd want to open them outside while the public watched. At the dollar store, I bought her 2 hairbrushes, tennis balls, plastic toys, chalk, sippers, a hat, a shawl, and a red satin purse. She watched closely as I wrapped the gifts. So did Elok. I put a banana and a mango in the purse. I made her a "cake" with thick oatmeal and raisins. I topped it with blackberries and a baby carrot as a candle. I added sliced bananas around the edge right before putting it on the exhibit. After putting everything outside, I went around to take photos when the keeper let them out. Chey hurried out, leaving Indah behind. (She stayed in the tunnel and whined like crazy. She finally went out about an hour and a half later.) Chey went to the window right away to drink her juice from her new sipper. Elok went for the cake which was on the structure so Chey got none of that. He also got the purse with the mango and banana. There were lots of people there, and I went around a couple of times to answer questions. People wondered what had been going on because the yard was a mess.

Being with my favorite orang mom was a terrific way to spend Mother's Day.

June 6, 2007

Went to help clean in orangs today. I took red satin purses for each one, but Chey and the kids went out early. I'll keep theirs 'til next week. I want to personally hand Chey hers. I put a lime in each. I gave Rudi a canvas, paints, and a straw. He amused himself for a long time. I had the ever popular pineapple for all of them to share. Lots of kiss squeaks.

June 14, 2007

I helped clean in orangs again. Gave Chey and the kids their red purses with the limes.

The keeper said she had a gift for me. She gave me the canvas that Rudi "painted" last week with the straw. She said he worked on it for some time. He kept it clean, and she thought I should have it as I'd given him the paints and straw.

Solaris was a wild child today. He's a very busy and active little boy. He'll be four years old on the 22nd.

July 26, 2007

Well, an exciting, but scary, day in orangs yesterday. Seems the tunnel door was inadvertently left open and Chey, upon returning from a conjugal visit with Rudi, got out into the aisle. She did hesitate, but only slightly, when the keeper said, "Get back in there." As per protocol, the keeper left the night house immediately. Chey had the run of the aisle for several hours. She got into all the masks and gloves. She gave Rudi a large plastic bag to play with, and he was very happy about that. (Kelly, Doc, and Solaris were outside at the time.) Elok seemed somewhat concerned but space cadet, Indah, was her la-ti-dah self. Chey got into the paints and spread paint around. She tasted the mineral oil, Joy dish liquid, and organized the bottles. Thankfully, she didn't bother the bleach. Surprisingly, she didn't open the fridge. Cindy hoped she could bribe her to the night house door and get her to present her arm for an injection, but no way. She did give Cindy a cherry pit. Maintenance came and cut through the skylight in cage D. Lynn and one of the vets went down through the skylight into the cage via a ladder. Rudi was in F. When the vet managed to dart Chey, it upset Rudi so he spit feces soup at Lynn. He also "nailed" another supervisor who had come into the building. She said it was on her face, in her hair, and she shampooed five times.

Chey was fairly mellow today. The hydraulics were broken so we could only clean the aisle. It was covered with beta chips to soak up the spilled mineral oil and dish liquid. The keeper gave Chey some gum and she loved that. She was letting Chey know she'd done nothing wrong, and that it was her fault because she left the door open.

Chey disciplined Indah. Indah peed in a large tub. Chey touched it with her finger, noted it was urine, and when Indah was going to get into the tub, she grabbed her out. Chey also spent a lengthy time hiding in a large barrel. Her hand was outside of the barrel, holding a prop. She couldn't see us so she thought she was hidden.

Elok grabbed a glove right off my hand today. We also had a tug-o-war over a bag of trash. I won but not without a struggle.

September 25, 2007

First week back after two months off. Just cleaned and didn't take time to play. Kelly is now allowing Doc and Solaris to play together. FINALLY!

October 2, 2007

Doc refused to go out today. I wonder if Solaris is wearing him out and he needs a break.

October 10, 2007

I took a pineapple today. Chey was probably wondering if I was <u>ever</u> going to bring one. After all, I've been back two weeks. I worked with Cindy which I always enjoy. Observed Doc and Solaris together. Solaris was trying to get a game going. At one point Doc gave him a shove, and he tumbled a few feet away. He was having fun playing with a big box and some balls. He put the balls into the box and then <u>he</u> would climb in. He'd then tip the box over and start all over. He is so cute!

October 24, 2007

We let Chey visit Rudi today. Didn't see any romantic action but it seemed they were just enjoying some adult time together. The kids played together with no real whining on Indah's part.

    The family went out and I went around to throw ice pops, Solaris grabbed two and ran to the other side of the exhibit where Doc was. Kelly extended her hand (begging) and I tossed her one. She stayed on the structure. I think Kelly enjoys not having to deal with Solaris, and letting him explore and play with Dad.

October 31, 2007

Just cleaning today. I took an Incredible Hulk toy Derek put in the pile of enrichment. Gave it to Chey and the kids. Chey tried to take it apart but no go. I gave Rudi a piece of sidewalk chalk. He broke it into pieces, put them into a little yogurt cup, and carried them about. ???? Doc refused to go out today.

November 2, 2007

Elok turned 7 yesterday. The yard was a mess because of his "party" but they said he got his cake with Indah swiping some of it. He was cute today. I gave him a large, (6-7") foam ball and he used it to scrub the floor, the wall, the mesh etc. Later, he and Indah were having a squabble. When I checked on them she started after him and he scooted away, climbed a barrel, and looked scared. She's discovered what her teeth can do and apparently he knows too.

November 7, 2007

I took two pomegranates today so Chey was kiss squeaking like crazy. She, the kids, and Rudi shared one. I left the other one for Cindy to give to Doc, Kelly, and Solaris when they came inside. Doc was a good boy today and went out. Of course we bribed him with peanut butter.
   Also, Elok has a new trick. Puts a rubber hose to his ear and gives us the other end to blow in or talk through. Cute.

November 14, 2007

We let Chey and Rudi spend time together. No sexual activity but a lot of togetherness, staring into each other's eyes etc. Indah was an especially whiny girl today because Elok was harassing her.

November 28, 2007

I had a cold so skipped last week. They said Chey was stressed two days ago due to workmen being around. She bit Indah. Elok helped by showing the keeper Indah's foot when asked. Indah stayed clear of Chey. But yesterday Chey seemed sorry and was trying to make it up to her. She sat close to Indah and all.

December 5, 2007

Rudi's 30th birthday is the 9th. So today I took him cooked rice with raisins and peanut butter and honey mixed in with it. I also gave him a whole pomegranate as his birthday gift. I think he enjoyed it a lot.

Doc refused to go out - <u>again.</u>

The keeper said Indah loved the red tote bag I took in last week. She played and played with it. When the keeper was trying to get her to shift, she noticed the tote was near the cage front. So she grabbed it. Indah had a tantrum and the keeper told her and showed her it was going into the next cage. Indah moved!

December 12, 2007

No funny stuff today. I took a pineapple so I was very popular. Lots of kiss squeaks.

December 19, 2007

Sadly, Chey's mother, Sandra, died this week, on December 17th. She died in her sleep at age 51. She had been surrogating baby Mahal for a few weeks and was very happy. She'd had nine of her own and we know how well Chey learned parenting from her. I'm so glad I went through Colorado Springs this past summer and met her at the Cheyenne Mountain Zoo. (Met Mahal at that time too. He was being hand raised then.) I cried last night when I got the email regarding her death. The photo of her and Mahal was so beautiful. I put a message on the memorial website.

Today I had a bag of assorted nuts so they loved that. I also took a stuffed orangutan that makes sounds when his hands are squeezed or his belly button is pushed. The orangs were really fascinated. When I first turned it on they all sort of froze in space. Too funny. Kelly's eyes got <u>so</u> big and she just stared and stared.

Indah has a cold and Rudi is all stuffed up.

I'll be off the next three weeks.

January 9, 2008

Back to the zoo today with loads of enrichment from Christmas; wrapping paper, ribbon, boxes etc. I put my boots on before I went into the night house. When I went in and said hello to Rudi he kept staring at my feet. Next time I'll have to let him get a look at my bare feet and painted toes.

Another volunteer brought some empty peanut butter jars. Chey was using a paper towel spindle as a tool to get any remaining peanut butter out. It was flimsy, of course. I had a stronger, narrower spindle from something with me. I told her, "Here, this one is better." She put hers down and proceeded to use the new one.

We didn't put a box out in the exhibit for Solaris this morning. So I went up on the roof with one. He was over by the window. I told him, "Here's a box for you," and threw it down. He immediately came to the box and climbed in.

January 16, 2008

Cindy was sick today as was Lynn. So another supervisor covered 'til a keeper arrived at 9. She wasn't familiar with the routines so she asked me a few questions. We finished cleaning by 11. Rudi refused to go out for her in spite of good bribes.

I took pine cones with cranberries pushed into them. They liked those. It seemed Indah couldn't quite figure out how to take them out of the cones. However, she eagerly grabbed any that fell to the floor.

January 30, 2008

Kelly was in cage A. She kept applauding all morning like she knew there was good stuff in the fridge close by. She probably hoped we would give her something if she kept trying to get our attention.

I had Rudi, Chey, and Kelly work on a painting for the church auction. I may have another one done next week as I'm not too happy with the way it turned out.

February 6, 2008

Today I had Rudi do another painting with a tiny brush and a small foam brush. It turned out better.

Last Friday (5 days ago) Chey hurt Indah's arm during a hormonal bad mood. The arm was not broken, just sore, and Indah is not showing any ill effects from the injury. Chey's Prozac was increased, and according to Cindy, she has been very quiet the last two days. She says she seems more herself today. She has kiss squeaked, climbed about the cage, and has interacted with the kids some. Poor thing. We think she feels bad when she lashes out. She just can't help it.

February 13, 2008

Today I took in some huge wardrobe boxes that Derek gave me. Elok took one to the top of the structure. Cute. Solaris was so mad because he was trying to pull one from cage A into cage B, and he couldn't get it through door #1. I thought Kelly was maybe playing rough with him when I heard him whining. She wasn't even close but playing in a huge tub. He was just whining in anger.

I gave them all treats of pine cones with cranberries stuffed into them today. However, Doc wasn't given any as he'd refused to go out. He got only biscuits and greens.

February 20, 2008

Nothing special going on today. Lynn worked in orangs. Doc refused to go out. Indah was a whiny butt early in the day. Lynn gave them soy milk today instead of juice. They were a little suspicious. All of them did drink it, even Doc. Indah loved it!

I'll be away for a few weeks. I'm going to Montana.

March 19, 2008

Interesting day in that when Tammy, a new keeper in orangs, opened door #8, door #4 also opened. It seems rats had chewed the wires in the "control room" causing a short.

It was good seeing my orange buddies again. They all behaved like "good little children" today. And I enjoyed working with Tammy.

March 26, 2008

I took a pineapple today. Doc and Kelly were in A and B, and we wanted to wait to give them some until they stationed to go outside. However, when we moved Chey and the kids into C and D, we rewarded <u>them</u> with pineapple. Therefore, until Doc and Kelly went outside, we had Doc kiss squeaking non-stop and Kelly applauding over and over. Funny!

Cindy said Chey put a straw on the licksit drinking water system to get a drink the other day. Smart woman.

April 2, 2008

Today Chey refused to leave the tunnel after she and the kids came inside. We tried all sorts of bribes. Finally just shut her in the tunnel and let the kids have C and D. She did eventually move and was then very playful with Elok. He will be moved to the Oklahoma City Zoo in a few months.

April 8, 2008

Did an extra shift today, watching Indah for four hours (3 p.m. – 7 p.m.) after an umbilical hernia repair this morning. She was a sleepy girl most of the time, but she ate and had sips of juice.

April 9, 2009

Tammy was the orang keeper this morning. Chey was parked in the tunnel and wouldn't move to B for her juice. I pulled the pineapple out of my bag and said, "I'm just going to wash this pineapple," and headed to the sink. Chey moved quickly into B. She was rewarded with a piece.

When Rudi came inside he was put into F. Chey and Elok were in C and D. Chey hurried into D and stared longingly across the aisle at Rudi. I told Cindy, who'd just arrived, I thought maybe Chey wanted to visit Rudi. Rudi put on a big display when he saw Chey was headed his way. They met in cage E. When we left the building they were sitting close together, and it appeared Rudi was caressing her arm.

April 16, 2008

Indah is back "home" but living separately for a few days. Her incision looks good. Nothing too special today. I had a pineapple so they liked that. Cindy said Rudi and Chey spent about 3 hours together last week. They love each other.

April 23, 2008

Indah is back in with Chey and Elok. Chey played with her some today. Guess it was just yesterday she was allowed back. She is two weeks post op.

I took some nuts for them today. Chey gave the almond back to me, wanting me to open it. I thought she'd be able to open the softer shell almond, even with the few teeth she has. She did manage to open some later. I think she even got the English walnut open.

Doc refused to go out so we gave him nothing but six biscuits. However, later on I did give him one nut.

April 30, 2008

I took a pineapple today. Doc refused to go out again, not even for pineapple. Strange. We gave him no treats, not even biscuits. He did a lot of kiss squeaking but we ignored him.

May 7, 2008

Cindy said that last Thursday, the day after we didn't give Doc any treats for refusing to go out, he fairly flew out the door to go outside. Funny boy.

I made Chey a birthday "cake" and brought it today. (Her birthday is May 13.) It was made with browse biscuits, oatmeal, raisins, and topped with cranberries. I made little ones for the kids. Elok took Indah's, of course. Chey shared some cranberries with her however.

Remley Babirusa is about to have her baby. So exciting.

May 22, 2008

Remley had her baby yesterday. Haven't seen it yet.

Luna escaped from her new exhibit in Tampa. They bribed her back with vanilla ice cream.

Cindy was sick today so Lynn was in orangs. I cleaned everything as I like to do when she's in there. That way it frees her up for her boss duties.

Nothing special happened and I finished at 11 a.m.

May 28, 2008

Usual day of orang housekeeping with Cindy today. The cages were a mess! They had alfalfa yesterday. Kelly and Solaris were in cage E which Kelly does not like. She always makes a huge mess of it.

I took a pineapple so there were lots of kiss squeaks, even little Indah. And then when I did give her pieces of pineapple, poking them into her mouth so Elok wouldn't steal them, she chewed them like she savored them so much, almost smacking her lips.

When Rudi came inside he was kiss squeaking for pineapple. Even flipped his lip back, smiled, and covered his eyes when I said, "Peek-a-boo." When I said it again he put his index fingers on his eyes, like "see no evil." Very funny. That's the first time he's done that with me.

Chey was also playful today, playing with the kids and doing somersaults.

The baby babirusa is adorable. Named Hadiah which means gift. We call her Haddie. She's one week old and about 8 inches tall.

June 4, 2008

I helped another keeper in lemurs and tamarins today as there was an intern needing orientation in orangs. However I did go in to visit and give pineapple treats.

June 18, 2008

I missed last week due to Derek's wedding on the 14th, and I had an out of town guest. I took cinnamon rolls for the keepers and a pineapple for my orange friends. Kelly was applauding, anxious to have some. We gave her, Solaris, and Doc some when they stationed to go outside. Chey kiss squeaked so loud you could probably hear her outside.

Elok is going to the Oklahoma City Zoo in a few months. His transport cage is locked into door #1 so he can adjust to it. So far Chey doesn't seem upset at the sight of it.

June 25, 2008

Today Remley and Haddie were given access to their pool. Haddie went nuts, swimming and swimming. She's 5 weeks old today and ever so cute.

Nothing new in orangs.

July 30, 2008

Back at the zoo after a month. I was on a mission trip 'til two weeks ago; then had "stuff" to do that must be done after a mission trip. It was good to be back. Another keeper got engaged.

I took three empty frosting containers, each with a tiny bit left in them. Gave Rudi one. Used another to lure Doc into the squeeze to go outside. (I did give Chey a little taste from that one.) I put one in a cage for Kelly but Solaris grabbed it. Kelly took it away from him. Mothering only goes so far.

I gave Elok a length of hose that Derek sent from cutting up a garden hose. He put it over a prop to swing. Then he gave me an end and put the other end to his ear so I could talk to him through it. He's so funny!

August 6, 2008

Elok seemed kind of punkish today, lying on a bundle of hay wrapped in a blanket. Cindy decided it might be because the opening between A and B wasn't big enough and he was stuck in A. However, even after they shifted and he ate, he still seemed a bit listless.
No other news. I just cleaned.

August 13, 2008

Lynn told me Elok has been playing with the turtles from the moat, wrapping them up and scooting them along like trucks. Just a boy!
Today he managed to grab a black trash bag in which I was putting stuff from the drains. Yuck! He emptied it and proceeded to play with it, in it, on it etc. He even tore some of it and put it around Indah's neck. He would not trade it for any goodie that was offered. However, when the door was opened and Chey was in the same cage, she took it away from him and gave it to Tammy. I always forget his very long arms can reach a long way.
I took a pineapple and they were happy about that.

August 27, 2008

I missed last week so it was fun being back with the gang, and armed with the ever popular pineapple. Cindy said yesterday, after Solaris ate his strawberries, he tried to steal his mom's. Kelly grabbed his arm and held it while she ate hers. Then she gave him a leaf. He was not pleased and spit it out. Cindy said it would have been a great video with the look on his face and all.

September 3, 2008

Nothing special today except we collected fecal samples. Rudi took his container from Cindy and actually used it correctly but wouldn't give it back to us. We did get a sample but he played with two sample containers all morning.

September 24, 2008

Back to the zoo after three weeks; other plans and Hurricane Ike. Doc refused to go out so no treats (pineapple) or extra attention. He kiss squeaked all morning! Cindy said Chey got hold of a broom from the Monday volunteer and swept her cage before giving it up.

October 1, 2008

Cindy is trying to train Elok to go into the travel crate, hoping they can crate him without sedation for the trip to Oklahoma. He cooperated 4 days ago and not since. Little toot! Yesterday even candy treats in the crate didn't work, but Indah went in and got the candy. Then Elok pried her mouth open and smelled her breath. Cindy was hoping sibling rivalry would work. Not yet. Later this morning he was screaming for no reason. Just mad, I guess.

October 15, 2008

Today was the last day to see Elok here as he's leaving on November 4th for the Oklahoma Zoo. And I'm leaving before then for several weeks in Montana. I had a pineapple and another volunteer brought dill pickles. There were very happy campers in the night house with lots of kiss squeaks.

December 16, 2008

I was back at the zoo after being in Montana and breaking my wrist while there. I only went to show the gang my blue cast before going to the doctor to get it removed. I knew they'd be fascinated. Rudi purred like crazy and stared. Kelly, Solaris, and Doc nearly stared a hole in it and wanted to touch it. Indah was busy in her own little world. Chey took a look and then looked at me like, "Okay, but where is the pineapple you always bring?"

December 24, 2008

I did work today with my brace on. That fascinated everyone and Rudi refused to go out for awhile. Guess he thought he'd miss something. I took in a pineapple and tons of enrichment.

February 4, 2009

It was good to be back in orangs doing housekeeping with my wrist all healed. I had lots of enrichment collected over the past month. I gave Rudi the wrist brace. Apparently he was quite pleased and Tammy sent me the following message by email.

"I wanted to let you know what Rudi did with the hand brace throughout the day. He would travel between cage E and F and always had it with him. When I finally shifted him into F for the evening, I saw him specifically pick it up and carry it from E to F and set it right next to his bowl of food. It was a treasured gift."

I also learned a baby was born to Noel Giraffe on Friday, January 30. His name is Miles and he weighed 110 lbs. and is 5' 9 ½" tall.

February 11, 2009

Fun day today. They did paintings. Rudi was very cooperative and then Chey added some to his painting. A lovers collaboration. He also painted lots of stuff in his cage. He was slow to go outside because he was dipping his brush in a container of strained peas and was painting the wall. He took his brush outside with him and we <u>think</u> he still had it when he came in. He also played peek-a-boo with me for extra pineapple.

When Kelly spotted the pineapple, after changing cages, I could tell she wanted some. So I gave brushes to her and Solaris so she could paint to get some pineapple. She did her bit and then broke all of her brushes. Doc added some to that canvas with pineapple rewards. I had to keep turning his brush around, however, as he kept trying to paint with the wrong end.

Chey did a painting and didn't want to give her brush back. I added two figs to the pineapple for a trade. Chey moved to Kelly's cage when Kelly went outside. She then traded every piece of the broken brushes she could find for bites of pineapple.

February 18, 2009

Nothing special today. Doc refused to go out, even for a little tub of peanut butter. Cindy said Indah refused to go out yesterday; stayed in the squeeze cage with a creep door to outside. Chey <u>brought her food</u>. No reason to cooperate as mom played right into her hand. Solaris decided to spit at us today – over and over.

February 25, 2009

Today three turtles came out of the moat when we were cleaning by there. They wanted their biscuit breakfast. We hand fed the whole herd later.

Rudi played peek-a-boo with me for pineapple. One time he held his hand over his eyes, and the next time put his index fingers over his eyes. He was not overly fond of the bird seed snack, so Tammy mixed granola with it to make it more intriguing. He dumped it all in a box, and then meticulously picked out and ate only the granola.

March 4, 2009

Short day today; only worked 'til 10. The orangs got a <u>huge</u> new hammock in the yard. Indah absolutely loves it! She swings and falls into it, over and over.

April 8, 2009

Back doing housekeeping in orangs today. (Was gone due to a mission trip and all that's involved before and after that.) I did work Zoobilee twice and a fundraiser for Sifaka lemurs last week. I had a pineapple today and that was a big treat as usual. I gave Rudi a tray of paints, a toothbrush, and a little canvas bunny. He painted everything <u>but</u> the bunny. At least he was entertained.

Carnivores had an open house today. It was fun touring their different buildings.

April 15, 2009

Indah and Solaris have diarrhea and Indah was not her usual active self. Chey dragged her to the squeeze to go out; probably wanted to get away from the smell. Indah lingered in the squeeze for awhile.

Kelly made a great one handed catch of an orange that Cindy threw across the moat.

April 22, 2009

A good day. Kids apparently over the diarrhea problems. Everyone cooperated in shifting.

April 25, 2009

After the volunteer appreciation party this morning, my guest and I went over to orangs. Rudi was out, sitting in the middle of the yard. When we went to the window he rushed over to stare at my feet. He's so funny!

April 29, 2009

Chey and Indah were sedated today for their checkups. Indah did great; seemed clueless afterwards as to what, if anything, had gone on. They had to pull one of Chey's teeth. When they turned her over for the second half of her exam, she started waking up and was trying to get off the table. Took three people to hold her down while the vet gave her a shot. I got to go to the clinic for part of the exam. That was neat. When they sedated her and carried her out of the night house on a stretcher, I got a lump in my throat. She is so special to me.

Rudi was a bit upset to see his "sweetie" being worked on but he settled down quickly.

May 13, 2009

Today is Chey's 37th birthday. I made her a "cake" of oatmeal, raisins, and carrots. Indah got it. Chey was happy to get the figs placed in the gift wrapped boxes that Tammy made. Tammy also made a huge Happy Birthday banner. I gave Chey a boa, a new hairbrush, a shawl, a large sponge, and some sidewalk chalk. (Indah also got that.)

Apparently Chey and Rudi had 6 hours of "sex time" on Friday. They love each other so much.

May 27, 2009

The group had BIG drinking straws today. Chey used hers to drink from the licksit. Solaris put his penis in his straw. Chey also cleaned the hydraulic door with hers, removing straw from the door.

I gave Chey a purple water gun after showing her how to use it. She thought it was a fancy way to drink water. She did put her finger on the trigger but couldn't get the hang of it. Indah whined because she couldn't have it.

I gave them all empty thread spools to play with today. That was something new and they all seemed to enjoy them.

June 3, 2009

Nothing special today. I had a pineapple for them so that was the usual hit. I will be gone for about six weeks and will miss my orange friends.

July 22, 2009

Back to the zoo today. Forgot to take the empty peanut butter jars I'd saved, but did take an empty frosting container for Chey. When I went to say hi to Rudi, he immediately looked at my feet. I removed my Crocs so he could have a good look at my feet and painted toenails. Kelly greeted me by spitting at me. Hmmmm…. It was good to be back.

July 29, 2009

I had a pineapple today so I was very popular. Chey kiss squeaked so loud you could hardly hear anything else. Cindy gave Rudi a long handled brush and he scrubbed and scrubbed. She also gave him a squirt bottle.

August 5, 2009

Chey and Rudi had together time today and they were happy about that. When Cindy asked Chey if she wanted to go see Rudi and opened the door, Chey raced into E from D. True love.

August 12, 2009

Chey and Indah went out first today. When I sat up Rudi's cage I gave him two small paint brushes and two cardboard pallets with paint on them. He was in a strange mood today and slow to shift. Cindy said Chey bit Indah yesterday and that upset Rudi as Indah was screaming. He does not like screaming kids. Then today there was activity in the service court. He was in A so he was fretting about that. Anyway, he finally shifted into C and painted and painted things in the cage. Several times, when his paint supply was depleted, I asked him to give me his pallet saying, "Do you want more paint?" He'd slide the cardboard out. He was so busy painting he ignored the empty peanut butter jar I'd put in the cage. When he shifted from C into E and F, he took a brush and a pallet of paint with him and proceeded to paint things in cage E. Rudi Van Gogh.

I put pineapple pieces in containers. When Indah and Chey came in, Chey stopped to potty in the moat as usual. Indah went into B and started collecting pineapple pieces, putting them into a dish. She headed into A. Chey picked up a bottle with a couple of pieces in it and was trying to get them out. She looked through door #1 into A. Indah glanced at her and headed to the high hammock with her dish of pineapple. Sometimes she's smarter than I think she is.

August 19, 2009

Nothing special today and I had no treats They all moved where they were supposed to, and Chey played very nicely with Indah.

August 26, 2009

I had a pineapple today. When I asked Rudi if he wanted some, he flipped his lip. I told him he had to do a peek-a-boo. So he put his index fingers over his eyes. A short while later he did the same thing. Then, even later, he was kiss squeaking. I turned and said, "What do you want?" He put his whole hand over his eyes. I gave him some pineapple. He's so neat!

September 2, 2009

I could only work three hours today. I did take a pineapple for bribes. Everyone co-operated. Rudi played see no evil, hear no evil to get some. (He doesn't know speak no evil.) He also put his whole hand over his eyes playing peek-a-boo. I gave him paint, a toothbrush, and a foam brush as enrichment. He kept very busy painting his cage.

September 9, 2009

Cindy said Indah lost one of her baby teeth and Chey gave it to her yesterday. Apparently Chey was kiss squeaking like crazy to get Cindy's attention. When she finally took the time to see what she wanted, Chey showed Cindy the tooth. She gave it up for some gum. Nothing else going on.

September 16, 2009

Kelly and Solaris were sedated yesterday for their checkups. He came through fine but Kelly had vomiting afterwards. She was "under" for three hours. She was still punky today. She coughed hard a few times when she first woke up, and spent the morning lazing around.

Rudi played peek-a-boo again to get pineapple.

September 23, 2009

Today Doc absolutely raced out door #3 because Chey, in cage B, was spitting at him. Rudi was cranky but didn't spit at <u>me</u>.

September 30, 2009

Cindy said Chey and Rudi had an "interlude" yesterday. She said Chey was kiss squeaking like crazy. There was no food in the building so she wondered what she wanted. She asked Chey if she wanted to visit Rudi and Chey went to the door. Cindy secured Indah in another cage and Chey fairly flew into F to be with Rudi.

As usual I had a pineapple so that was a plus. Rudi did the lip flip, peek-e-boo, and see no evil, hear no evil routine. I also gave him paints again for enrichment.

October 21, 2009

Well, it's been a few weeks so I took pomegranates as a special treat. When we moved Rudi he must have been bored because he started tearing paper like Cindy had been doing; tearing it to put in the cages. I gave him a piece of chalk to play with, and he chalked the white part of the cage door.

October 22, 2009

I worked again today. Cindy was sick and Lynn was in orangs. We finished by 11 which was a good thing. We were having a bridal shower luncheon for one of the keepers who is getting married next month.

I gave Rudi a tray of paint. He proceeded to paint doors, and passed the tray out to me when he needed more paint.

November 4, 2009

I took little pumpkins for the group today. (My church had a pumpkin patch and they offered them to me.) Solaris threw them around like balls. Rudi ate some and handed the rinds out to us. He's a tidy one. Chey didn't eat the ones I sliced for her but did finally get one opened herself and ate that. Guess she thought that would taste better.

November 11, 2009

Kelly was funny today. She wouldn't come to the cage front to drink her juice so we put it into a bottle. She dumped it into a bucket and drank it through a straw while back in her tub nest. Then she went back to sleep.

As usual, I had a pineapple. When I walked down the aisle toward Rudi to give him some, he flipped his lip and did a peek-a-boo with his big hand over his eyes BEFORE I said a word.

I also watched while Tammy had him paint a Christmas ornament using a pineapple leaf.

November 11, 2009

Rudi was sedated yesterday. 332 lbs. He started to wake up during the exam and reached for the gas mask. It all worked out. He is okay and was anxious to go outside today.

When Chey was given access to Indah's cage (the door between them is always "creeped" at night), she went right to her, loved on her, and gave her kisses.

Kelly went back to bed this morning which is not unusual for her. She's so funny!

We gave Chey some of Rudi's hair that was combed out yesterday during his exam. She did lots of sniffing.

November 25, 2009

Nothing special. I took pumpkins and gave Rudi a huge one. He opened it (didn't see him doing it), and then spent the morning eating the seeds.

November 26, 2009 Thanksgiving Day

I worked again today as my kids are all out of town. Lynn was in the building so I let her not feel guilty about doing other things. I finished by 11:30 and headed home to put up outside Christmas lights.

December 2, 2009

No juice today and soy milk was the substitute. Rudi took several swallows and then turned away. But he did finish it later.

When it was time for Chey and Indah to go out, Cindy opened door #6 and Chey went into the squeeze. Indah stayed in D. Cindy told her to go outside. She didn't. Then Chey was told, "Go get the baby." She marched into D, grabbed Indah by the arm, and dragged her into the squeeze. So smart!

December 9, 2009

Rudi's 32nd birthday. I took him oatmeal with raisins in it, a pomegranate, an ear of corn, a bucket, scrub brush, shower gel, and a stuffed Santa. He "washed" his hands thoroughly with the gel, smelling his hands as he did so. He scrubbed his cage, and when I'd ask him if he needed more soap, he'd push the bucket to the front so I could squirt liquid soap into it.

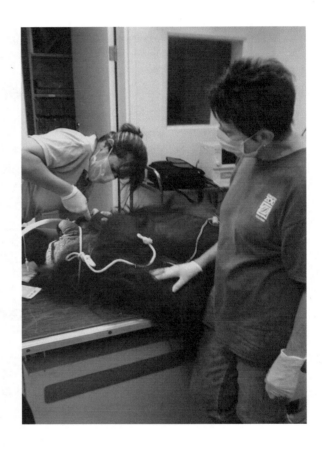

Chey was sedated today due to a bad tooth; one of her lower incisors. We noticed last week she was messing with it. She did not want to present her arm, and seemed to know something was up. Probably thought, "My tooth hurts, they want me to present my arm, and I'm going down." The vet had a tough time digging it out as it was broken. She also took out the one next to it. It was bad too. That one came out easily. I went to the clinic during the procedure as Tammy and I were done cleaning. Was able to love on Chey a bit and had my photo taken. That was neat. When back in the night house she was slow to wake up. Rudi was concerned, but we kept him busy with his birthday goodies.

Chey pooped big time during her sleep, prior to waking up in the squeeze. When she tried to sit up by grabbing the bars of the squeeze, she couldn't get a grip due to her arthritic fingers. She fell back right on the poop, and bumped her head on the metal door. Poor thing. She doesn't like to be dirty.

Tammy called this evening to say Chey finally left the squeeze, ate a couple of soaked biscuits, crawled into a black tub, pulled a blanket over herself, and went to sleep.

December 16, 2009

Chey seems to be doing okay. In fact Cindy didn't offer her any pain med today. And she seems to have no problem eating. ☺

I had a pineapple so was popular as usual. Kelly couldn't get our attention by applauding. Therefore, she started banging the padlock against the cage. So smart and very effective.

We noticed Rudi scrubbing with no water, using a piece of paper. I told him I was going to get a bucket for him. By the time I got back he'd pushed a small dish out for me to put water in.

Cindy opened doors so he and Chey could be together. He carried his bucket into D where she was, and proceeded to scrub the barrel. She went into F and started scrubbing the door with the water he'd left there. They are so funny!

December 23, 2009

Today I took spaghetti that I'd dyed red and green. I also took cranberries and put some into pine cones.

I put some pasta outside and Solaris was scared of it. I guess he thought it was snakes and made a wide berth around it. He did want a pine cone with the cranberries in it so he quickly grabbed one and ran. When he came inside he was over his fright and ate the pasta in his cage. Of course Chey was ready to eat the pasta right away. Food—yum! Indah liked it too.

I gave both Rudi and Chey scrub brushes and soapy water. Rudi took his outside with him, but I left before I could see if he washed things out there. He was eating his fruit when I left. He'd scrubbed plenty inside, including the inside of a big swim pool a volunteer brought. Chey scrubbed her cage.

December 30, 2009

I took lots of Christmas wrap, bags, and boxes today for enrichment. Another volunteer brought blue and red cello wrap in on Monday and some remained intact. The kids were having lots of fun with that. Doc continues to love playing with the plastic swimming pools. He was sitting under a pool, turning around, and vocalizing. He still sounds like a teen whose voice is changing. He spent most of the morning under the pool.

This morning I noticed Kelly with her hand firmly planted on her forehead as she rested in her tub. I wonder if she had a headache.

Rudi extended his hand when he saw Cindy get a brush to do some cleaning. When she finished she gave it to him so he could scrub things. He's so funny. He washed the hydraulic door, the walls, and the barrels. However, I couldn't convince him to push a bucket to me to give him more water.

January 6, 2010

It was cold today so they had access to the building when they took their turns to be outside. Rudi was "out" but was in the tunnel. He was "scrubbing" the track of door #3 with his hand. (He has seen me cleaning that track.) I gave him a wet, soapy rag so he could clean better and he did. I also showed him I was putting a new scrub brush and a bucket of water in the cage he was going to move into. So more and more scrubbing. He even delayed eating his goodies to scrub.

Then Kelly and Solaris were let outside with access to the tunnel. Solaris proceeded to scrub with the rag Rudi left there. First time we've seen that. And when Chey moved to C, she started scrubbing with a piece of paper so I gave her a sponge. They love to scrub!

January 13, 2010

Not too much going on today. Early on, we had some workers in the building. They left, but Rudi wouldn't shift until he could no longer see them in the service court. Also had to give him gum to get him to move. He tried to blow bubbles with the pack of Dentyne gum. Didn't work. Then we gave him paint and a toothbrush to keep him busy. Later, when he was up on a prop and his pallet was empty, I asked him if he needed more. He came down and pushed his pallet out. Such a smart guy.

Rudi paints the door track

Because of the workers the family fairly flew outside. Kelly took Solaris by the shoulders and herded him out.

January 20, 2010

When we first entered the night house this morning we heard a tiny whine. We naturally thought it was Indah at first. No. Chey had a baby rat clutched in her hand and it was not happy. We traded some pineapple for it. I don't think she wanted to hurt it; just have it.

Doc was sedated yesterday. He weighed 266 lbs. A cardiologist saw him and discovered a heart problem. One side is not functioning properly. Apparently he's had a heart attack at some point. He stayed inside today to rest and seemed a bit subdued. I fixed him some Gatorade. Well, Indah threw a tantrum when she saw me do that. She screamed so loud Chey came from the next cage to check on her.

January 26, 2010

Rudi took the wonderful new hammock that has been in cage A completely apart. He traded bolts for bubble gum and also surrendered the PVC. I don't know what possessed him. He's been in that cage numerous times since the hammock was installed a few months ago. When he moved I gave him a bucket of soapy water and a new brush to keep him busy.

Indah turned six yesterday. I brought her two shiny gift bags (she likes shiny things), a soft doll which she promptly tore apart as I knew she would, a stuffed dog, and some crinkle wrap. Early in the morning I gave her a little tray of oatmeal with raisins in it. I brought all of them jello with peaches in it. Yummy!

February 3, 2010

Nothing too special. Chey was in a mood, Indah made a lot of noise rattling the cage door, and I was popular because I had a pineapple. Kiss squeaks everywhere.

February 10, 2010

Nothing too interesting today. It was too cold to let anyone outside. I gave them all large sheets of red plastic to play with. Rudi had a bucket of soapy water and a new brush so he kept busy cleaning. Cindy gave Chey a brush so she was busy too. Indah whined, thinking <u>she</u> also needed something. Kelly spent most of the morning back in bed.

February 17, 2010

Another uneventful day. As I had a pineapple Chey nearly wore her kiss squeaker out. Tammy gave Rudi a sponge with soap so he could scrub. A short while later I turned around and noticed he'd pushed a bucket to the cage front, requesting more soapy water.

February 24, 2010

Doc refused to go out. He was put into cage F with very little as he gets no rewards for bad behavior. When he saw Kelly and Solaris go out, he picked up a handful of hay, "packing" like he does before leaving a cage, thinking he'd go too. Nope! Too late. He'd missed his chance.

Kelly spit at me couple of times today for some reason. Was she mad because I didn't bring a pineapple?

March 4, 2010

Doc refused to go out again so Rudi ended up with his treats of figs and pineapple. Doc ended up in cage F with only biscuits and greens. He made quiet kiss squeaks for some pineapple but we ignored him.

March 10, 2010

I worked in lemurs and tamarins today as they didn't need help in orangs.

March 17, 2010

Today Chey had an empty peanut butter jar and was using a cardboard tube to try and get any that remained from the bottom. Then she switched to a toothpaste box as a tool. I offered her a ½ inch wide drinking straw, telling her it would work better. She took it, used it, and it <u>did</u> work better.

March 24, 2010

Nothing worth recording today.

March 31, 2010

Lynn was in orangs today. I took Easter baskets with treats in plastic eggs. We finished by 10 as Lynn had a sedation to do.

April 21, 2010

Back after a three week break for an out of state conference etc. It was an interesting day, but many are.
    Rudi hesitated to go out. We even had pineapple on the stool by the squeeze as his shifting treat. Then we added gum to the stool. But first he had to get up on the bench in D

to poop. Meanwhile Chey was in cage E across the aisle, spitting at the treats. She'd gone to door #8 first, thinking she was going out. Rudi finally went into the squeeze, got his treats, and then just sat there after Cindy opened the door. After awhile she said, "Rudi, I'm going to close the door," and he left.

We were waiting for the PR people to do a photo shoot for Earth Day so delayed the family going out. Kelly kept applauding. She got gum. Applauded more. I asked her, "Where did the gum go?" She handed me the wrapper like, "It's all gone. Duh."

At least when it was time for the family to go out, Doc didn't give us any grief and went without a problem.

Chey got the hose today and we gave her gum for giving it to us. Not sure how she got it, but we think Indah grabbed it. Chey also kept begging for more and more pineapple.

It was a fun day!

April 28, 2010

Nothing too special today. I had an empty frosting container with just a tiny bit stuck to the sides. Gave each orang a little taste. Then I put it outside as Chey and Indah were going out first. When they came in Chey brought it in with her. Big prize item.

Poor Rudi. He thought he was going out when Chey and Indah went; was waiting at the door. Then he thought he was going out when the family went. Sitting at the door again. He was not pleased.

May 5, 2010

Nothing special today.

May 12, 2010

Today when it was time for Chey and Indah to go out, Chey went into the squeeze. Indah was lying prone on the floor near the squeeze. She was looking into the squeeze, arms outstretched, wiggling her fingers, bobbing her head up and down, as if to say, "Mama, help me. I can't get there without your help." Chey obliged. Then Indah didn't go out for awhile but sat in the squeeze looking pitiful. Of course Chey was already out.

Chey will be 38 tomorrow. Today I took her a dish of oatmeal and raisins. I also shared it with the others.

May 20, 2010

I didn't have a pineapple today. Chey kiss squeaked like crazy. She probably thought there must be one somewhere. I let her look inside my bag, showing her there was none in there. I gave her a bit of rice cereal.

May 26, 2010

We sent Chey and Indah out early this morning. Why? Because Kelly was sedated today and also intubated inside the night house with National Geographic Wild filming it all. She then was taken to the clinic for her regular exam and to have her birth control implant removed. It was my job to keep Solaris entertained during the sedation and intubation. I had soap bubbles, a water gun, and a water toy that I could not get to work properly. Rudi and Doc were in the building. Rudi worried and was tearing up paper. Cindy said it was too bad he didn't have water to boil. Kelly came through her exam with no difficulties. As she came up from the anesthesia she coughed, and Doc displayed. At least this time, however, she didn't have vomiting afterwards.

June 2, 2010

I had a pineapple today and they all loved me. I also had a new water toy, a water pillar that worked well. Solaris had a blast and was thoroughly soaked. Kelly took a nap while he played. Doc stayed back in the cage corners so he wouldn't get wet. Rudi was in A, put a cloth over his head, and kept backing up if the tiniest bit of water got in his cage.

June 23, 2010

Back to the zoo for one day after a mission trip. I'll be gone until August after today. Rudi left some poop pieces in a plastic cup and wrapped one in cello wrap. Mr. Tidy.

August 4, 2010

It's been six weeks since I've seen my orange buddies. Rudi looked at my shoes immediately. So of course I took them off to show him my pretty, newly pedicured, feet.

Chey was in a very playful mood with big grins. Basically toothless grins.
And lastly, KELLY IS PREGNANT! Baby # 3 due about March 5, 2011.

And that seems a perfect way to end this book. It all started when Kelly had her first baby, Luna. She didn't nurse her and I was one of the very fortunate ones to get involved. Of course there are more entries in my journal; some very brief, and others in great detail. To include a few...............

I made a visit to the Oklahoma City Zoo in May, 2008, to visit Elok. As they were doing some training in the back area, the keeper took me to visit him in the public area. When he saw me he came forward immediately and pressed his hand against the window. I put my hand on his at the Plexiglas. Then he put his head against the window. So did I. As people were saying "Awww," the keeper told them I helped hand raise him and he remembered me. I had a cardboard tube and placed it against the window. He then put his ear against the tube. It was a wonderful moment, and I got some good photos of him trying to look pitiful. I might add that one day Elok made an escape from his exhibit in Oklahoma City. He just strolled through the zoo. He kept checking to see if the keeper following him was still there. A short time later he climbed into a maintenance truck and was driven back to where he belonged. Apparently, Chey taught both Luna <u>and</u> Elok about escapes.

Elok at Oklahoma City Zoo

Malaysian, Fly River, Painted Terrapins, Red Eared Sliders, and Yellow Headed Temple turtles make up the turtle herd in the orang exhibit moat. They come up almost daily to be hand fed monkey biscuits by the keepers.

Solaris has a great fascination with the turtles, and has been known to pick them up if they are out of the moat. He occasionally turns them onto their backs and Kelly has to "right" them. Once he inserted his "personal part" into one's shell. Not a good idea for a future valuable breeding male. Fortunately, no harm was done.

There's the day Rudi and Chey were together and didn't consider privacy important and moved their love making to cage C, near the night house door. They were right in front of us and thoroughly enjoying themselves. Tammy and I left the building, pulled the curtain which is at the night house door, and placed a sign that said they were together.

Also, as Kelly's third pregnancy advanced, "her fuse shortened." One day she had to go into B from A to retrieve Solaris as he wouldn't move over on demand. As she pried his fingers and toes from the bench pole and pushed him across the floor and then over the threshold into A, the look on her face was priceless.

Life is never dull when working with orangutans. It's an ongoing adventure. Volunteering in Primates, and for other zoo events, continues to be the best non-paying job in the world.

Addendum September 1, 2011

Kelly gave birth to a healthy baby girl, Aurora, on March 2, 2011. Unfortunately, she rejected Aurora, and she is being hand raised by a group of zoo staff and volunteer caregivers. So here we go again! I'm not keeping a diary this time; just enjoying the experience as much as I did with the other three.

Doc, Solaris and Aurora's father, was diagnosed with cardiomyopathy and was receiving treatment. Over the past few months, however, his condition worsened and he passed away on August 30, 2011. He was a gentle giant, full of fun and mischief, and a great dad. He will be missed so very much by all who knew and loved him.

Aurora

Made in the USA
Thornton, CO
02/28/23 20:33:12

1f9e4486-b668-4795-9372-f111c8b5103dR01